In Tune With Heaven Or Not

Series Editor

JUNE BOYCE-TILLMAN

PETER LANG

Oxford · Bern · Berlin · Bruxelles · Frankfurt am Main · New York · Wien

In Tune With Heaven Or Not

Women in Christian Liturgical Music

JUNE BOYCE-TILLMAN

PETER LANG

Oxford · Bern · Berlin · Bruxelles · Frankfurt am Main · New York · Wien

Bibliographic information published by Die Deutsche Nationalbibliothek.
Die Deutsche Nationalbibliothek lists this publication in the Deutsche National-
bibliografie; detailed bibliographic data is available on the Internet at http://dnb.d-nb.de.

A catalogue record for this book is available from the British Library.

Library of Congress Control Number: 2014936229

ISSN 2296-164X
ISBN 978-3-0343-1777-1

© Peter Lang AG, International Academic Publishers, Bern 2014
Hochfeldstrasse 32, CH-3012 Bern, Switzerland
info@peterlang.com, www.peterlang.com, www.peterlang.net

This publication has been peer reviewed.

Printed in Germany

Contents

List of Figures   vii

Acknowledgements   ix

Introduction   1

CHAPTER 1
Controversies in Musicology   11

CHAPTER 2
Vignette One – Narrowing the Vision: The First 600 Years   65

CHAPTER 3
Vignette Two – Ecologising Music: Hildegard of Bingen   95

CHAPTER 4
Vignette Three – Encloistering the Angels: The Renaissance
Nun Composers   113

CHAPTER 5
Vignette Four – Radicalising the Vision: Ann Lee and the Shakers   139

CHAPTER 6
Vignette Five – Hymns or hers: Hymnody past and present   169

CHAPTER 7
Vignette Six – Inning and Outing: Contemporary Practices   209

CHAPTER 8
Conclusion: Musicking Wisdom's Ways   263

Bibliography   295

Discography   309

Interviews   311

Index   313

Figures

Figure One	People in Positions of Power	21
Figure Two	Dominant Ways of Knowing	25
Figure Three	The Musical Experience	26
Figure Four	O Virtus Sapientiae	27
Figure Five	Turning Song	151
Figure Six	From the Moon	152
Figure Seven	A Mince Pie or a Pudding	152
Figure Eight	Marching Tune	153
Figure Nine	Solemn Song	153
Figure Ten	Shuffling Song	154
Figure Eleven	Mother's Love	158
Figure Twelve	Drink ye of Mother's Wine	159
Figure Thirteen	Sweep as I go	162

Acknowledgements

This book has taken many years to write and even longer to be published. I am extremely grateful to the Episcopal Divinity School in Cambridge Massachusetts for my time as a Procter Fellow there which enabled me to do the primary research. Here I was helped particularly by Professor Carter Heyward, Professor Kwok Pui Lan and Jane Ring Frank. I am also grateful to all the people who have been interviewed for this book and the research students whose work I have quoted. These have enabled current hidden voices and hidden stories to be made more public. They are the primary sources which balance the use of more secondary sources in other areas of this study. The use of secondary texts was necessary because of the considerable historical period covered by the book. Other parts of the book have been drawn from over forty years of sharing in alternative liturgy groups in the UK and beyond. I am extremely grateful to all the members of these who encouraged my creativity and were often the first people to sing my pieces. I owe a particular debt to Catholic Women's Network – now Women Word Spirit and WomenChurch, Reading.

Various friends have encouraged me to persevere when the project ran into problems and affirmed me and the need for such a publication, such as Professor Mary Grey, Professor Tina Beattie, Professor Michael Finnissy, the Rev Dr Janet Wootton and Professor Lisa Isherwood. I am grateful to Ianthe Pratt and the Association for Inclusive Language who enabled me to disseminate my material first, Dr Carol Boulter who funded my first recording and Hannah Ward who compiled the index. Stainer and Bell have played a significant part in my journey in publishing my hymns, songs and chants and for permission to use those that are their copyright in this book (Boyce-Tillman 2006a). My good friends the Rev David Page, Dr Carol Boulter and Susan Lawes have helped my journey through the difficult times and Elizabeth and Stanley Baxter at Holy Rood House have enabled me to try out new ideas and supported and critiqued them. My two sons – Matthew and Richard – have also encouraged and helped me.

I am grateful to Peter Lang and Lucy Melville for enabling it to be published and to Oliver Osman for helping me to prepare my final manuscript. At the University of Winchester I am grateful to my colleagues in Foundation Music and The Centre for the Arts as Well-being for their encouragement and Professor Elizabeth Stuart and Professor Joy Carter for their continual support in the process.

— THE REV DR JUNE BOYCE-TILLMAN MBE,
Professor of Applied Music,
University of Winchester, UK. February 2014
Convenor of The Centre for the Arts as Well-being
Extraordinary Professor, North-West University, South Africa

Introduction

Gender stereotypes have been challenged in many musicological texts; but the alliance of theology and music in the Christian liturgical tradition has taken much longer to interrogate the challenges posed by the gendered nature of church leadership in many areas of its life. The title of this book draws on the Report of the Archbishop's Commission on Church Music from 1992 which was entitled *In Tune with Heaven*. It questions the absence of women's voices and experiences from the literature and attempts to redress this.

This is all the more perplexing because the patron saint of music in the West is a woman. It is now a disputed story; but St Cecilia has held her place and is celebrated in many churches on her feast day by means of music of one kind or another. However, her image has not been altogether helpful as Susan Cook and Judy Tsou pointed out in 1994:

> St Cecilia was in many ways the *patronized* saint of music, limited, by her sex, to a passive role, idealized, even swooning, muse or performer but not as an active creator. Cecilia thus presented cultural notions of acceptable female practice; she played the organ but she did not compose organ symphonies. St Cecilia presents just one example of gendered musical activity. (Cook and Tsou 1994 p. 1)

Discovering this writing clarified my own journey into church music in the UK in the Anglican tradition in the 1940s, 1950s and 1960s. Cultural role models of this kind had dug deeply into the world into which I was being initiated.

When I first started the research for this book while a Visiting Fellow at the Episcopal Divinity School in Cambridge, Massachusetts I thought I was driven from a story from my childhood: at the age of eight a singer was required to sing *O Jesus I have promised* in the Church Hall as part of a play. Various children came forward, both girls and boys. A girl was selected for the role. When she offered herself as a chorister for the liturgy she was told that only boys sang in CHURCH. No explanation was offered. She could only assume that a [male] God preferred the sound of boys' voices.

This story epitomises a deep controversy in church music and for much of my life it represented a deep woundedness in my experiencing of music. Why did God not want my voice? Why could I not be part of the church musical ritual? Why could I not sing in the beautiful cathedrals and have that wonderful education? Why can I still not sing in a cathedral ensemble? Why has it been so difficult to get pieces by women composers into the repertoire of churches? Why do women do many of the unpaid musical jobs in churches and the men take the paid ones? Are women not in tune with heaven (Archbishops' Commission 1992)? These questions strike at the heart of the powerful alliance between a patriarchal theology and a theology of music. When I related this story I was accused by some more traditionalist church leaders of starting from a position of anger. I have spent many years examining these remarks and now see that it was more a position of lament and initially of incomprehension. This book may be seen as an attempt to understand this position. Also, further reflection and encounters with not only the joyful stories of the choral world of the Church but also the sadnesses of the less appreciative participants, have led me to reflect that I may have been spared a quite bruising culture. I might also have been given a chance to see the dominant tradition more clearly by being placed outside it. This book therefore is a reflection by an outsider. In it, I hope to set out some frames for viewing the tradition and illustrate them by various vignettes from church history. It will attempt to make the hidden voices of history more audible as well as showing how entrenched cultural patterns were and how we might reconstruct heaven so that women's voices might be heard.

My Theological Background

My story described above took place in the context of rural Anglicanism in which I explored a number of different theological positions ranging from a fairly conservative evangelicalism to a quite liberal Anglo-Catholicism.

While working in London in Notting Hill post the 1960s race riots, I worshipped with the Methodists for seven years – quite 'high' Methodists who tried a great deal of liturgical experiment and innovation. I have enjoyed Quaker worship, but in the end have re-housed myself back in my home tradition of Anglicanism and am an ordained priest. The journey to this was long and complex and involved exploring several other faith traditions and some of the more 'New Age' variety before finding this resting place along the way.

My main spiritual nurturing has been received through a variety of 'alternative' liturgy groups listed below, that all embrace a strong feminist theology (although not all of them are composed exclusively of women). However, I write hymns and liturgical music which are finding a place worldwide in more 'mainstream' Christianity (Boyce-Tillman 2006a). The discovery of the Wisdom traditions has been very important for me. Julian of Norwich was an important guide in the journey. She came at a time in my life when I was sort of at a crossroads and experiencing quite severe depression. Largely through the ministrations of the Beatles, Transcendental Meditation came to the UK with the Maharishi; and I learned it in the same way as hundreds of others from diverse backgrounds. Despite being brought up in the Church I had encountered nothing like the peace of the twenty-minute practice and there was no one to talk about it to in Christianity which seemed to regard it as devilish. Then I found Gonville ffrench-Beytagh, ex-Dean of Johannesburg, with whom I discovered the Christian contemplative tradition, the way of unknowing and of darkness. That for me was the beginning of the Wisdom journey, which was tightly tied up with the aspect of the feminine in God. I think, as with so much of my life, at first I did it my way. For me it was to do with finding the other half of one of the binary divides that characterise the Christian tradition:

- The darkness that balances the light,
- The unknowing that balances the aggressive pursuit of knowledge which has led theology in patriarchal form to reduce God to a series of creedal statements,
- The feminine images to balance the male images,
- The accepting God to balance the judgmental God that had peopled my childhood fears,

- The intuitive God who cannot be held by the reasoning mind alone.

I think I would describe her (Wisdom) at that time as a blessed all-embracing darkness where I could take refuge from the worst of the excesses of the so-called Enlightenment that took its stranglehold on Europe in the late eighteenth century (Boyce-Tillman 2007b). Thanks to this rediscovery I was able to pursue (with much struggling) my route into the Anglican priest-hood that resulted in my ordination to the priesthood in September 2007.

My Musical Background

Musically also the patterns of knowing that had been presented by my education were very limited. Trained as a musician at Oxford University in the 1960s where sexist jokes were the common currency of the lecture hall and, in general, unquestioned by men or women, I am now attempting to bring together in this book insights from theology and musicology. This is because for most of pre-Enlightenment Europe most 'high art' music was written for the Church, the 'objective' underpin of much musicology can be laid at the door of the notion of God as constructed by mainstream theologians during that period.

My further musical exploration represented an embracing of a musical freedom; this was not true of the classical training I received at Oxford University, consisting as it did of history, analysis, and written composition in the style of composers from 1550 to 1900. My grandfather had been the dance band pianist in a New Forest village and played by ear; but he wanted his granddaughter to enter the world of classical music (epitomised by his 78rpm recording of Jose Iturbi playing Chopin's *Fantaisie Impromptu*). I was too young when he died to realise what I had missed by not learning his skills. In fact, as a child, I was glad of the containment of the classical tradition. I knew where I was by learning how to read the notes and enjoyed the poise and elegance of Mozart and Haydn who were my favourites at that time. I was terrified of improvisation in any form. The printed notes offered the security that I needed. It was later through exploring sound with children in school that I found that freedom to improvise; and this was followed by playing folk guitar and (much later) buying a djembe. Twenty-five years after leaving Oxford I dared to improvise in public and felt that I could claim that musical freedom.

My route into Oxford consisted largely of a set of challenges called examinations and as a child I remember my musical life as a series of hurdles. No sooner was one surmounted the next one loomed on the horizon. The notion of using music for relaxation was not a possibility and indeed was discouraged by teachers of musical analysis who despised what they called 'wallpaper' music. They used to set listening up as something to engage the whole mind and certainly never to be indulged in while doing something else. It took the discovery of therapeutic massage to introduce me to the use of music to nurture and heal, as an accompaniment to other activities.

Although I composed a few original pieces at Oxford (not as part of the academic course) I wrote few classical pieces for the next twenty years. Oxford had taught me that composers were usually male, German- or Italian-speaking and dead. It was during a prolonged illness that I started to compose again. The process of doing so was actually part of my own healing process, that in combining and recombining the ideas musically I was actually changing parts of myself. At this point composing was essentially an individual activity done at the piano or on paper, as I had been taught it to be. I was a pianist, an essentially individual instrument. I enjoyed accompanying but the examination system dictated that I was always examined as an individual. My parents could only afford for me to learn the cello in a class, so advanced orchestral playing was not available. Choral singing was the only communal music-making experience open to me. Playing folk guitar for large gatherings in the 1960s offered me an experience of communal music-making that had largely been denied.

My first move into other musical traditions was the protest song movement in Notting Hill in the 1960s. I remember the sense of rebellion in going back to Oxford to sing at my college and using a song entitled *O that greedy landlord* which I accompanied on the guitar in my essentially classical programme. The scene was set for the embracing of musical diversity as a way of exploring different parts of my own psyche. It has led me through various New Age groups, into ethnic traditions and an exploration of the tenets of music therapy. At first I was concerned about the diversity and discrepancies between what was the dominant tradition for me – classical music – and the other ones. Now I rejoice in the diversity and realise that each represents a different aspect of my persona and can be respected in the same way as I taught respect for difference in the course on World Musics. This is as true internally as it is externally in terms of society.

Through these other traditions, especially the drumming, I discovered a much greater awareness of the role of my body in music-making. Although I necessarily spent much time on technical exercises in learning the piano and was aware of how the state of my physical health affected my singing, the tradition I was being initiated into did not show a great concern for the role of the body and concentrated largely on the role of the mind which was seen to be the ruler of the body. I sang in church (but not in the choir) for as long as I can remember and was a deeply religious child. When later I did sing in a choir that included girls, I found that most of the members of the church choir had little sense of the religious meaning of music (less so often than the congregation). It took explorations into Hinduism and New Age to discover a group of people who genuinely believed in the transcendent power of music and indeed, sometimes linked this with the embodied art of dancing.

What Does this Book Hope to Do?

It was in those various journeys that this book was born. It seeks to examine the values that underpin Christian musical liturgical traditions primarily in Europe and the USA with a view to understanding where women are situated within or without these traditions. It does not set out to be a definitive history of women in these traditions but simply to give some small vignettes that illustrate a variety of positions that they have occupied in various denominations – and thus make their often hidden contributions more visible. It will examine these through a particular set of lenses developed from my philosophical understanding of the nature of the musical experience – like what musical materials are used, what expressive character is created and how it is constructed. Before the Enlightenment there would have been a congruence between the value systems of music and the prevailing spiritual frame. Various contemporary writers like Noirin Ni Riain (2011) have attempted to restore this relationship in her book *Theosony*:

> Through the ear, although not exclusively, revelation from God can freely enter and be completed. One important way of being with God is through sound; the auditory is a direct invitation out of oneself towards the Divine. Sensory perception of God's self-communication is vital for humanity and no one sense exists or operates in isolation in the work of the divine communication. (Ni Riain 2011 p. 34)

This book will look at the value systems and the spiritual experience separately and also try in the final chapter to bring them together again. It will examine how the value systems and the spiritual frames have served the work of women working in liturgical and religious music.

The tradition of Christianity in its first three centuries saw women in positions of authority liturgically and musically in some traditions as well as a fluid theology which included feminine figures in the notion of the Divine. The subsequent loss of the feminine in the Divine and women's authority in the Church are inextricably linked together. After this came a male trinity which dominated theology with characteristics such as triumphalism, clarity, order, eternality and unity. People looked in this divine mirror and saw male values. When the Church lost its power post-Enlightenment these values passed into the apparently ungendered world of aesthetics. Although there has been evidence of a feminine Wisdom tradition that has surfaced occasionally in Christianity, this has often been more hidden and less public. Women have been systematically excluded from public music-making traditions in Christianity. The last half of the twentieth century has seen an attempt to unearth the hidden theological tradition and to encourage women to write liturgical material. Although this is finding some expression in publications, the mainstream of the Church protects its patriarchal structures. As churchgoing declines in the UK, it is often the more liberal thinkers that leave the Church, leaving behind them a more conservative rump and a growing number of Christian fundamentalists anxious to preserve the maleness of God as a core belief justified by Jesus' regular use of the term Father for God. The centrality of hymnody to many traditions means that it is important that the insights of feminist theologians are encapsulated in the songs of Christianity, if they are to be disseminated. Inclusive language is slowly being accepted. Folk material (which necessarily includes women in its process of oral transmission) and material by women is appearing, although there is a perceived lack of musical expertise among the women. The conflux in the late twentieth century of a belief in a God that is partly or wholly feminine and women in positions of authority is the first time the two have coincided in Church history since the first three centuries of Christianity. This may herald the beginning of women's entrance in the public musical traditions of the Church. However, there is no sign of the acceptance of the mature women's voice in the choral traditions of significant churches and cathedrals in England. The women's voice choir does not have the standing of the male voice choir in secular society if we consider, for example, the way that Women's Institute choirs are rated alongside the Welsh male voice choir tradition.

The most accepted public corporate voice of the Church has been a group of men. Here, as in other areas, the model of the Body of Christ is constructed as male. Much of the material by women is being used primarily in small liturgy groups and services concentrating on what are perceived as feminist or women's issues. There is great difficulty in getting material by women better known. I hold to my basic belief that it is for women to realise their creativity and have courage to sing, to play, to compose, and to improvise within the Church; for music is power. It is in this courageous spirit of empowering women by making their stories visible that this book was written.

The first chapter sets up a frame for examining musical activity through a variety of lenses (Boyce-Tillman 2006b). This will be used for the analytical work in the rest of the book. It draws on a variety of theorists – some from feminism, some from cultural studies and some from ethnomusicology. I have chosen here to concentrate on the musicological literature as this gives a frame for thinking about the music and assumptions of more popular music literature and musicians outside of the Academy that are often drawn from these sources. The music itself will be encountered and viewed through the frame developed here in the subsequent chapters. Traditional musicology has looked at music primarily from the point of view of how it is constructed. Ethnomusicology caused a revisiting of the materials used for music-making with the study of organology. Expression has been in general downplayed despite the fact that it is an emotional bond that holds most people to music. Its study is often confined to the area of music therapy. So different academic traditions have valued different aspects of the musical experience; this book suggests that there is a need for it to be regarded once again in its entirety. Until developments in cultural studies were included in musicology in the late twentieth century there was little attempt at dealing with the values that surround music or are implicit within it, except passing references to the end of the age of patronage in the nineteenth century. Music was traditionally presented as value-free. Spirituality had already disappeared from the academic agenda (except for departments of theology or religious studies) when the discipline of musicology as we know it now was being developed.

The next chapters are vignettes of times in Christian history when women have held positions of authority in the tradition and therefore some control in shaping the dominant musical tradition. It will examine the early years of Christianity, Hildegard of Bingen (as a woman who not only composed liturgical music but also wrote about music), the Italian nun composers of the sixteenth and seventeenth centuries, Ann Lee and the Shakers, women hymn-writers and a variety of people now working in liturgical music (drawn largely from interview material from the English-speaking world) – both women and men. Some of these are well established within the mainstream churches but others have left it, are challenging it, or hanging onto it by a fingernail. The final chapter draws all of these together and suggests ways forward.

The book will show how the prevailing value systems in the areas of theology and music have controlled the way in which liturgical music has developed and will be of interest to all who wish to examine how the dominant culture values are reflected in liturgical practice (Foucault/Gordon 1980).

Summary

The route into this book has been a journey that has included academic scholarship, personal friendship and musical performance and composition. It is only a beginning in examining what a narrative of Christian liturgical music that includes women's contribution might look like. It will be of interest to any concerned about women's systematic exclusion from positions of authority in the Church (particularly in the area of liturgy) and show how what is true of admission to the priesthood is also true of the musical aspect of liturgy. The narratives in this book will show how the alliance of Christianity with the surrounding musical culture has not served women well.

The limitations of size and cost has meant that certain choices have been made as to which areas (called vignettes) of the history of liturgical music are explored; but I hope the scene is set for a more comprehensive historical survey of a tradition that has largely been hidden. I have indicated some of the signposts that might direct such a journey and I look forward to continuing on it with old and new companions – both supportive and infuriating, both dead and living, from the human and the natural world. The past is always with us and is always shaping the present. I hope that this book gives some pointers as to how it can be seen as a source of energy and power for men and women – in fact, as the Music of Wisdom – a tradition that is truly inclusive and can contain these controversies within itself.

CHAPTER I

Controversies in Musicology

Story

> When the men in New Guinea are away at war, or on a long journey, their women beat upon booming gongs and sing to hasten the coming of the new moon ... No man composed the music ... No audience listens ... They are not doing this to entertain anybody, even themselves. This is woman's music made by women only, for a woman's purpose ... Theirs is an incantation of singing to invoke the powers that govern the rhythm of life ...
>
> — DRINKER 1948 p. 3

About 500 BC [sic] there fell on these hopeful civilizations of our earth a kind of creeping blight. It did not come all at once, but slowly in a change here and a change there that may have seemed at first a great improvement in the organization of life or a correction of local abuse ... But the men, in taking over, did it crudely. Their idea of making sure that their children were their own was to shut women up from the moment they could bear a child ... In China they achieved this in the end by so crippling the women that they could not move beyond their homes ... As exemplified by the Chinese, Hindus, Jews, and Greeks – four widely separated peoples of the ancient world – women's authority in music waned at the same time that it weakened for emphasizing her special way of life ... A new theory was persuasively expressed by Aristotle to the effect that *only* men transmitted the spark of life and that women were merely incubators of the male seed. 'The Father alone is Creator; the Mother is but the Nurse.' He even taught that woman was man in arrested development – a deficit of nature ... Woman's fundamental assumption for symbolic thinking has always rested upon her faith in herself as a creative being, pre-eminently potent in the making of both children of the flesh and those of the imagination ... It was only gradually that the serious consequences of women's altered value to civilization affected women musicians. Changes in religious and musical customs did not occur everywhere at the same time, nor did women suddenly lose their prestige in the religious ceremony ... Finally, when the mother-musician became denuded of her musical heritage, wedding songs and laments – always womens greatest contribution to song – no longer appeared in the lists of new compositions. And it is an undeniable fact that the quality of music was vitiated for several centuries until men developed another idiom from an entirely different inspiration ... One of the direct results of the revolution, and one which profoundly affected women in relation to music, was the twilight of the goddess.

— DRINKER 1948 pp. 127–42

The opening story from a remarkable book by Sophie Drinker looks back to a golden age based on archaeological artefacts from various sources and some of the hidden women's musical traditions today. There are some who would rubbish such historical utopias for women, but there are within the story hints at what the subjugated ways of knowing for Western music might look like.

This chapter will explore the value systems of western musical culture – dominated as they have been for some time by the western classical canon – a patriarchal theology leading to the implicit assumption that women cannot be 'in tune with heaven'. We will start with a form that expresses this most clearly because here text, drama and music are combined so the themes are more clearly discerned:

Opera is not forbidden to women. That is true. Women are its jewels, you say, indispensable for every festival. No prima donna, no opera. But the role of the jewel, a decorative objective, is not the deciding role; and on the opera stage women perpetually sing their eternal undoing. The emotion is never more poignant than at the moment when the voice is lifted to die. Look at these heroines. With their voices they flap their wings, their arms writhe, and then there they are, dead on the ground. Look at these women who fill the theatre accompanied by penguins in uniforms that scarcely vary: they are present, they are decorative. They are present for the dispatch of women like themselves. And when the curtain closes to let the singers take the last bow, there are the women kneeling in a curtsey, their arms filled with flowers; and there, beside them, the producer, the conductor, the set designer.

> Occasionally a ... But you wouldn't know how to say it: a produceress? A conductress? Not many women have access to the great masculine scene surrounding this spectacle thought up to adore and also to kill, the feminine character. (Clement 1989 pp. 5–6)

Because of the systematic persecution of the feminine in Western culture we find the same forces operating in theology and music. There are as many stories to be found now of the ridiculing and marginalisation of women's music on the Internet as there are in the area of women priests. A member of the International Alliance of Women in Music[1] describes an adjudicator's disparaging description of Karen Tanaka's piano piece as 'just a mood piece' lacking in musical content which resulted in students who performed it being marked lower than those playing the 'standard' repertoire.

This chapter will examine the writings of people (mostly women) critical of the traditional field of musicology to see how their critique of the traditional value systems of western classical music relate to those of feminist theologians on western theology and how these relate to subjugated ways of knowing and the values of the musical academy which have increasingly dominated the musical scene. The development of this elite academy has had disastrous consequences for music-making in Western culture. One of these is that most people – both women and men – define themselves as failures. In a recent conversation with a woman at an interfaith gathering she defined herself as a musician by these standards: 'I am not really a musician, I mean, I don't have Grade 8 or anything like that.'[2]

So this chapter will unpack the values of the Academy. To do this it will set out a model of musical experience as having four domains and show how the expansion of the traditional limitations within the domain of Value will affect other areas of the total musical experience. It will then examine how revisiting this domain will affect the other domains of the experience.

Since the Enlightenment, Western thought (especially as Music struggled to hold its place in the Academy) followed the valuing of objectivity of the dominant value system and concentrated on the cognitive aspects

---

1　Becky Billock, DMA candidate, University of Washington in mailing list discussion March 2003.
2　Unpublished conversation in Tooting, London in 2006.

of music and therefore devalued other aspects of the musical experience. Notions of beauty and aesthetic excellence have been based in the area of the way in which music is constructed – the cognitive aspects of music – rather than the way in which it is experienced. Similar charges have been made about the relationship between academic theology and experience by feminist theologians. It would be interesting to speculate what would have happened to our approaches to music in Western culture, if the basic premise of the dominant culture had been 'I feel therefore I am' or 'I pray therefore I am' rather than 'I think therefore I am' with its concentration on rationality as the hallmark of 'humanness'. What, however, happens if we look at a model of the musical experience that tries to reclaim a rounded approach to music?

Feminist theorists have charted the growth and increasing dominance within the classical music tradition of the concept of the musical canon (Goehr 1992, Citron 1993). This is a construct in the area of what is 'valuable'. It set up a model of Western Art Music moving smoothly from masterpiece to masterpiece and master composer to master composer in an orderly sequence moving continually forward by means of a process of innovation from about 1550 to the present day or at least 1950. However,

> Women have exercised minimal power in the formation and semiology of the canon in Western art music. (Citron 1993 p. 40)

The construct of the master composer underpins the model based on philosophers like Nietzsche (Citron 1993 p. 49) who claimed ephemerality as the characteristic of women's creations. Creativity has traditionally been linked with male potency

> Creation, which involves the mind, is reserved for male activity; procreation, which involves giving birth, is applied to women ... God is actualized as male and referred to as He, Lord, and King. This forms the basis of the connections between creator and male, divinity and creativity, and divinity and male. Created in God's image, man assumes the potential if not the actuality of these characteristics. (Citron 1993 pp. 45, 46)

The result of this is that a woman composer often feels isolated and without a past (Citron 1993 p. 66). Virginia Woolf (Citron 1993 p. 68) sees a general problem for female creators who have to resort to such justifications of herself as being 'only a woman' or as being as 'good as a man' and thereby rejecting her female identity, sometimes very dramatically by using a male pseudonym.[3] These refrains run like a leitmotif through women composers' accounts of their lives and works.

In this construction, Bach and Beethoven are often regarded as the Old and New Testaments of the musical Bible and have often been treated as such by the historians of western music. Elisabeth Schüssler Fiorenza writes powerfully of the role of androcentric interpretations of the Bible in the history of women's oppression (Fiorenza 1990 p. 32). The way in which the Bible functions as an oppressive document for women is very similar to the role the figures of Bach and Beethoven have played in constraining women in the Western classical tradition. Still, for example, when I am asked to think of 'a composer' the immediate image is of the busts of those two composers that sat on my music teacher's piano. How similar is this to the role that God as Father in the Bible – with its associated visual images – has played in the position of women theologically?

The notion of the canonical progress of musical history is based on a Darwinian view of history which sees the processes as 'objectively' sifting what is good from what is bad. Carr's book on history in general challenged this in 1963:

> The facts are really not at all like fish of the fishmonger's slab. They are like fish swimming about in a vast and sometimes inaccessible ocean; and what the historian catches will depend partly on chance, but mainly on what part of the ocean he chooses to fish in and what tackle he chooses to use – these two factors being, of course, determined by the kind of fish he wants to catch. By and large, the historian will get the kind of facts he wants. History means interpretation. (Carr 1963 p. 26)

3   Rebecca Clarke (1886–1979) had pieces rejected under her name that were accepted under her male pseudonym Anthony Trent. Some of Fanny Hensel Mendelssohn's songs were published in the name of her brother, Felix.

Feminist musicologists took up the opportunities offered by this decon-struction of traditional views on the nature of history. In 1986, Jane Bowers and Judith Tick compiled a collection of historical studies about women – the 'first written by musicologists from different specialisations within the discipline' (Bowers and Tick 1986 p. 4). They included work by scholars focusing on a variety of time periods. In this way they were able to evalu-ate women's contributions to Western Music over an eight-hundred-year period – a period that roughly coincides with the development of nota-tion between 1150 and 1950, including four essays on music before 1600. Their book reflected new criteria for what is 'valuable' in the history of western music. It was an inspiration to many scholars to search for female role models in the Western Art music traditions.

As feminist philosophies developed in other areas, musicians worked them out in musicology but more often in areas around the edge of it like music education. Roberta Lamb runs a listserve for those interested in this area. Drawing on the writings of Audre Lorde (Lorde 1984) and bell hooks (hooks 1994) she identifies the following as what she has learned:

- The value of passionate knowing
- The power of self determination
- The need to create space to 'protect [women's] genius'
- The significance of feminist insights for men and women (Lamb 2000)

The insights of sociologists and social philosophers of music started to create a new view of history which identifies the processes of marginali-sation within it and how they function. Carol Robertson, in her revisit-ing of theories underpinning ethnomusicology interestingly entitled *The ethnomusicologist as midwife*, writes how the marginalised have developed strategies for survival:

> I want to approach these issues by looking at the relationship between what we have valued in scholarship as *mainstream* and as *marginal* and by examining the ever-shifting relationship between the *center* and the *periphery* ... Cultural synergy may rest in the hands of those who are willing to wear many masks, play many roles, and defy the stasis of the mainstream. Change, when seen as a constant in any living

tradition, always seems to yield a fool or a trickster who embodies the paradox of experience and who transforms the perception of truths in order to open discourse between the center and the periphery. (Robertson 1993 pp. 108, 124)

Ethnomusicology, based as it is in the discipline of anthropology, has from its beginning paid more attention to context than traditional musicology. Marcia Herndon (Herndon 2000) describes, in the book *Music and Gender*, the creation of the Study Group on Music and Gender by the International Council for Traditional Music with the declared aim of including gender in all musical analysis:

> Most approaches thus far have been less theoretical than descriptive, definitional and methodological. The study group's initial efforts often focused on women's music, or women's roles in music cultures [this anthology includes the role of tea-maker in its analysis of roles in a Pelaminni music group], because this information had often been neglected whether the scholar was male or female. Considerable time and effort were also expended in distinguishing sex from gender, as well as exploring concepts of androgyny and more ambiguous areas of gender blurring [as is hinted at in the literature on older women in some cultures]. Now that scholars have filled some of the gaps, particularly with the women 'missing' from the literature on various musical cultures, this volume begins to situate gender in its proper place as a major factor in musical exegesis and analysis. (Herndon 2000 p. 348)

She sees ethnomusicologists as dealing with 'living musics in a synchronic way', whereas musicologists deal with 'historical musics in a diachronic way.' She sees the beginning of a merging of the fields (Herndon 2000 p. 357). This has resulted in a division in the ranks of the theoreticians of music between those upholding the values of traditional musicology and those in the 'alternative' musicology camp, some of whom see the entire music experience as a question of values. Rose Rosengard Subotnik, identifying the problems of the career of a woman with children in academe, stresses the problems of finding a 'middle' ground (Subotnik 1996 p. xxvi), a position that I have tried to embrace with the ideas set out in Chapter 8. The result of this is that many feminist musicologists present articles that include a variety of readings of the same situation. In her book each article is 'an argument between two views' Rose Rosengard Subotnik struggles to retain the 'autonomous and nonautonomous views of music' (Subotnik 1996 p. xxviii).

But the ideas of feminist theorists have notably failed to influence the mainstream of musicology in the same way as mainstream theology has chosen to ignore the insights of feminist theologians:

> Indeed one of the signs that the discipline has even noticed the challenges feminism has presented elsewhere is that musicology appears to be in the vanguard of anti-feminist backlash. Norton's specially reprinted collections from The New Grove Dictionary of Music ... are entitled 'Masters of Italian Opera' 'Masters of the Second Viennese School'... There was also a prestigious new series of books and videos on the various periods of music history from Prentice Hall called *Man and his Music* ... If music has lagged behind in admitting feminist criticism to its list of legitimate areas of inquiry, it is way ahead of the game in its efforts to expunge all evidence that feminism ever existed. (McClary 1991 pp. 5–6)

So the central questions of the literature are summed up by Bowers and Tick:

> How have prejudice and discrimination – roughly parallel to belief and behavior – shaped the history of women in music? (Bowers and Tick 1986 p. 11)

Values and Patriarchy

I have written more fully about this elsewhere (Boyce-Tillman 2006b, 2007a). In my earlier writing (Boyce-Tillman 2000a) – based on the work of the philosopher Foucault (Foucault/Gordon 1980) and the work of anthropologists like Gooch (Gooch 1972) – I built a notion of subjugated ways of knowing. These are ways of knowing that are not validated by the dominant culture of the time. The trick of the controllers of a culture is to make these meanings/values seem fixed and given – even God-given – when, in fact, they are cultural constructs. Many writers have identified the role of myths in the maintenance of the apparent truth of the dominant values, which suggest a fixed version of a value system that transcends temporality. The role of mythologies is carefully explored by Barthes (1972) and Mary Midgley in *The Myths we live by* (2003). They represent a sort of pattern or grid that gives meaning to a range of experiences (Pollock 1984). Gender relations, in particular, are often supported by myths. In western culture the Odyssey and the Aeneid have played a significant part in the roles which women are expected to occupy.

Michael Kirwan in reworking mimetic theory sees the possibility of transformation by means of reworking literature (Kirwan 2004 p. 123). This book explores how this might work in reworking the music. What we need is 'in place of a transcendent myth, any emotionally satisfying narrative that speaks to our humanity, we have created a materialistic religion that leaves us, as people, empty of an emotionally satisfying, shared purpose' (Clarke 2002 p. 233). The absence of such a myth Clarke sees as the deep root of human stress and 'may well be responsible for most fatal violence on others (murder) and in self (suicide), as well as for the much more frequent instances of lesser violence' (Clarke 2002 p. 306). I tried to set this out in a song:

> There stood in heaven a linden tree
> Whose leaves would heal the nations
> Of many colours, many shapes
> And each contained a story.
> CHORUS We'll tell the stories that heal the earth (×3)
> And bring it to rebirth
>
> Some stories fell as binding rope
> To keep the people tightly bound
> With laws and morals and beliefs.
> These stories had no hope
> CHORUS (Boyce-Tillman 2006a p. 158)

Nowhere is the power of the myth in Western society more clearly seen than in the area of motherhood which has played out in such myths as around men making artworks and women making babies. Myths associated with maternal instincts have been a cause of guilt for many women (Rye 2003 p. 6). Stephen Hunt (2005) explores how the Alpha course is maintaining powerful gendered myths within the Church and women's essentially domestic role. Kristin Aune also sees how the charismatic movement New Frontiers International (NFI) uses the Bible for the maintenance of these myths (Aune 2005 p. 2). Margaret Myers in her work on women's orchestras in Europe looks at the origin of the myths in the wider society:

The latter day Aristotelians – Schopenhauer, Nietszche, Weininger and in Sweden, Strindberg – were all the rage in the late nineteenth and early twentieth centuries. They were published and republished in cheap popular editions and quoted in daily newspapers and the popular press. Their ideas permeated most educated people's thinking. They were all thoroughly misogynist and denied women all creative and artistic capacity, as had their forefather, Aristotle, whose ideas had survived into modern times because they resonated with the ideas of the Church Fathers.

These misogynist ideas were projected on any woman who embarked on a public, professional career in occupations defined as masculine or creative. Such a woman had to be prepared for ridicule and castigation. She might be accused of being essentially male or essentially immoral. (Myers 2000 pp. 206–7)

Although many of these quotations are taken from feminist literature of one discipline or another, my use of the term subjugated ways of knowing rather than women's ways of knowing acknowledges that there are a variety of subjugated groups of which women are only one. There is a clear link between those who hold power – who in western culture have, in general, been patriarchs – and which ways of knowing will become subjugated. In a passage resembling that of Sophie Drinker at the opening of the chapter, this linkage was identified by Matilda Joslyn Gage in *Woman, Church and State* in her remarkable analysis in 1893:

The difference in civilization between Christian Europe and pagan Malabar at the time of its discovery was indeed great. While Europe, with its new art of printing, was struggling against the church for permission to use type – its institutions of learning few; its opportunities for education meager; its terrible inquisition crushing free thought and sending thousands each year to a most painful death; the uncleanness of its cities and the country such as to bring frequent visits of plague; its armies, its navies, with but one exception, imperfect; its women forbidden the right of inheritance, religious, political or household authority; the feminine principle entirely eliminated from divinity; a purely masculine God, the universal object of worship – all was directly opposite in Malabar. Cleanliness, peace, the arts, a just form of government, the recognition of the feminize – were found in Malabar ... under the missionaries sent by England to introduce her own barbaric ideas of God and man, this beautiful matriarchal civilization soon retrograded and was lost. (Gage 1893/1998 p. 7)

The Church has been a publicly masculinist organisation after the first few hundred years of Christianity as will be discussed in Chapter 2. This has had a devastating effect on generations of women. The Church has sought to control, for example, women's creative processes. Elizabeth Stuart Phelps Ward (writing in 1869) describes powerfully the effect that the patriarchal nature of the western Church had in her experience of church which was, significantly for this book, carried by its hymnody:

> For it came to seem to me, as I pondered these things in my own heart, that even the best and kindest forms of our prevailing beliefs had nothing to say to an afflicted woman that could help her much. Creeds and commentaries and sermons were made by men. What tenderest of men knows how to comfort his own daughter when her heart is broken. What can the doctrines do for the desolated by death? They were chains of rusty iron, eating into raw hearts. The prayer of the preacher was not much better; it sounded like the language of an unknown race to a despairing girl. Listen to the hymn. It falls like icicles on snow. Or, if it happen to be one of the old genuine outcries of the church, sprung from real human anguish or hope, it maddens the listener, and she flees from it, too sore a thing to bear the touch of holy music. (Ward 1896 pp. 97–8)

Carter Heyward (2003)in this diagram shows clearly the effects of patriarchy and shows the variety of those who are likely to become subjugated knowers.

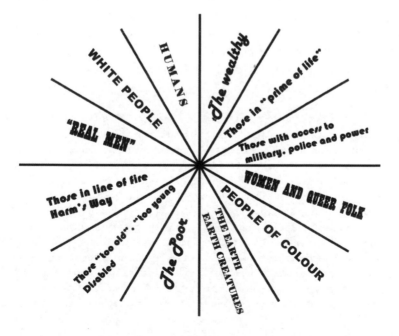

Figure One – People in Positions of Power

It is the value systems of these people, often linked together by the term patriarchy or heteropatriarchy, that will become dominant and these groups will put systems in place to see that they remain dominant, like prisons, mental hospitals and redundancy. As we see here it is not only women who are subjugated but a range of different people as well as the natural world; and, as such, the calls to examine the subjugated ways of knowing have come from many sources. Dominant ways of knowing develop into internalised 'self-policing' practices in subjugated knowers who imbibe the negative and disempowering mores of the surrounding culture:

> The gendered nature of socialization processes ensures that males and females internalize different *and unequal* self-understandings. (O'Grady 2005 pp. 6–7)

The people in power in a state often resort to violence to maintain their position as we shall see in the story of Mother Ann Lee and the Shakers in Chapter 5. In relation to women Helen O'Grady reworks this as internalised violence (O'Grady 2005 p. 2) which happens when women take on within themselves the dominant values of the surrounding society. We shall see how this still affects contemporary female musicians. The effect of the often violent enforcement of western values on indigenous culture has been devastating – musically and theologically as well as politically. My own experience of staying with native Canadians illustrates the differing value systems very clearly:

> I was privileged to spend some time with a native people in North America. I had been present at several sweat lodges at which a particular medicine man had been working. I had also purchased a small hand drum and he had consented to beat the Bear Spirit into it for me. One evening he was preparing for a sweat lodge and said that he needed a powerful woman to help him and sit alongside him. This would usually be his wife but she was unable to be there so would I help him. I was both honoured and terrified; but he said he would help me with the ritual and so I agreed to the role. The first round of prayer took place and he concluded it by saying that now June would sing a song about the eagle and the sunrise. It was here that I thought that I had met an insuperable problem. I knew no songs from the culture. But I remembered that in the songs I had heard each phrase started high and then went lower in order to bring the energy of the sky to the earth. So I started each phrase high and took it lower while singing about the eagle and the sunrise. It was

a powerful experience for me and my voice seemed to come from a place of power deep inside that I had not experienced before. With the prayer round ended we went outside to cool in the night air. 'Great song, June' said the leader of the sweat lodge. I was about to say that, of course, I had to make it up and then remembered from my previous conversations with some of the women singers that in this culture everything is given not the creation of an individual. So I replied: 'The Great Spirit gave it to me when I was in the Lodge.' (Boyce-Tillman 2007a pp. 23–4)

Here I was in a culture where the intuitive way of receiving musical material – construed as coming from a connection with a spiritual source – was the dominant way of knowing, not the individualistic, humanistic way of the individual composer creating an individual song from their own experience in their own personal subconscious. I had previously been in a women's sweat lodge after which the leader had said that she thought the Great Spirit had given her the whole of the song when she was in the Lodge and that previously she had only received part of it. In the West we would probably have said that we had not yet finished it and were working at completing it. However, the notion of receiving music in this way from a Divine source would not have been remarkable for Hildegard of Bingen in medieval Europe as we shall see in Chapter 3. She saw herself as composing nothing herself but receiving everything directly from God. In medieval Europe intuitive ways of receiving material were more acceptable than in contemporary secularised western culture.

The contemporary challenges to the dominant patriarchy come from a variety of groups with a variety of agendas; but the feelings of the subjugated knowers are often similar. Grace Ji-sun Kim calls it *han*:

> *Han* is not only an experience of women; it is a typical prevailing feeling of the Korean people, for the nation as a whole has endured many defeats and disasters ... *Han* is 'the suppressed, amassed and condensed experience of oppression caused by mischief or misfortune, so that it forms a kind of "lump" in one's spirit' (Kung 1990 p. 30). (Kim 2002 p. 57)

This links with notions of internalised self-policing, which will have more devastating effects on those who belong to a number of the groups of subjugated knowers – so that black women will be more disadvantaged than white and so on.

So what values are dominant in western culture? I have developed a model to identify some of them. Drawing on a wide variety of literatures from music, education, humanistic psychology (particularly Myers and McCaulley 1985, Myers 1993 and Assagioli 1994), sociology, gender studies and theology I have identified certain polarities which are in dynamic relationship.[4] This model identifies a number of polarities that are in dynamic relationship both within the self and within society (Boyce-Tillman 2007a).

The model presents a way of looking at the health of a society and a person. In a balanced person and a balanced society all the possibilities are held as of equal value but in most people and societies this is not the case. This will be because of the issues of power identified above and the establishment of a normative dominant discourse and internal self-policing. However, the more dominant one of the pairs that make up the polarities becomes, the more the alternative value system will tend to be projected onto the marginalised 'other'; which will consist of groups who have less power or whose power is tightly constrained.

In the model, these polarities are drawn as having a constant flow between them. Balance is defined as being when that flowing is fluid and dynamic. The subjugated and dominant knowings have to be in dialogue with one another to achieve a wholeness but this book will show how they have been more often in opposition rather than dialogue in the area of liturgical music. In this drawing the dominant values are on the right of the diagram.

---

4   There are dangers in what might be seen as a syncretic or 'hybrid' approaches to the various disciplines on which I have drawn, but it does serve to make the findings of one discipline accessible to others and in the Introduction I have drawn attention to the anthological nature of the book. This is line with the developments of the methodology of crystallisation (Ellingson 2009).

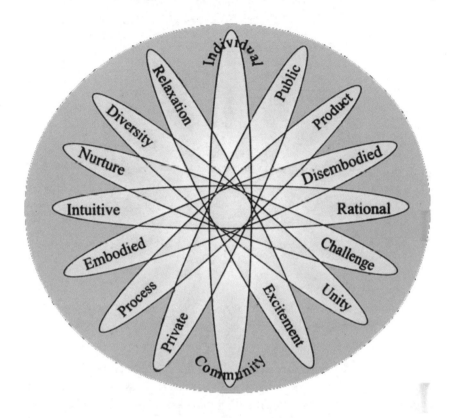

Figure Two: Dominant Ways of Knowing

To understand how these values have played out in music, I am using a model of the musical experience that I have developed growing out of research into children's musical development (Tillman 1987) and music and culture (Boyce-Tillman 1996b and 2000a). I have attempted to deconstruct the musical experience in a way that is, at the same time, both holistic and analytical. The model set out below identifies four interlocking domains – Materials, Expression, Construction, Values – which act as lenses through which the musical experience may be viewed and which come together to create the spiritual or liminal experience (Turner 1969, 1974):

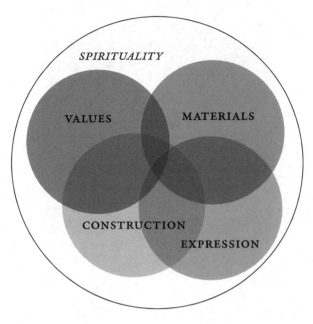

Figure Three: The Musical Experience

To take Bach's B Minor Mass, in the domain of Materials it uses a large choir, soloists and an orchestra. In the domain of Expression, it uses a variety of characters to represent the changing moods and atmosphere of the text for the Mass, like the gentleness of *Et incarnatus est* and the power of *Et resurrexit*. In the domain of Construction it uses a variety of different forms like fugue in various movements; and the scale of the forms means that it is unlikely it was designed to be used in a liturgical context. In the domain of Value it is held as a masterpiece within the western canon of music, is frequently recorded, and has maintained its place in classical music charts. It is a male piece with a patriarchal view of God and a patriarchal view of performance practice. In the Spiritual domain it represents an important statement about the liminal nature of the Christian Eucharist.

Now let us take Hildegard's antiphon (see Chapter 3) to Wisdom *O Virtus Sapientiae*:

Hildegard of Bingen   Hildegard of Bingen

Figure Four: O Virtus Sapientiae

Here we find much simpler Materials, an unaccompanied single vocal line designed for a medium sized community of women or a soloist using the church modes of the day. The Expression is closely related to the text as the two were received together from Divine inspiration (the way in which Hildegard's music was received the Divine source). There is clear word painting so that when the text speaks of a high wing the tune is at its highest whereas the wing that sweats in the earth is nearly the lowest point of the chant. The Construction has an improvisatory feel about it using small motifs which recur throughout the piece. The Values are that of a nurturing Wisdom figure using clear feminine imagery. The Spirituality is conceived within Hildegard's developing understanding of the image of God as interconnected with the entire universe and the relationality generated by that understanding. It has been used by contemporary feminist scholars as an example of the interface between feminist theology and musicology. I have explored it more fully in relation to congregational music in *Tune your Music to your heart* (Boyce-Tillman 2013).

As the problems for women's place in liturgical music lie in its reflection of the value systems of Western culture, I shall start with this area.

Values

If we look back at the model of value systems set out above we see that community is the subjugated value and the individual the dominant. This is based very heavily on the value placed on the male heroic journey in such myths as those of Odysseus and Aeneas where a young rich (usually European) male hero finds himself by means of negotiating a series of challenges. These he faces largely on his own and survives by following his own individualised destiny which is sometimes associated with Bildungsroman or maturation narratives. Such a journey was never open to the poor or women whose task was to stay at home doing the circular community-building tasks of maintaining the domestic community. This has been reflected in a variety of ways in music. First of all music is seen as disconnected from its environment; and this has led to Western classical music often regarding itself as value-free. In fact, the work of feminist theorists and sociologists of music has attempted to show that music is as much a particular language contextualised in a particular time and place with its associated Value-systems, as it is a universal language.

Musical performances contain both implicit and explicit Value systems, both of them associated with its place in the surrounding culture. The implicit Value systems are within the sounds of the music themselves and result from the mores in which the music was created. For example, a single conductor controlling a group of performers represents the benevolent dictatorships that characterised the political structures of many European countries when the music of the canon was created. The notion of a single composer who constructs a piece alone and hands it to performers who mediate it to an audience reflects notions of a transcendent God creating the universe and handing it to human beings. The rooting of musicology in this tradition links it tightly into these elitist,[5] exclusive structures:

> *The Magic Flute* is an opera in which structures idealized or even consecrated as universal are selective and exclusionary to the end. (Subotnik 1996 p. 34)

This awareness of the relationship of music to community is a very significant event in the development of Western musicology (Subotnik 1996 pp. 209–10).

The idea of explicit Value is concerned with the way music is placed within the culture – the context – such as how much money is involved or the intention of the music – like for therapeutic or charitable purposes and, significantly for women, who controls the gates to large public spaces like churches and concert halls. However, these two areas of Value interact powerfully. We shall see below how heated debates become about the intrinsic meaning of instrumental music; but as soon as a text or story

---

5   Jazz and many ethnic traditions are more democratic in their creating processes and the New Age and community-making traditions have egalitarianism at the heart of their principles.

are present, Value systems will be explicit within it, whether these are the heterosexual values of the traditional love song or the maternal love of the lullaby. All musical pieces stand in relation to the culture in which they are created, even if that relationship, like the protest songs of the sixties, is to challenge that culture. Various forms in the history of music theatre have reflected the racism, sexism and elitism of their cultures, as illustrated in opera above. We have also already seen women dedicated to making people aware of these Value systems (Ring Frank 2003). This link with positions of privilege and power makes the absence of issues of gender in these debates more serious (Kisliuk 2000 p. 26), particularly in the Church:

Our society places a high premium on unity and nowhere has this been clearer than in liturgical music. Various denominations have maintained their unity by assuming a single musical style and diversity has been *between* various denominations rather than within them. The gatekeepers of a particular tradition have often exercised an almost fascist control on what is or is not acceptable using words like 'good' as if there were some 'objective' measure of musical 'goodness' somewhere in the universe, when in fact, it means subscribing to patriarchal value systems. This was clear in the attempts made to get the dundun drum into a contemporary Christian Church (Eluyefa 2010), where it was not seen as an acceptable instrument.

The embracing of egalitarian approaches to music potentially means the embracing of a more diverse approach to musical judgements rather than the monolithic value systems that have characterised musicological analytical systems designed to help with these judgements. Susan McClary sees 'those fused and confused, messy, paradoxical, and contradictory cultural practices' created by capitalism as a cause for delight (Shepherd 1993 p. 65).

Many theorists have seen musicology as inextricably linked with middle-class value systems. Musicologists come from the middle-class; they are indeed likely to be moving up within its spectrum. It is middle-class values that they project and seek to protect (Kerman 1985 pp. 11 and 36): 'Why do our idealistic western conceptions of human universality too often end up as apologias for the privileged?' (Subotnik 1996 p. 191).

The assertion of the possibility of a united, universal view of music has caused problems for other cultures:

> Those arguing for an Elect find it hard to grasp the relationship of their own uni-
> versalistic ideals to cultural experience that is different from their own. (Subotnik
> 1996 p. 191)

And yet, male composers are still extolling the virtues of unity as the main
spiritual purpose of music. The metanarratives that underpin such statements will be revisited in this book. Jonathan Harvey in his book on *Music
and Inspiration* writes:

> At the root is the interest in order which we have observed in all the composers [which
> are all male] discussed. Many would sympathize with Stravinsky's view that music
> is peculiarly well equipped to create a vision of an ideal order. (Harvey 1999 p. 137)

John Sloboda, in identifying a number of barriers to achievement in
Western society, includes elitism of this kind:

- A reduction in societal scaffolding like music in the home and village
- A discourse about music 'in terms of talent, achievement and success, rather
  than community, fulfillment, or transcendence' (p. 455), reflecting a consumer
  society. (Here he highlights the dangerous culture of competition encouraged
  by music colleges and conservatories.)
- The barrier and elitism of high art, adding that 'The academy in most of its
  manifestations promotes the classical performance tradition as the paradigm
  and paragon of what music *really* [author's italics] is and what it is to be a musician.' (He highlights the gap between notion of the good in the academy and
  the values of the majority and the high level skill necessary to perform the 'core
  exemplars of the form'.)[6] (summarised from Sloboda 1999 pp. 454–5)

The failure to embrace diverse value systems because of the stranglehold
of the Academy has not served women well. Certainly in the area of funding they have often been marginalised by funding bodies on such grounds
as their failure to secure commercial recording contracts (Harris 2002
pp. 7–8). This failure to get funding often prevents women's products from
reaching the very public arenas of music. The result is that they are often
private in their conception and dissemination. They are conceived for their

---

6   This is what feminist theorists have called the musical canon and is discussed above.

own performance. The singer/songwriter is still a favourite role for women composers. To a certain extent the structures of capitalism especially the Internet are allowing a freedom for new structures:

> The 'industrialization of music' can't be understood as something that happens to music but describes a process in which music itself is made – a process, that is, which fuses and confuses capital, technical and musical arguments. (Frith 1987 p. 54)

These messy processes are allowing for more ephemeral events more linked with their context. Here the experience of ethnomusicology in producing frames to analyse these events may be helpful:

> Some scholars now examine performance not as a product but as the process of realizing other social goals for example, as part of the negotiation of identity, the symbolic mapping of space and relationship, or the transformation of consciousness. (Moisala and Diamond 2000 p. 21)

Our society is wedded to products; indeed capitalism depends on it. It does not matter if the processes involve human (or indeed animal) suffering providing the product is good. Nowhere has this more clearly been seen than in the way 'excellent' musical performances are produced with brutalising treatment of choir members who have not yet grasped their part (and this could include cathedral choirs) or children who cannot meet the demands of Associated Board exam pieces.

By concentrating on process as well as product, new motivations for musical activity can emerge. Improvisation can find a place and this can be for its own sake rather than as simply a staging point on the way to a fixed product. This has always been part of black Pentecostal traditions but has seldom found a place in the dominant western notated tradition.

Challenge has played an important part in western culture, based on the heroic journey myths described earlier, where overcoming challenges leads to greater self-realisation. However, challenge separated from nurture often leads to collapse and earlier in this chapter we have seen how people regularly defined themselves by which Associated Board exam they failed rather than the ones they passed. This failure may signal the end of any musical activity.

To find a place in the musical canon as described above, a piece had to be innovative which often meant challenging – a value system based on a misconstrued Darwinian progress myth.[7] These innovation-based Values that were required for pieces to find a place in the musical canon can be balanced by more nurturing approaches to musical activity. The conductor, Jane Ring Frank, sees that the two are brought together. By nurturing the mostly middle-aged women in her choir, she challenges them to leave behind their stereotypes of womanhood in her concern for social justice and altruism:

> I feel like the text and the experience of the challenge is teaching them something about the way women are and can be and have always been, different from giving to the kind of stereotype of what's written for women's voices. (Ring Frank 2003)

She also sees herself as both nurturing and challenging them about the relationship of their bodies to music (see below), asking them to:

> Be present in their own bodies. I think it's very hard ... for the older women that I work with. It's just not even in their experience to become incredibly conscious of the bodies they walk in ... The stress on thinness and the stress on being invisible ... I try to teach them to take up space ... [and] having a body full of breath is part of that. (Ring Frank 2003)

In the area of embodiment, Christianity fused with Graeco-Roman thought to effectively split mind, body and spirit. The valuing of mind more highly than the body and spirit was completed at the Enlightenment. Our music-making has become disembodied. Western Art Music has followed western culture in embracing the split. Audiences are seated so that little movement is possible; the link with the dance is broken. Feminist theorists have worked to return the centrality of the body to the musical experience, whether it is that of the performer, composer or audience. The application within theories of music of ideas from feminists like Kristeva has resulted

---

7 'The ideology Dawkins is selling is the worship of competition. It is projecting a Thatcherite take on economics on to evolution. It's not an impartial scientific view; it's a political drama.' Jackson, Nick. Against the grain: There are questions that science cannot answer, *The Independent*, 3 January 2008.

in the inclusion of the body in musical meaning. In these debates we see the notion of plurality of meaning developing, already examined under Expression above. At the end of a complex argument, Barthes comes to the role of the body, concluding that in music 'the referent is the body' (Barthes 1985 p. 308). To understand this, he says we need 'a second semiology, that of the body in a state of music' (Barthes 1985 p. 312). In this writing the way is open for the physiological response to music being a meaning in its own right. By drawing the body into the debate about musical meaning it is possible to see music's meaning as closer to the world of action than that of signs (which constitute the world of language).

There is a sense of movement within musical discourse, but whether that is simply a movement in the area of Expression or actually of the body is a subject for much debate. Theorists like McClary (2003) write about their own need to move while listening and sees music as an embodied experience. She sees the baroque as a physical time, and the embodiment being lost in the nineteenth century. More contentious than this is the association of music with sexuality which we have seen above (Leppert and McClary 1987 p. 154).

But, whatever, the implicit Value of music is, it is clear that the body and sexuality are important for the image of women performers in the domain of explicit Value. The association of public performance with sexual availability has dogged women performers for much of European history. For example, the father of the seventeenth-century composer, Barbara Strozzi, ensured she had a good musical education; but despite the fact that she was talented, she was still seen as a courtesan. It was impossible for women to be publicly involved in music at that time without acquiring this label. Her father also required her to pose bare-breasted for a picture. She was also faced with the dilemma that she must sing 'desire based' songs to prove her capabilities but that to do so would only fuel the gossip about her lust. McClary traces the complex sexuality of the rise of the castrati in the seventeenth century and locates it in a time when women were getting some reputation as performers. The Duke of Ferrara set up a women's voice choir in the late sixteenth century. The Ladies of Ferrara became famous as they pushed their voices to new limits which led to other courts developing similar ensembles. The Ladies of Ferrara were virtuosic singers, accompanied with appropriate facial gestures and choreography. There is an unusually high level of detail in the music written for them – including how ornaments were to be sung. This led to professional musical employment for women. At this point the soprano voice becomes fetishised. McClary sees the male jealousy of the position of these women leading to the development of the castrati, the first of which appeared around 1599, as the public wanted to hear music in that high register. The castrati were seen as virile and representing a new meaning for manhood. It was also at this time that the division of performers, composers and teachers began. This division became deeply engrained over the next four centuries.

The issue of image including sexuality is central to contemporary women in the world of opera and pop music:

> The prima donna is a male constructed fantasy image (indeed, an image that often approaches that of the campy female impersonator); the demands of the public are that the singer conform to their ideals of femininity, temperament, sexual behavior, beauty and weight. (McClary in Clement 1989 p. xvi)

> Attractiveness is not something owned by the singer. Rather it is built up around singers, through their engagement with other networks of meaning including fashion and, of course, through the type of display they enact ... Attractiveness becomes part of the delineated meanings of music ... The more she [the female singer] goes in for displaying her body, the less likely it is that she is a 'good' musician. (Green 1997 p. 39)

The connection/disconnection between soul, mind and body is also seen in the area of ethical action. Some cultures have seen a clear link between music and ethical belief and action. Deep in Greek thought was the notion of the controlling power music held over human behaviour. Classical literature is filled with stories embodying the potential power of music. Jamie James in *The Music of the Spheres: Music, Science and the Natural Order of the Universe* cites the incident from the biography of Pythagoras where he comes across a violent man listening to tunes in the Phrygian mode. He changes the mode and the man calms down. He links this with the notion of enchantment (James 1993 p. 32).

The sixth-century theorist, Boethius, drawing on Plato, had similar ideas in defining modes by what they incite in the listener like lasciviousness and

violence (Godwin 1987 p. 45). These ideas were revived in the Renaissance
with such writers as Ficino looking at the power of image, perception and
language as revealed in the arts, science, rhetoric and culture as

> the ground for knowledge of and action within the wider world, whether social,
> material or spiritual. (Sullivan 1997 p. 1)

Today the idea of such a link is returning both in the work of theorists
cited at the beginning of this section and in the work of theorists using
notions of improvisation and aesthetics in the area of morality. The theologian, Richard Holloway, uses improvisation as a metaphor for the way
we operate morally in his book, *Godless Morality* (1999). Foucault used
the notion of the aesthetic in his work on ethics (Foucault 1980 p. 203).
In bringing aesthetics into his discussion of the technology of the self he
offers a possibility of work linking value systems with aesthetics or indeed,
spirituality (Carrette 2000 p. 150).[8]

Lifestyle becomes the public face of aesthetics or a morality governed/
engendered by aesthetics. So music regulates the self both at a personal
and a collective level. We become what we listen to. Music can now be
seen as taking the place of the transcendent deity in shaping our lives. It
has then the qualities of immanence and transcendence that we associate
with God. It is only fleetingly present in an evanescent form; it appears to
be disembodied (although it has once been embodied which has interesting parallels with incarnational theology). It becomes re-embodied in its
effect upon the self of the listener.

To summarise, the patriarchal value systems have disadvantaged
women, especially in relation to their nurture, sense of self in relation to
community, identity and embodiment.

8   I have discussed this much more fully in Boyce-Tillman, J. (2001b).

Construction

This leads us well into the area of Construction where women are traditionally regarded as being less accomplished. Effective Construction often depends on the right management of repetition and contrast within a particular idiom. The way in which contrast is handled within a tradition – how much or how little can be tolerated – is often carefully regulated by the elders of the various traditions – be they the composers or theoreticians of the Western classical tradition or the master drummers of Yoruba traditions.

Musical forms in various cultures have approached this balance in a variety of ways. For example, the degree of repetition in Western popular traditions is often much greater and more overt than in avant-garde Western classical music. This is one reason why the audiences of the two traditions differ. Construction issues are well documented (probably overdocumented) in the pieces that make up the classical canon (Goehr 1992). Most academic courses that include church music in the West have concentrated their teaching in this area. The compositional side of my music education at Oxford University, for example, consisted largely of the reproduction of empty shells of the musical forms of High Art European Music between 1540 and 1900 (Lovelock 1952). Systems of musical analysis such as those of the German theorist Schenker (in which the cathedral organists who control much liturgical music-making in the UK will also have been reared) concentrate on this area for their Value judgements. The centrality of the musical score to this has resulted in a devaluing of improvisation and all forms including it. The stress on the product ('doing' rather than 'being') reflects the dominant values of western culture, as we have already seen.

However, in the area of early childhood music work, adults (often women) do make up songs about anything, such as puddles or seeds or traffic lights. I watched an amazing lesson where a female teacher of six-year-olds conducted a whole afternoon's teaching through improvised song. It was a lesson in November and was a wonderful musical dialogue about Fireworks with imaginative sounds included to represent the fireworks themselves. Interacting with young children, either as a parent, grandparent or teacher, can free that improvisational capacity for an adult, if they have the courage to take it. It is an area where adults can play and take risks without serious real life consequences. The jazz musician Keith Jarrett talks about jumping in as a jazz technique (Jarrett 1997 pp. 80–2), by which he means relating quickly to the musical utterances of another player in the group. Such value systems are in stark contrast to the notated traditions of the West which have pride of place in the music canon.

Instrumental lessons in the Western classical tradition have traditionally concentrated on sight-reading as a key skill. This has been reflected in the training of church choirs. This involves the decoding of notation to realise the 'products' that make up the Western musical canon. Improvisation is less often taught and often discouraged and described in such terms as 'messing about'; it has been devalued in the interest of reading the dots. I once had an eleven-year-old bass recorder player who said five minutes before a concert: 'I've got some bad news for you, miss. I've forgotten my music.' It was a part of which I had no second copy and did not know what we could do. 'Don't you worry, miss,' he replied, 'I'll busk it!' He was also the drummer for the local Assembly of God Church, and so regularly improvised every Sunday for over two hours. He had both skills. He had retained both because he could function in two differing traditions. He was a real example of a musician who valued both ways of knowing – the oral, based on process and the literate, based on product – equally.

The development of Western musical notation caused literacy to be valued over oracy. Many world musical cultures are, or have recently been, essentially non-literate or orate.[9] That is, they have not used visual notational means of recording details of human transactions. There are many contrasts to be made between the ways in which literate and orate musical cultures function. Here are four broad proposals about the effects of the availability of notation:

9   I shall use the term orate throughout this book for cultures without a notation system, drawing on the work of Walter Ong (1982).

1. The existence of written notation allows lengthy verbatim recall of complex meaningful material.
2. Notation allows proliferation and migration of material so that it exceeds the capacity of any one individual to know it all.
3. Notation encourages the separation of the content of an utterance from its context, and makes it easier for an utterance to be treated as a 'thing in itself'.
4. Notation selects certain aspects of sound for preservation, and, in doing so, both embodies current theory and also tends to restrict the future development of music in certain ways. (Sloboda 1985 p. 242)

The decontextualisation of music was made possible by means of musical notation. Pieces can be inappropriately moved from one context to another and put into a permanent and definitive form, which is impossible in the constantly evolving products of an orate culture. The fact that access to learning about musical notation was for a long time limited to rich men, meant that subjugated knowers were disempowered, and still are. The process of sound recording has served a similar function for popular musics in that it provides a once-for-all version which becomes definitive and intervenes in the process of the oral transmission of musical material.

In a musical culture that values the permanence of the written score and the size of the performing ensemble required, women have suffered from their inability to get their works notated. Recording catalogues have a similar effect. In the Introduction to their seminal text *Women making Music: The Western Art Tradition 1150–1950*, Bowers and Tick highlight how the absence of manuscripts of women's music and the lack of interest in the sociology of music has, in itself, marginalised women (Bowers and Tick 1986 pp. 3–4). Diane Harris highlights how self-perpetuating this is. Without a commercial recording, women composers cannot get funding: 'Women have rarely been allowed out of the changing rooms let alone reached the starting blocks' (Harris 2002 pp. 7–8).

The centrality of innovation and permanence to this approach has served to exclude women and all who would

- use more nurturing or circular forms
- delight in a variety of ways of looking at music
- favour orate traditions which lack the permanent products of the notated traditions.

Because the domain of Construction, with its concentration on notated masterpieces, has dominated the Value judgements of Western classical traditions, the principles and terminologies developed in this area have often been applied to other cultures, without sufficient regard for how thinkers within those traditions have regarded their own processes of musical Construction. For example, the more circular structures of improvised traditions often sit uneasily with the use of the terminology associated with the more linear notated traditions. How musical form is perceived in orate musical cultures differs markedly from its perception in literate musical cultures.

The problem for challenging assumptions in the area of Construction is that many of the conventions have been in place for a long time as the title of Susan McClary's book *Conventional Wisdom* indicates:

> Although musicologists and theorists often grant these formations the status of 'purely musical', I will start with them as conceptions – albeit conventions that so permeate human transactions that we usually fail to notice their influence ... Yet my title also means to acknowledge the fact that genuine social knowledge is articulated and transmitted by means of procedures and assumptions concerning music. (McClary 2001 p. 5)

Many of these 'normal' structures put a high stress on unity and unification (sometimes associated with transcendent Values like the unity of the universe or God Himself). In such a scheme women or the feminine often had a place – as a minor as opposed to a major chord, as a gentler subject following a masculine first subject and as the ending of a phrase on a weak beat. This is epitomised in this quotation from the eighteenth-century theorist Georg Andreas Sorge:

> Just as in the universe there has always been created a creature more splendid and perfect than the others of God, we observe exactly this also in musical harmony. Thus we find after the major triad another, the minor triad, which is indeed not as complete as the first, but also lovely and pleasant to hear. The first can be likened to the male, the second to the female sex. (Quoted in McClary 1991 p. 11)

Susan McClary delights in the process of deconstruction of such conventions showing a delight in the chaos of a chapter entitled *Reveling in the Rubble* (McClary 2001 pp. 167–8). The rise of diverse forms from different traditions and the fusing and synthesis of these has resulted in more repetitive, circular forms finding acceptance. This is particularly clear in such areas as the rise of an interest in chant in the New Age traditions and also the development of minimalist techniques in Western Art Music. Nevertheless there is a problem with getting new forms accepted in the repertoire in the world of classical music. Ensembles (in the domain of Materials) are still organised along traditional lines and are looking for a repertoire in the line of the classical forms:

> Works that do not fit into any category are less likely to be performed. A major weakness of generic classification: the exclusion and implied devaluation of works that do not fit the categories within the system. (Citron 1993 p. 125)

Without a place in the mainstream repertoire there will be no reviews:

> Even if the assessment is negative, and implied significance is present that is missing when a work is not reviewed. Attention in print can lead to further performances and potential canonicity. (Citron 1993 p. 186)

Reviewers also tend to concentrate on the larger musical forms such as operas and symphonies. Access to these performing ensembles has often been exclusive of women (Bowers and Tick 1986 pp. 3–4).

The defining of canonic status has been in the hands of men working in patriarchal structures of which the methodologies are part. These have often concentrated in the area of Construction, often to the reduction of other areas of musical experience. Marcia Herndon critiques traditional methodology for its reliance on scientific procedures and accuses it of concentrating on tertiary analysis rather than on primary analysis which is closer to the data itself. She calls for a focus on whole systems rather than on deterministic, equilibrium or generative models (Herndon 2000 p. 251). Jane Bowers looks at a new approach to the notion of biography in *Writing the Biography of a Black Blues Singer*. She draws on the work of Harriet Ottenheimer to show some of the problems in the writing of biography:

> We need to forgo our expectation that there be a single, true account of a life rather than several conflicting ones ... Indeed, it is not only in orally transmitted life stories that we find evidence of multiple or contradictory selves. (Bowers 2000 pp. 149–50)

Feminists favour approaches that include diversity. Pirrko Moisala in *Gender Negotiations of the Composer Kaija Saariaho in Finland* very helpfully uses a number of lenses to examine the biography of the Finnish composer Kija Saariaho drawing on the concept of the 'nomadic subject':

> The analysis of Saariaho's gender negotiation, her 'nomadness', is presented in two parts. The first section discusses gender as a factor in the construction of her identity as a woman composer, and the second focuses on her negotiation of gender in relation to her social environment, particularly to the Finnish press. (Moisala 2000 p. 185)

Subotnik sees the need to abandon the traditional hegemony of reason which has characterised this area as a moral issue:

> If our marriage to abstract reason has produced not just an Elect team of winners but also ... moral malformations, then maybe it is time for us to commit bigamy and add a second standard of reason to our household. Whether we work in classrooms or boardrooms or in smoke-filled rooms, surely it is time for those of us already inside the American dream to do the right thing and open up that dream to all Americans. (Subotnik 1996 p. 192)

To summarise, this section has linked how Construction has been the dominant area in musicological discussion. This dominance has resulted in the 'it does not matter who wrote it but whether it's good' debate which makes its judgements almost exclusively within this domain.

Expression

The domain I have called Expression was traditionally designated in performance assessment as 'musical'. There is an urban legend of a private piano teacher who charged one rate to teach the notes of a piece (the Materials of sound) and another if you wanted to learn the Expression! This area is concerned with the evocation of mood, emotion (individual or corporate), images, memories and atmosphere on the part of all those involved in the musical performance. The composer and performer will often use variations in the speed and volume level of the piece to create changes in this area together with other aspects of musical Construction like metre and scoring.

We have limited vocabulary available in which to express nuances of Expression. Despite Langer's (1953) work, academics have only recently started to address this mismatch between the ways the academic world regards music and the way the wider public does. John Sloboda's work in the psychology of music has shown the need to see both the technical, constructional and motivational (emotional) aspects brought together in understanding the power of music. In reviewing why so many love music as listeners and yet so few acquire the necessary skills to play it in Western culture, he sees motivation as devalued in relation to cognition and technical skill (Sloboda 1999 pp. 450–1): it is the place where academic words often fail and in the context of sacred music, pieces of a marked expressive character have often been labelled sentimental.

This domain is where the subjectivity of composer/performer and listener intersect. Drawing on Lucy Green's books *Music on Deaf Ears: Musical Meaning, Ideology and Education* (1988) and *Gender, Music, Education* (1997) I define two different meanings associated with a piece – extrinsic and intrinsic. The intrinsic meaning of the music reflecting the subjectivity of composer and performer is often completely changed by its intersection with the subjective experience of the listener – the extrinsic meaning. For the listener this is meaning that has been locked onto that particular piece or style or musical tradition because of its association with certain events in their own lives. (Sometimes there is an overlap between the two forms of meaning, setting up tensions and questions in the mind of the listener.) Popular music, in particular, often conjures up a range of associations. The phrase 'They are playing our tune' reflects the association of certain emotional events with certain pieces. A song associated with a particular event can recall that event in great detail including powerful associated emotions. This is often called involuntary memory (Mace 2007), a term first explored by Proust in *In Search of Lost Time (À la recherche du temps perdu)* (Proust 2002). So familiar pieces of music become like familiar pieces of furniture and old friends, places that can be used for exploration of the self in relation to various communities. The advent of recording techniques enabled music to be fixed in space and time. A recording is a virtual place that can be revisited at will. Our record collections could be seen as a collection of sites that we have at some time found to be sacred; but older than this is a song, hymn or a chant that we reproduce ourselves as performers.

These well-known pieces can assume the properties of revisiting places of significance, like a pilgrimage (Boyce-Tillman 2001b). Most of us use music in this way. This area of musical meaning has often been downplayed by classical theorists (Rahn 1994 p. 55). What is clear, however, from people's accounts of their listening experiences, is that extrinsic meaning – that is, expressive meaning drawn from the listener's own previous experiences – is an immensely important component in this area that has often been ridiculed or ignored by classical musical theorists.[10]

It is not as easy to secure the place of gender in the area of intrinsic meaning, as it is in the area of extrinsic meaning. Since classical musical theorists have concentrated on the intrinsic meaning, this had helped the process of marginalising women. By including the notion of extrinsic meaning as central to many people's experience of music we re-establish the notion of identity construction as an important part of the musical experience. The association between music and the arousal and channeling of desire (McClary, 1991 p. 53) makes it become an important part in socialisation; and is all the more powerful because few listeners realise the way it functions. It appears to reach our most private emotions (McClary 1991 p. 53).

The conductor Jane Ring Frank confirms how she deliberately challenges cultural archetypes in her programming of concerts by looking at how women have treated the great themes such as love, family, war and conflict (Ring Frank 2003) rather than the male view. This would include the effects of war on family life in the home, the notions of the effect of models of family life on women's experience of aspects such as motherhood.

The absence of role models in music has a significant effect of whether women musicians feel able to develop their creative powers (Citron 1993 p. 13). This debate opens up the area of who is allowed to function in

10   But not by music therapists where the use of music, particularly with the elderly, to aid reminiscence is well established.

public spaces and who in private. Fanny Mendelssohn, for example, was allowed to perform in their large performing space in their private garden, whereas Felix Mendelssohn, the better known male sibling, was allowed to travel freely. In this respect, Fanny, was more restricted in the nineteenth century than her medieval counterpart the 'enclosed' nun Hildegard of Bingen (Chapter 3) who was allowed to travel freely disseminating her ideas. Marcia Citron identifies how the cultural placing of women in the home and their consequent inability to travel has affected their ability to get their pieces known to a wider audience (Citron in Bowers and Tick 1986 p. 241). Women's exclusion from the notated traditions, because of their inability to access a musical education, compounded this phenomenon.

Clara Schumann who had written a number of very successful pieces before her marriage describes it well:

> The separation has once more made me aware of my peculiar and difficult position. Shall I neglect my own talent, in order to serve as a companion on your journeys? … You took a companion with you and I returned to the child and my work. Thus I torture myself with thoughts. Yes, it is absolutely necessary for us to find some means by which we can both utilise and cultivate our talents side by side. (Reich 1986 p. 261)

Eventually she draws the following conclusion:

> I once believed that I possessed creative talent, but I have given up this idea; a woman must not desire to compose – there has never been one yet able to do it. Should I expect to be the one? To believe that would be arrogant. (Clara Schumann's diary 1839 quoted in Reich 1986 p. 267)

The composer Nicola LeFanu in an article entitled *Master Musician: an Impregnable Taboo?* writes about the effect of the lack of role models on girls' construction of their identity as composers or conductors:

> Composers develop through hearing their music played. How are women composers to develop if they are denied access to the leading professional outlets? Taboos on conducting and composing are particularly difficult to shift. 'Schoolgirls are not presented with models of female composers.' Ridicule is the traditional weapon against someone who challenges sexual stereotypes. (LeFanu 1987 p. 5)

Jane Ring Frank describes the importance of one teacher who had faith in her as a conductor, because he:

> promoted most of the men around him to be conductors, but he promoted me and stepped over his own natural inclinations to support the work that I wanted to do. ... But I will say that I still believe today, at forty-two years old that being a conductor and being a woman ... I still think that I fight the kind of school marm perception, and that ... I fight very hard to not be a mommy ... I don't resist being humorous or warm, but I resist being 'mommy' and taking care of things. (Ring Frank 2003)

And yet in the wider world of music making she encountered the stereotypes:

> I was a very successful repetiteur in Los Angeles, and ... I'm able to conduct opera and have quite an affinity for it. I grew up with opera ... I worked with a very famous opera conductor who has since passed away – ... who looked at me one day, very, very – without batting an eye-lid, and said, 'You know, it really doesn't matter how talented you are, you're never going to be able to do anything because of who you are, and no men in opera are ever going to be interested in hiring you. You know, it's a shame that you're a woman.' (Ring Frank 2003)

She goes on to describe how with all the varied ensembles she forms and directs, including *The Boston Secession*, she is looking for issues of gender that will often translate into promoting the works of women composers in some of those settings (Ring Frank 2003).

The role of education is clear in this story and educationalists like Roberta Lamb have analysed how education can aid the establishment of a musical identity for her pupils by dealing with the following areas:

1. Music history;
2. Music is not an absolute knowledge,
3. Music as a product of identity. (Lamb 2000)

In the area of history she makes women composers, performers, conductors, teachers and patrons visible. She challenges views about the purity of music as an abstract art and a product of talent. The aesthetics and structure of music must be identified as context-specific and not transcendent. She identifies the problem of what constitutes a curriculum when previous concepts of canons and transcendent values are exploded:

> In the face of this shifting terrain some prefer to hold tighter to older traditions (such as great masterworks, ta's and ti's, singing in head tone, the absolute authority of the music director), as do some state-mandated curricula. I would rather practice a more inclusive, creative thinking and, like Audre Lorde, flourish within the 'intimacy of scrutiny' (Lorde, 1984, p. 36) of my beloved music in order to find a greater passion and power for living through new knowledge and expectations. (Lamb 2000)

In the area of identity, she identifies the need for constant scrutiny by the people controlling the gateways of musical power:

> It isn't simply a matter of treating everyone fairly or the same. It does require constant examination of cultural values. It does mean recognizing and appreciating differences, seeing the value in treating people differently but fairly, and going further than noting the difficulties when deep-seated and/or unexamined prejudice and beliefs interfere with that fairness (e.g., racism, sexism, homophobia). The interfering beliefs most often relate to that which is outside any individual's personal experience, so these identity-driven issues are not addressed once and forgotten, but become part of an on-going process of scrutiny and learning. (Lamb 2000)

In all of these areas she sees that the role of music educators is to challenge the existing patriarchal stereotypes. Challenging musical patriarchy is not just a question of making women's achievements visible but also a fundamental rethinking of the nature of musical meaning and identity – all musical conventions (Citron 1993, p. 8). The male domination of musical culture has meant that our conceptual thinking is therefore gender specific.[11] Homans sees the roots of this in Judeo-Christian myths:

> Eve, and the women after her, have been dislocated from the ability to feel that they are speaking their own language. They could not speak with a right to personal usage of the godlike powers of the mind. (Homans 1986 p. 173)

---

11   Because, following Lacan, language is a male construct.

And yet it is into this world that women must enter to start on a musical career; but women are traditionally preservers of order and many find this process of challenge unacceptable. They tend to acknowledge their debt to the surrounding culture rather than possess their own work as the male composers do. They are conciliators, not fighters, whether by nature or enculturation. An anonymous respondent to a questionnaire about women's compositions wrote: 'Biggest problem for women composers: not enough emphasis in woman's upbringing on ego, courage, and independence. [...] This is a bigger problem than outside prejudice and/or male chauvinism.' This highlights the way women are reared leads to the establishment of internal self-policing through the internalisation of the dominant value-systems, as we saw earlier.

The absolutist position with its concentration on intrinsic meaning has disadvantaged other cultures as much as women. Other traditions like those of the Far East have been far more comfortable with more referen-tialist approaches concentrating on the relationship of musical meaning to the wider world. Instrumental pieces with such titles as *The Crane's Story* and *Water on a Lotus leaf* are common. Western music, particularly post Enlightenment, has used titles concentrating on the Construction area like *Sonata* and *Symphony*. Indeed, children have often seen pieces with such titles as being of greater Value than those with titles in the area of Expressive character. As a child I felt much prouder of being able to play a piece entitled *Sonata No 2* than one called *A Passing Storm*.

The work of feminist theorists like Susan McClary, in the area of intrinsic meaning has been hotly debated:

> But these new claims about gender in music force open again a Pandora's box of questions about musical aesthetics that used to be debated without resolution and about which there has been, in the mainstream of musicological activity, tacit agree-ment to let them lie. I wonder whether we are really meant to stir them up anew. I am talking now about grand questions: whether music possess a content beyond its purely musical syntax and structure (for example, the 'erotic imagery' that informs 'the tonality that underlies Western concert music'); or whether music imitates action and experience ('assaultive pelvic pounding'); of how music affects the lis-tener ('music after the Renaissance ... appeals to libidinous appetites'); or whether it expresses feeling (the 'throttling, murderous rage of a rapist incapable of attaining release')... (Treitler 1993 pp. 38–9)

Here it is the supposed sexual meanings of music that have raised the writer's ire. But feminists have supported her:

> What I did on the second half of the programme was to talk about the female sexual cycle and to liken music in a different kind of way using kind of distance and release models within harmony or longer, extended distance release models ... The female one is a longer cycle because the cycle is much more drawn out ... And there was a way within that, using Hildegard, using a lot of female composers ... a way to draw some kind ... of natural, original from the body, a kind of way to look at what this could sound like ... hearing it in this new way ... I put it in the context of fore-play and very kind of strong language. ... The audience spent the first ten minutes tittering ... over the actual concept of the programme; tittering over however many times I said orgasm. And then there was a settling ... into how the body, how we listen. (Ring Frank 2003)

It is debates about women's sexual nature that have underpinned, as we have seen, the thinking that led to the establishment of the western canon:

> In the Renaissance, male sexual potency was considered the basis for creativity, which could be depleted if expended in sexual acts. There are two interesting implications for women. One is that they cannot be creators because they lack a male's sexual equipment. The other, more indirect, is that as the recipients of sperm in the sexual act women are somehow robbing a man of his creative powers. (Citron 1993 p. 51)

The essentialist notions of identity based on a particular arrangement of the genital organs have been applied to many aspects of the process of musical composing and performing:

> women have been considered too "emotional' to create – an ironic observation given that emotion is arguably a major component of art. Emotional meant irrational, and the dualism rational – irrational emerged alongside mind – body. (Citron 1993 p. 53)

It is from such assumptions that the stereotypes women=weak and men=strong come. These assumptions have stereotyped music written for women:

> I'm a believer that ... most of the music that's written for treble voices for children or for women is what I always call 'fairy music'. Kind of celestial, heavenly, angels, chorus of angels, fairies – the kind of music that doesn't allow women to be rooted

into the earth, and it angers me. Holst's *The Planets* being the great example.[12] So my
focus with this fifty-voice women's choir is to find material that allows them to be
powerful – allows them to be strong... I have found... strong composers... like Libby
Larsen, [who] are writing on strong themes of personal power, personal discovery
that defy the sort of fairy/angel approach to love, family, conflict, war, that demand,
I think, of the singers and of the instrumentalists a deeper level of commitment and
skew the norm. (Ring Frank 2003)

Dame Ethel Smyth (1858–1944) suffered from this stereotype as a composer. Her operas impressed critics for its strength and its architectural
proportions; they wrote that it was: 'Virile, masterly in construction and
workmanship [and lacking] the qualities usually associated with feminine
productions' (Beecham 1943 p. 137).

To summarise, in this section I have examined the Expressive aspects
of music, drawing on notions of emotion, meaning and identity. It has
re-evaluated traditional Western musicological judgements in this area
especially those concerning extrinsic meaning and identity.

Materials

All music consists of organisations of concrete Materials drawn both from
the human body and the environment. These include musical instruments
of various kinds, the infinite variety of tone colours associated with the
human voice and the sounds of the natural world. What is used in a particular piece or tradition depends on the availability of materials in certain
geographical locations and the technical abilities of those involved. The
choice of instruments and vocal colours and ranges will also dictate musical
pitches and rhythms – the keys and scales that can be used and associated
motifs and melodic and rhythmic patterns. Different traditions also value
quite distinct vocal and instrumental colours. The development of certain

12   A women's voice choir is used here to denote the ethereal.

technical skills on the part of players and singers of various traditions is associated with this area and intimately linked with the development of instrumental shapes and vocal tone colours.

We have already seen how the development of instruments was associated with men and permanence. In many cultures women had no access to instruments or only to the most simple and peripheral like rattles, tambourines and bells (often strapped to their bodies as they danced). For women the voice was paramount and often related to the dance. The musical canon, which, as described above, forms the basis of the conventional histories of music, covers the period by the development of the Western symphony orchestra and the instruments that make it up, which almost acquire a canonic significance. The rise of ethnomusicology and historical musicology in the second half of the twentieth century led to the revalidation of instruments from other historical and cultural locations at this time. It also included a renewed awareness of the area of organology (the instruments of the Western symphony orchestra were no longer a 'given'), as instruments from different cultures became available to Western eyes and ears. There was also a revisiting in the worlds of composing and education of the Materials of music. Titles of pieces like Stockhausen's *Mixtur* and books like *Exploring Sound* (Tillman 1976) reflected this trend.

The history of the western orchestra has been one of exclusion of women and the Vienna Philharmonic was very proud of this policy. But even if they are not actually excluded, the musicians' pattern of working including touring – has made it incompatible with the traditional women's roles of home making and child bearing. Lucy Green (1997) has shown how girls in UK schools choose the classical instruments while boys tend to choose the rock and pop instruments; this finding supports the point already noted that women, in general, have supported the cultural norms rather than challenging them. And yet the world of the classical orchestra is dominated by men. Women who choose to enter the musical profession tend to end up teaching, either privately, or in schools.

Traditionally the teaching of instruments has concentrated on technique which is the ability to control the Materials of sound. Instrumental and vocal performance studies show a concentration on this area of the musical experience. There is a television cartoon that portrays a sad 'virtuoso' violinist sitting sadly a corner before a concert. When asked by a puzzled friend why he is so sad, he replies that he can play all the scales and arpeggios very fast, but that in the pieces they are all muddled up! Here is someone able to handle the Materials area of performance very well but unable to use these technical skills to enter any of the other areas of musical experience. This is evident to some degree in some contemporary performances that display a pyrotechnic level of technical skill with little Expressive understanding or grasp of the Construction of the music. There are some aspiring performers who wait in this position for a lifetime with their books of studies, unable to move from this area into the others, waiting till they have sufficient technique.

Philosophers of music education are looking to restore the relationship between the areas of musical experience and not to see them as a linear progression (Boyce-Tillman 2004). It is possible with the most basic technical skills to enter the totality of the musical experience if these areas are regarded as interlocking and not hierarchical. A good example of this is the instrument called the singing bowl. The instrument itself comes from Middle East and requires the mastery of the technique of running the stick around the outside of metal bowl to produce a 'singing' sound full of complex overtones. This sound produced with reverence, an understanding and connection with the 'feel' of a particular group and with the intention of calming and healing the people present, can have an amazing effect. I similarly remember a young boy of about 9 years old, who attended a workshop of mine preceding a performance of my one-woman show based on the life of St Hild of Whitby. He brought with him a Scottish pipe that he wished to learn to play. As part of the workshop he learned three notes. These he used in a piece depicting the element of air in the performance which took place in an ancient chapel, full of intense atmosphere and lit only with candles. In this piece he used his very limited and newly acquired technical skill to make unbelievably expressive sounds within the structure we had worked at in the workshop. His father attended the performance and looked across at his son with an attitude of rapt attention that drew father and son together in a moment that I guess neither will forget. It was a deep spiritual and personal experience that involved all the five areas in the model above but which was entered with limited expertise in the domain of Materials.

The acoustic space is an important part of the Materials of music, but one often ignored by the dislocation of work from its environment that characterises the classical canon. Composers for ancient cathedrals knew that each building accentuated certain tones – the resonating frequency – and wrote their pieces with this in mind. There is now a return to including the venues in the natural world for musical performances including the natural sounds found in them as part of the piece. Composers like Pauline Oliveros have demonstrated their concern for acoustic space by recording in spaces like the old cistern used for her CD entitled *Deep Listening* (Oliveros 1989).

In an age of recording techniques we are aware of the need to create acoustic space artificially. In recording an opera of mine we had the singer stand at different distances from the microphone to simulate the movement on the stage; in a recording I made of my own songs we used three different levels of reverberation to suggest a small room, a concert and a larger, sacred space. Such techniques have become an important part of the Materials of sound.

In this area also, the relationship between the body of the performer/composer and the environment is established and is found in the work of some musicians working in the area of New Age spiritualities. The Materials from which instruments are made provide an intimate link between human beings and the natural world. In traditional societies, the process of making an instrument involved a reverence towards, for example, the tree that gave its wood for the making of the drum, and the player would regard him- or herself as continually in relationship to that tree every time the instrument-maker was played. Our industrialised society with its production lines for musical instruments dislocates the connection between the natural world and the Materials of sound. The role of instrument maker is dislocated from the roles of composer and performer.

The developments in this domain show the effect of the restoration of some of the subjugated ways of knowing. The sense of connection with the environment shows the establishment in the area of community of the presence of the environment. The opening of a variety of ensembles shows a change in the fixity of the ensembles that make up the pieces of the classical canon. On the other hand, it is difficult for pieces using alternative ensembles to find their way into the classical programmes that attract the attention of the press and media. And these ensembles can still market whole programmes without a single piece conducted, composed or performed as a soloist by a woman. The alternative ensembles are to be found in alternative venues. But the use of a variety of acoustic spaces including outdoor locations also characterises a rediscovery of other ways of knowing. The re-establishment of the relationship between movement and music shows a re-establishment of the role of the body as a significant part of the materials of music. The use of venues for performance other than the concert hall also allows the bodies of listeners to be in different positions from the 'trapped upright' position of the western concert.

Spirituality

Music in many cultures is associated with Spirituality generated by their Value systems. In post Enlightenment Western culture, this is often not declared, but, I would claim, is often present as a negotiated experience between the music and the performer/listener (Boyce-Tillman 2006b). I am defining Spirituality here as the ability to transport the audience to a different time/space dimension – to move them from everyday reality to 'another world'. 'Liminality' would be another possible term, as defined by Turner (1969, 1974) or the 'limit experience' (Tracy 1975). In this experience one is in non-ordinary reality and there is often a sense of *communitas* in which 'the participants feel joined together in a unity that lies outside of ordinary social structures and that expresses the prior flux and even formlessness out of which those structures have emerged' (Zuesse 1987 p. 417). Academic postmodernism with its mistrust of met-anarratives has attempted the marginalisation of this area, already started by post-Enlightenment suspicion of anything concerned with magic or belief (reflecting the dominant value system described above) (Hay with

Nye 1998).[13] This is in line with David Hay's thinking related to his work with Rebecca Nye on children's spirituality (Hay with Nye 1998). From this research, Hay draws the conclusion that spirituality or, 'spiritual awareness' a term that he prefers, is a universal feature of human experience. He calls it a natural predisposition, drawing on the work of Alister Hardy (1966). It is overlaid with cultural constructs but in the end he relates it to *biological reality*. The central aspect of this 'spiritual awareness' is *relational consciousness*. Hay supports this with a study of children's responses to research interviews. He maintains that children express their spirituality through their use of narratives whether fictional or autobiographical. In the process of analysing these narratives, Hay identifies the central aspect of spiritual awareness as *relational consciousness* which he sees as an antidote to the dominance of the competitive ethos.

Anthony Storr in his book *Music and the Mind* (1993) sees the creation of community as the main reason for the presence of music in world cultures. This experience of being united with others and the wider cosmos is a feature of the spiritual experience and central to the musical experience. Music makes people physically more like one another because of the effect of music on the body (Boyce-Tillman 2000a). Storr sees parallels between religious and warfare rituals and western coronations and state funerals (Storr 1993 p. 23). The act of singing together therefore has a spiritual dimension as in the school assembly. The nature of the song here may have changed over the years. Initially in the 1940s it was a Christian hymn like *Praise God from whom all blessings flow*. This moved towards more secular traditions, as topic work became the basis of the assembly so songs like *Waltzing Matilda* found a place. As schools addressed intercultural issues, songs from other traditions like short chants from African traditions found a place and the Educational Reform Act (1988) has resulted in a return to the Christian hymn. But the importance of the song lies in

13   There is a real need for academe to reconsider its position with regard to this area – to consider, for example, the possibility of a plurality of in the area of metanarrative. Debates about the area of liminal experience in the arts may well facilitate this process, which is clearly developing in areas such as Spirituality at Work and Spirituality in Music Education.

its capacity to bring a group of people together in a unique way. Hills and Argyle (1998) studied subjects who were members of both a church group and also a music-making group like a choir. They reported greater intensities in music-making in the areas of 'joy/elation', 'excitement', 'feeling uplifted' and 'loss of sense of self'.

So it is possible to see music as producing experiences similar to those traditionally associated with religious rituals. These are experiences involving belonging to wider society including the natural world or the transcendent. It involves the imagination which can function like a religious ritual in its contact with Otherness and its transcendence of the limitations of time. The development of a notion of transcendence as part of self-actualisation contributed to the idea that the musical experience is the last remaining place for the spiritual in western society (Hills and Argyle 1998). Maslow included the notion of transcendence in his hierarchy of human needs and his concept of self-actualisation. To some extent this links with the trance experience of other cultures, but the failure to approach it by means of bodily movement sets it apart from many trance ceremonies (Rouget 1987 p. 11). In Maslow's definition, peak experiences include characteristics associated in the past with religious experience like self-forgetfulness, concentration on the present, the absence of fear, increasing of strength and courage, trust and the breaking down of boundaries (Maslow 1967 p. 43). This notion has systematically been explored by Csikszentmihalyi in his concept of 'flow'. Here he sees enjoyment as central. His list of characteristics of the experience is similar to Maslow's:

- intense involvement
- clarity of goals and feedback
- deep concentration
- transcendence of self
- lack of self-consciousness
- loss of a sense of time
- intrinsically rewarding experience
- a balance between skill and challenge
  (Csikszentmihalyi and Csikszentmihalyi 1988, as summarised in Haworth 1997 pp. 84–5)

Descriptions of a unitive experience as part of the musical experience do resemble that of religious mystics. This often takes the form of a feeling of being united with the universe, other beings and the natural world. Nicholas Cook (1990) in the Introduction to *Music, Imagination and Culture* develops the idea by seeing the formal structure of the music as a container in which the imagination of the listener can flow free which is bounded by the limits of a culture (Cook 1990 p. 170).

The perceived effectiveness of a musical experience is often in this domain – the sense of a connectedness to all of the cosmos – and it is open to those attached to a particular religious system and people attached to none. Insofar as a musical experience takes us out of 'everyday' consciousness with its concerns for food, clothing and practical issues and moves us into another dimension we regard the musical experience as successful, whether we are a composer, performer or listener. Indeed some would see music as the last remaining ubiquitous spiritual experience in a secularised western culture (Boyce-Tillman 2001b).

This spiritual dimension to all musical performance is linked with myths, aesthetics and religious belief and notions of transcendence and here interfaces with the domain of Values which includes religious belief codifications. In music written within particular religious traditions the nature of this world will be more tightly defined with ideas of God, heaven, and spiritual beings articulated in forms appropriate to the relevant tradition. This would have been true of Medieval Europe and is true of many indigenous traditions. But these are simply religious frames provided to validate the liminal experience and linked with particular cultures with their associated religious beliefs.

It is the theorists of the Western Classical tradition who, in general, have had problems with this area and composers', listeners' and performers' accounts of the musical experience regularly include it. Handel, for example, recounts experiences of angelic figures surrounding him, during the composition of Messiah. Here is a listener's account of his first experience of sitar music where this element is clearly present at the end:

> For the first twenty-five minutes I was totally unaware of any subtlety ... whilst wondering what, if anything, was supposed to happen during the recital.

> What did happen was magic!
> After some time, insidiously the music began to reach me. Little by little, my mind all my senses it seemed – were becoming transfixed. Once held by these soft but powerful sounds, I was irresistibly drawn into a new world of musical shapes and colours. It almost felt as if the musicians were playing me rather than their instruments, and soon, I, too, was clapping and gasping with everyone else ... I was unaware of time, unaware of anything other than the music. Then it was over. But it was, I am sure, the beginning of a profound admiration that I shall always have for an art form that has been until recently totally alien to me. (Dunmore 1983 pp. 20–1)

Altered states of consciousness associated with the phenomena of Ecstasy Culture and Acid House are the subject of Matthew Collin's book (1997) entitled *Altered State*. Here we see an attempt to revive traditional rituals within the context of a society that has outlawed them:

> The eighties were a long way away now, almost innocent in hindsight. For the children of ecstasy, gulping down their first pill in pleasure domes of the late nineties, the euphoric frontiership of acid house must have seemed like ancient history, its roots in black gay culture all but forgotten. Many weren't even ten years old during 1988's Summer of Love. But for all that had changed, old uncertainties and contradictions remained – between a commodified culture and the illicit drugs that fuelled it, between rhetoric and reality, between knowledge and ignorance. And underpinning it all, still, was the restless search for bliss. (Collin 1997 p. 316)

Here he underlines that the fundamental search in ASC's (Altered States of Consciousness) was for transcendence. However, in traditional societies the use of the hallucinogens was under the control of experienced elders. The commodification of Western society has produced a situation where money is the only value system. This has opened the way for the exploitation of what Maslow saw as a fundamental need in human beings – the experience of transcendence. The alliance of drugs, music and dance to produce this is not a new phenomenon. What is new, however, is its alliance with a capitalist economy and its associated value systems, which allow for the exploitation of human need.

It is true that in these traditions transcendence has been commodified by a monetary value system. There is also no shared spiritual frame in which the young participants can place their experiences of the spiritual/

liminal; indeed they may have no frame at all. At least there needs to be examination of these as a cultural phenomenon to explain their popularity and investigate their relationship to the area of Spirituality within the areas of musical experience. The churches need to examine an area where one might have expected them to be engaged.[14]

So myths – religious and otherwise – play a significant part in people's capability to have a liminal experience. Many of these are linked with high art notions of music and notions of canonicity explored earlier. Many of these concern women's relation to music. Ethel Smyth sees that mountains of women's musical products need to be built to support women in their search for a musical identity:

> You cannot get giants like Mt Blanc and Mt Everest without the mass of moderate-sized mountains on whose shoulders they stand. It is the upbuilding of this platform that is impossible so long as full musical life is denied to women. (Neuls-Bates 1996 p. 295)

Sophie Drinker links this with the domain of Spirituality:

> Almost none of the music we sang was composed by women ... It is not necessary to emphasize the value of music in relation to spiritual stature ... It is generally recognized that music gives access to regions in the subconscious that can be reached in no other way ... Women's failure to think in terms of their own creative music has the inevitable result of causing a kind of feminine spiritual starvation. (Drinker 1948 pp. xv–xvi)

Marcia Citron sees the link between criticism and the creation of these quasi-transcendental realities:

> The role of critic implies authority. It connotes mind, wisdom, and judgement: an epistemological foundation for dispensing knowledge to others. This foundation hearkens back to the notion of God as the ultimate authority figure. But God is male, and thus women cannot hope to acquire the necessary moral foundation for dispensing knowledge. (Citron 1993 p. 192)

---

14   However, experiences like the 9 o'clock service in Sheffield in the 1990s have made church leaders less willing to engage with this area.

These debates resonate with ideas about women's link with nature, while men control culture; for women do have a quasi-transcendental role in the canon but only as idols and inspirers. Such debates set up a construction of women, particularly in Romanticism, as idols and re-producers and precluded them from creating their own music. So men dealt with the threat of female creativity (Citron 1993 p. 71). Kimberley Marshall traces this position back to the Muses of Ancient Greece. She sees the name Music as originating in the power of the female Muses. She then describes how in the late Middle Ages they were still depicted as strong women playing musical instruments:

> Unfortunately, during the intervening centuries these powerful female archetypes have been reduced to an insipid allegory for artistic inspiration ... In rediscovering the original meaning of the word *music*, we uncover a vital female creative force. (Marshall 1993 p. xix)

Marcia Citron sees real possibility in the destruction of these myths of powerful female archetypes with a new aesthetic created by women:

> For women creators a potential means of expurgating the negative myths of women in works by men is the construction of a female aesthetic: women composers creating their own definition of self. (Citron 1993 p. 75)

This discussion shows how cultures develop mythologies to support the status quo in the area of gender relations; for there is a clear relationship between the Value domain and Spirituality. Stanley Tambiah in his *Performative Approach to Ritual*, claims that all performances have the following elements:

- A commonly acknowledged procedure ordering the actions
- A sense of collective and communal enactment that is purposive
- A communal 'awareness' that makes the performative acts different from 'ordinary' everyday events. (Tambiah 1979 pp. 116–17)

Clearly the first two of these are linked with Value. Lucy Green's (1988) concept of inherent and delineated meanings are important here for as we saw under Expression, the delineated meanings play a significant part in whether the liminal state is engendered by the musical event. Feminist understandings can interrupt the meaning of a previously meaningful work and a disruption in any of the areas listed above will mean a loss of the spiritual dimension. The liminal experience involves what the theologian Martin Buber (1970) called encounter. Through the experience the musicker encounters the environment through the Materials of sound, the feelings of another in Expression, the world of abstract ideas in the area of Construction and the value systems of a culture in the area of Values. If the musicker is unable to negotiate that process of encounter for whatever reason then the liminal state will not be reached and the sense of fusion that characterises the liminal experience will not happen (Boyce-Tillman 2006a). For some feminists all male performing groups are so at odds with their own Value systems that they are unable to make that encounter. That is particularly true in the male choir tradition of some liturgical music. We shall see this emerging in Chapter Seven.

Some cultures declare the spiritual nature of their music as did pre-Enlightenment Europe. It not only linked humans with the Divine but also was sometimes seen as giving control over the Other whether this is the Divine Spirit of Judaism and Christianity or the multiple deities or spirits of other traditions (Werner 1959 pp. 7–8 et passim). The union of words and music is seen by some theorists and religious traditions as the union of body and spirit (Koskoff 1993 p. 152). We shall see in Chapter 3, Hildegard's view of the centrality of music to God's purposes in the universe. In Renaissance thinking we see the shift from the Christian view of music to the more contemporary view by a new synthesis of Graeco-Roman ideas with Christian thought. In this process Ficino is a significant figure. He is not only a great humanist whose thinking laid the foundations for much contemporary thinking but has also influenced the development of postmodernism and significantly influenced the thinking of Michel Foucault as we have seen above. In the hands of the philosophers of the Enlightenment the link between music and the spiritual became weakened and the search for the spiritual which had characterised the musical tradition of Europe for hundreds of years became an essentially human search.

The notion of the connection with the Divine now reappeared in the human sphere and music and the aesthetic came to be about the highest expression of human achievement. Although an element of the sublime remained in the thinking, the notion of the spiritual was lost. Music came to be associated exclusively with the human mind. The location of the Divine was no longer outside the self somewhere in the universe, but within the human mind which can be probed and searched. The outward search of theology was replaced by an inner search. In theological language, the transcendent Divine was replaced by the immanent sublime. The spirits of the outer world were now identified as human personality traits and emotions. Later texts, like Vitz's *Psychology as religion or the Cult of Self worship* (1979), reflect this shift. But the aesthetic principles espoused by the elite were still those of a male God. The philosopher Rosi Braidotti although claiming that feminist theory does not need to engage with metaphysics, does acknowledge the power of the legacy of metaphysical symbols in her provocative statement: 'God may be dead but the stench of his rotting corpse pervades all of Western culture' (Braidotti 1995). Nowhere is this truer than in what is regarded as aesthetically satisfying.

To summarise, despite the fact that I have drawn on many male theorists, it is nowhere more important than in this aspect of the musical experience to recognise the role of both narratives and metanarratives in the way in which they construct and make sense of reality. There is a real need to collect narratives (particularly of women) in this area to examine the role of myth, religious beliefs and relational consciousness in the musical experience.

Summary

The theorisation of music – that colours much popular thinking about music – has been carried out by academe in the context of Cartesian ways of knowing. These have disadvantaged women and resulted in an imbalance within the conceptualisation of the musical experience, particularly its Expressive character and Spirituality. The area of Values has often been denied completely. Yet there are contemporary signs of both the acknowl-edgment of the presence of Values both intrinsically and extrinsically within the musical experience. This has made it possible to include a greater diver-sity of Value systems which has effected how the other areas function. The main controversies centre on the patriarchal favouring of:

- A structuralist approach seeing music as separate from its surrounding context, a separation from the surrounding community
- An emphasis on the musician's control over the Materials of music
- Formal structures that favour unity
- Disembodied practices like written notation (reflecting the mind/body dualism and devaluing oracy)
- Hierarchical systems for control of musical act

Subjugated ways of knowing (linked with the Wisdom tradition) in a musical tradition value:

- Connectedness with the community both human, natural and spiritual
- More cyclical, curving forms of Construction rather than linear narratives
- Collaborative forms of working in which musicians collaborate with one another and with the Materials of sound
- Embodied approaches to music making
- Ethical ways of understanding at music

These themes will now be traced through the following chapters looking at women in particular contexts in the Western Christian tradition.

CHAPTER 2

Vignette One – Narrowing the Vision:
The First 600 Years

Our sisters also were strengthened by you to give praise;
For women were not allowed to speak in church.
Your instruction opened the closed mouths of the daughters of Eve;
And behold, the gatherings of the glorious (church) resound with their melodies.
A new sight of women uttering the proclamation;
And behold [these women] are called teachers among the congregations.
Your teaching signifies an entirely new world;
For yonder in the kingdom, men and women are equal.
You labored to devise two harps for two groups;
You treated man and women as one to give praise ...
You (women) put on glory from the midst of the (baptismal) waters like your
    brothers,
Render thanks with a loud voice like them also.
You have partaken of a single forgiving body with your brothers,
And from a single cup of new life you have been refreshed.
A single salvation was yours and theirs (alike); why then
Have you not learned to sing praise with a loud voice?
Your silent mouth which your mother Eve closed,
Is now opened by Mary, your sister, to sing praise ...
Uncover your faces to sing praise without shame
To the One who granted you freedom of speech by his birth.
                              — JACOB OF SARUG in Amar (1995) pp. 35–53

Perhaps women were originally permitted by the Apostles and presbyters to join
in singing so as to prevent their gossiping in church. But later this permission
was withdrawn since it was learned that they did not gain any salutary fruits of
penance from divine song, but used the sweetness of melody for disturbances
of every kind, since they looked on in exactly the same way as theater music.
                              — ISIDORE OF PELUSIUM in Quasten (1983) p. 23

Introduction

It is impossible to understand the traditions of early Christianity without contextualising it socially, culturally and religiously. We need to understand the Jewish and the pagan practice of the day. Both theologically and musically the early years of Christianity saw the emerging Christian Church establish its position as distinct from its Judaic roots and the surrounding pagan traditions. Christianity started as a small non-Roman religion in a remote part of the Roman Empire and by the fourth century it was the official religion. We know that women were present liturgically in the development, but the evidence we have is diverse, patchy and sometimes contradictory, as the opening two quotations show, and therefore the subject of much controversy.

Christianity was regarded with disdain by the surrounding community because the earliest spaces it used were domestic; early Christian gatherings were in homes:

> Early Christianity is [seen as] a religion of women's spaces. Religion, which should properly be tied to the public domain of men has become privatized and feminized. Church groups are offensive because in them the public sphere is swallowed up by the private and women play a major role in defining the new ethos. The true purpose of the home is negated when it shelters church meetings and male responsibilities in public affairs are ignored or subverted. (Macdonald 1996 p. 217)

Theologically, the early days of Christianity saw a cultural struggle between the Hebrews with the all-powerful Yahweh, the Christians who claimed that the Messiah had come, the followers of the unconquered sun, Sol Invictus, often called Mithras, the followers of Isis, and the followers of the Great Mother, Magna Mater, Mother of the Gods, Mater Deum. Margaret Lindley in her fascinating article *Competing Trinities: The Great Mother and the Formation of the Christian Trinity* (1995) charts how gradually the concept of a male Trinity was constructed in order to present a credible challenge to the worship of the great mother. She describes how the first three centuries of Christianity show:

a preoccupation with three issues: the formation of a trinity ... the formation of authority, and the ministry of women ... By the time of Constantine the Christian church was led by men who had indicated their willingness to exclude women from ministry whilst retaining them as subjects within their congregations. (Lindley 1995 pp. 32–6)

When we examine the history of women in church music we see that in these early days the construction of the male Trinity went hand in hand with the exclusion of women from the musical ministry of the Church. From then on, the music of the Christian Church has been as tightly in the hands of men as the priesthood. The history of Christianity has been, until the end of the twentieth century, that of the systematic exclusion of women from both the central mysteries of bread and wine and from the central mystery of music.

In the Jewish traditions of the day women's choirs are in evidence, particularly at festivals celebrating such stories as the Exodus which includes Miriam's dance after the flight from Egypt. Jacqueline Lapsley sees a strand of distinctive women's traditions running in a somewhat hidden way through the Old Testament. She starts this with Eli's condemnation of Hannah's apparently drunken ecstasy in I Samuel 1 vv 12–15 (Lapsley 2001 pp. 3–12). Julian in the Dictionary of Hymnology includes the following description of the vigils of a sect called the Therapeutae who appear to be related to the ancient prophetic guilds of Israel:

> To this (the singing of the Son of Moses) the chorus of the male and female Therapeutae afforded a most perfect resemblance with its variant and concordant melodies; and the sharp and searching tone of the women together with the baritone sound of the men effected a harmony both symphonious and altogether musical. (Julian 1925 p. 206)

The pagan traditions of the day saw a variety of practices. In Greek traditions choirs of women participated in processions honouring the gods. Women could participate publicly in worship, except in blood sacrifices. There were some women priests (Bruit Zaidman 1992 pp. 338–76). This is recorded at the spring sacrifice on Delos and at Olympia where a choir of virgins and mothers sang a hymn in honour of the goddess. They seem to have been responsible for the hymns invoking the particular god or goddess. They had been present in the Egyptian traditions for a long time. Men and women are mentioned in temple records and women and girls entered the temple service with the specific role as musicians or singers. They were called 'the harem of the gods' (Quasten 1983 p. 76).

In Roman rituals, choirs of women are mentioned in processions of both expiation and petition. Horace details special occasions at the Sibylline oracle when choirs of virgins or chaste boys were required (Quasten 1983 p. 76). However, in Roman society, although the roles of women differed greatly (the life of a slave differed greatly from a Roman matron) no woman was considered equal to a man in status (Sawyer 1996 p. 31) and with the exception of the Vestal virgins, they were not allowed to perform priestly functions (Scheid 1992 pp. 377–408).

Although there is little detail in early Christianity it is likely that women were included in congregational singing. It is likely that in the early Church the rites of baptism, confirmation and the extreme unction at death were celebrated by women as well as men, possibly because some were celebrated in the home. The religious dance was present, clearly seen in the Hymn of Jesus (from the Apocryphal Acts of St John). Music was clearly important in the early Church. At death the purpose was to lead the departed spirit to the grave and have an influence over the soul of the dead. Traditions taken from the rites of the cities of Rome, Alexandria, Edessa, Antioch and Byzantium were taken into Christianity. The Gnostics retained the worship of Sophia, divine mother and her two daughters and she was invoked by hymns from women's choirs. The defining of Gnosticism as heresy was a significant step in the outlawing of women from singing in public worship.

The rest of the chapter will examine how the Value systems explored in Chapter 1 are reflected in the limited records we have of women's music-making in the early centuries of Christianity.

1a Individual/Community

Ignatius identified a high stress on communal singing as an expression of unity in early Christian worship. The 'singing of all with one mouth' was seen as lending particular power to intercessory prayer. But somewhere between Ignatius and Chrysostom the solo singer seems to have appeared, for Chrysostom writes in a homily

> Shall I name still another treasure chest that has been robbed of its original beauty? In times past all came together and sang psalms as a community. This we no longer do. Formerly there was one heart and one soul in every one, but today we can no longer perceive such harmony of soul and everywhere there is strong discord. (Chrysostom quoted in Quasten 1983 pp. 77–8)

In the early Church it is likely that the role of cantor was open to anyone who wanted to lead a psalm or hymn. As the offices developed and the liturgy developed from a freer to a fixed form, this role came to be devolved onto a single person and the separation of the more elite musicians from the congregation began. Eventually the role of the congregation audibly disappeared (Smith 1962 p. 35).

Egeria (c. 386 CE), a Gallican pilgrim confirms that this community included both men and women in the Church of the Holy Sepulchre in Jerusalem:

> Every day before cockcrow all the gates of the Anastasis are opened and all the monks and virgins ... descend – not merely they but lay people, men and women, as well ... And from that hour until the break of day hymns and psalms are sung in alternate chant, and so too are the antiphons. And after each hymn a prayer is said. (Quasten 1983 p. 79)

The practice of antiphonal singing developed very early but was not fully established in general use till the end of the fourth century. It was known in Jewish worship and practised by the Therapautae (see above). Ignatius claims to have received the idea from a vision of angels singing in heaven, while the development of antiphony in Milan is credited to Ambrose (Smith 1962 p. 37). Basil writes (c. 330–79 CE) that the custom of singing the psalms was in vogue and was in harmony and accord with all the Churches of God. He described how people were divided into two groups and sang antiphonally. This was a way of passing the night so that when the day began they were all in tune with one another.

The use of antiphonal practices is interesting to reflect on theologically. It is a form of singing that allows one the experience of dependence within the singing Body of Christ. Whereas singing in unison a person can get lost in singing and forget the rest of the community, in antiphonal singing there is a constant sense of the dependency of one group upon the other and the handing of the authority across the body of singers. It also allowed longer periods of singing to take place. However, White links its rise to the development of monasteries and professional choirs, as he claims it demands more skill than that of the simple response (Smith 1962 pp. 37–8). By the fourth century congregational singing had disappeared and the initiatives described by Tertullian in c. 197 CE that allowed everyone to take the initiative in song or prophecy (Frend 2002 p. 104) had been discontinued.

Whether women sang or not was an important way of identifying particular communities within the early Church or separating the Church from the surrounding culture. For example, because the heretics Bardesanes and Harmonius had a great following and included choirs of women, Ephrem decides to include women's choirs in his church:

> When the holy Ephraem[1] saw how all were being torn away by the singing [of the heretics], and since he wanted to keep his own people away from the dishonorable and worldly plays and concerts, he himself founded choirs of consecrated virgins, taught them the hymns and responses whose wonderful contents celebrated the birth of Christ, his baptism, fasting, suffering, resurrection and ascension, as well as the martyrs and the dead. He had these virgins come to the church on the feast of the Lord and on those of the martyrs, as they did on Sundays. He himself was in their midst as their father and the citharist of the Holy Spirit. And he taught them music and the laws of song. (Quasten 1983 p. 79)

However, there clearly were moves to separate men and women while attempting to unite them in worship:

[1]   Ephraem is an alternative spelling of Ephrem.

> This differentiation functioned more and more as a means of enforcing gender
> boundaries to the liturgical disadvantage of women. There is, to put it differently,
> evidence of a 'liturgical muting' of women within the New Testament itself ... There
> is, however, no trace of women being excluded from such fundamentals of early
> Christian worship as the Sunday assembly, the breaking of the bread, or penitence.
> (Berger 1999 p. 36)

The Church also tried to control the music of the secular society. Women
were often associated with these. Bishop Caesarius of Aries (Sermon XIII)
complained in 542 CE:

> How many peasants and how many women know by heart and recite out loud the
> Devil's songs, erotic and obscene. (Duchesne 1909 p. 10)

But the desire to control secular music had started earlier. Roman civilisa-
tion regarded music and dancing as vices, unlike Greek society which had
developed the theatrical use of music to a high level. The vulgar role of music
in pantomime came in for much attack; but the Christian condemnation of
it was on the grounds of its association with idolatry. The flutes of the cult
of Cybele are likened to 'the sound of the castrated man'. Women citharists
and lyrists who played at pagan banquets were condemned. The *Canons of
Basil* of around 400 CE emphasise the division in a period of purification:

> A woman who dances in taverns and allures people by her beautiful singing and
> her deceitful melody which is full of temptation, shall, if she renounces her profes-
> sion, wait forty days before she communicates; then she may receive the mysteries.
> (Quoted in Quasten 1983 pp. 125–8)

Theatre music is seen as consecrated to idols; and Christians were banned
from participating and priests from attending or having friends in the theatre trade. The tunes were very popular and formed the musical backdrop
to everyday life in the city. The Emperor Julian's failure to take a stronger
line on this issue led to a battle between church and theatre that lasted for
centuries. The Church fathers recommended regularly the substitution
of psalms for the music of the theatre. Christian families are exhorted to
avoid pagan songs at their meals, being encouraged to 'erect a fortress of
psalms, against him [the devil] and when leaving the table to sing holy songs

with your wife and children. They also served to invite Christ to the table'
(Quasten 1983 pp. 130–1). And so the Church took control of the home
and regulated it. Customs that had included women's contributions were
increasingly controlled by men.

This included wedding ceremonies that included songs celebrating
fertility and procreation and where music and dancing were present in
abundance. The *hymenaios* accompanied by flute and cithara was sung by
the bride's supporters, leading her to her husband's house. Early Christians
seem to have enjoyed it; but Chrysostom attacks it vehemently, along with
hymns to Aphrodite sung at wedding feasts which he links with 'filthy songs'.
Clearly his decrees met with opposition as he describes people laughing at
him and reproaching him. He particularly attacks the *licentia Fescennina*
which accompanied the bringing of the bride and groom to the market
place with torches and flute music. Participants were inflamed with a 'dia-
bolic rivalry' and had competitions in lewd songs:

> Although everything happens at night, darkness does not draw a veil over this atro-
> cious scene ... What shall one say of songs that breathe forth nothing but sensual-
> ity, dishonourable passions, forbidden relationships and the downfall of families?
> (Chrysostom quoted in Quasten 1983 p. 133)

From the canons from the Council of Laodicea (c. 380 CE) we see that
the Church was not entirely successful in its condemnation of the feast of
sensuality; for priests are told not to look at shows or banquets and leave
before the actors come. So clearly the injunction in canon 53 that 'It is
not permitted for Christians to go to weddings and dance, but only in all
propriety to eat or take a light collation' (quoted in Quasten 1983 p. 134)
was not followed by all.

Music played a significant part in pagan funeral ceremonies. Mourning
songs and chants were sung originally by the family and accompanied by
gestures but later by hired professional women mourners who employed
antiphonal performances. There seems to have been antiphonal singing
between men and women in Babylonian funerals. In Greece, women
mourners beat their breast, pulled out their hair and scratched their cheeks
until blood came while others joined in the laments. The songs included

reference to the body and the spirit of deceased and were accompanied by flutes. The Greeks used lyres and citharas while the Egyptians used the flute, sometimes the double flute. In Jewish traditions flutes were also used, as evidenced in the story of the Raising of Jairus's daughter in Matthew 9:23. From the first century comes a relief from a mausoleum with an excellent portrayal of the lamenting rites:

> A dead woman lies in solemn state on a bier. The man at the head of the bier, who is bringing a garland to adorn the deceased, may be the pollinctor, whose duty it was to prepare the corpse. The other people standing about the bier are striking their breasts with their hands as a sign of mourning. To the left at the foot of the bed is a woman flutist, seated on a stool, accompanying the mourning with a double flute. (Quasten 1983 pp. 149–51)

Music was not only part of the domestic rites but also the funeral procession itself. Here it was originally seen as having an adjuratory and preventive effect on the dead. The music had to be performed in the presence of the corpse as the soul was seen as lingering nearby. The significance may or may not have been lost in the accounts of historians but what is clear is that women played a significant part in these rituals. Egypt used the sistrum[2] to accompany the dirges, and the Greeks used flutes. There are references to trumpets, horn players and musicians of various kinds in Greece and Rome, but these were not part of the burials of the poor. The lamentation ceremonies continued at the grave where flautists and trumpeters played. It is clear that music also played a significant part in preventing the return of the dead. Bells were used over graves and even in them. In Christian graves whole sets have been found and it is likely that the rituals described under the heading Public/Private below were concerned with preventing the returning of spirit and keeping the area free of demons.

Christianity attacked these practices on several fronts. The authorities saw their doctrine of resurrection as changing the nature of the ceremony from mourning to rejoicing and they also associated the rites with idolatry.

---

2   The sistrum was a shaken percussion instrument which consisted of a metal frame on which are hung metal rings. It produced everything from a soft clank to a loud jangling sound.

They attempted to replace the dirges and lamentations with psalms (the answer to everything musical!). The bodily gestures were discouraged. Chrysostom used the story of Jairus's daughter to cast out the flautists like Jesus did. The writings emanating for the synods show how difficult it was to draw people away from the customs, particularly the use of pagan women as mourners. The prohibitions were mostly directed at women who were accused of excessive expressions of sorrow. So Shenute of Atripe said that burials of nuns can only be carried out by monks. Women were banned from entering houses in mourning or participation in the rites.[3] In the 4th century St Chrysostom attacked traditional mourners: 'Anyone who hires these wretched women shall be excluded from the Church for a long time, like an idolater' (Bright 1903 p. 33).

There were divisions within the Church in this area. For example, the Donatists were called The Church of the Martyrs and exercised less control over the rites than the Roman tradition, writing new hymns and songs for martyrs and renewing the receptacles for the relics in a practice that differed from the Roman (Frend 2002 pp. 106–16).

The Nestorian synod is more specific – banning cutting hair, tearing clothing, lamenting, beating drums, singing and cutting branches. Sometimes nuns were excluded from the prohibitions. Quasten describes a contemporary Melchite custom that clearly embodies the feeling of this time:

> A woman mourner in dark veils takes her place near the head of the person who has just died; the women of the house, as well as other female relatives, sit about the corpse and respond with sobbing and lamentation to the threnody of the mourner. Then one or more priests come and drive her out. (Quasten 1983 pp. 160–4)

The notion of music helping the dead in some way is attacked. Commodian denies the efficacy of the pagan rites in helping the dead, calling Christian participation in them a sin; but it is clear that the practices continued.

---

3   There are still a few remaining examples in western culture. In some research I was doing into women priests and funeral music in the UK, two women priests referred to funerals involving gypsies and black women that involved wailing.

Gregory of Nyssa acknowledges that lamentations accompanied the psalms on his sister's funeral procession and that there was a choir of virgins led by a deaconess in the procession. Hymns were composed and Ephrem wrote some for his choir of virgins. Consecrated sisters clearly were now used, thus retaining some link with the female mourners of the pagan tradition, even if their contribution was restricted to hymns and psalms without the traditional mourning bodily gestures.

The Christians tried to replace the all night vigils (pervigilia) of the pagans with their own commemoration of the dead. These were intended to be festivals of splendour and joy. The Christian rituals both for the dead and to commemorate martyrs included the celebration of the Eucharist, a meal at the grave and psalm singing. Songs were written for the martyrs which were very popular. The most determined attempt was the establishment of the Paschal Vigil, which Augustine calls 'mater omnium vigiliarum'. What is clear is that the ordinary people saw no distinction between them and produced syncretic rituals combining the two belief systems. Prohibitions against using the same profanity and self-indulgence as the pagans clearly did not work. Dancing was particularly condemned and in the end Basil of Caesarea writes that at the Paschal Vigil, licentious women:

> removed the veils of honor from their heads, contemned God and the angels, displayed themselves shamelessly for every man's eye to see, shaking their hair, dragging their garments and tripping their feet; with lustful eyes they rushed about with unrestrained laughter as if mad, ... dancing in every place before the city where the martyrs had shed their blood and making the holy sites the workshops of their shamelessness. They have sullied the air with their lewd songs and the earth with their unclean feet. (Basil quoted in Quasten 1983 pp. 175–6)

The number of edicts around this area continued into the Middle Ages and because of these dangers, monks were prevented from attending. It was finally in the thirteenth century when East Barhebraeus decrees:

> Women who dance in pagan fashion for the dead and go to the grave with drums, dancing the while, shall be admonished not to do that. But if they do not discontinue they shall be forbidden entrance to the Church. (Quasten 1983 p. 177)

What is clear is that it was around the rituals to the dead that the biggest struggle between the dominant patriarchy and the resilient pre-Christian traditions involving women were played out.

To summarise, during this period women's authority was systematically eroded; the worshipping community became more exclusive both theologically and musically as it defined an orthodoxy that excluded women from positions of authority.

1b Unity/Diversity

Early accounts of singing emphasise the effect that it has in creating unity from diversity. Ambrose writes:

> The Apostle commands women to be silent in church, but they may sing the psalms; this is fitting for every age and for both sexes. In this singing, old men lay aside the rigor of age: downcast middle-aged men respond in the cheerfulness of their heart; younger men sing without peril of wantonness: youths sing without danger to their impressionable age and without fear of being tempted to pleasure; tender maidens suffer not damage to the adornment of their chastity, and young widows let their rich voices ring out without endangering their modesty. ... For it is a powerful bond of unity when such a great number of people come together in one choir. The strings of the cithara are of unequal length, yet they all sound in harmony. Even with the very small number the virtuoso still sometimes mistakes his touch. But when all sing in community the Holy Spirit, as the Artist, permits no dissonance. (Ambrose quoted in Quasten 1983 p. 78)

But the history of the early Church is one of the systematic elimination of theological diversity. The diversity of practice in the earliest church communities reflected the diverse theologies that made it up. Walter Bauer in 1934 claimed that what were later defined as heresies were more widespread than orthodoxies in the first two centuries. When one considers the number of heresies that were created by the dominant group of Fathers this is very likely. The dominant orthodox group were not as large as those who subscribed to the many diverse practices that were systematically declared heretical (Bauer 1971).

There were, however, certainly in the third century traditions with a variety of practice and the practice of allowing women to sing was a subject of controversy:

> Clearly, any facile label such as 'liberating' on the one hand, or 'patriarchal', on the other, does not do justice to complex realities of women's liturgical lives in the earliest Christian communities. (Berger 1999 p. 39)

While Ambrose argues *for* women singing the psalms, others attack the practice. Werner sees the variation in practice as linked with the 'licentious' practices of the secular world. Here female singers and musicians had bad reputations. Quasten sees music as a defining principle for heresies who 'unscrupulously used female choirs as a means of popular attraction' (Werner 1959 p. 324)

In terms of the style of the music used, the shape of the early music was necessarily syncretic, drawing together Jewish practices with those of Greece, Rome and Egypt. This had started in Judaism in the years leading up to the birth of Christianity especially in the Diaspora. The very fact that the texts were sung in Greek rather than Hebrew necessitated this.

To summarise, diversity is clearly an important part in the early practice of the Church but was systematically eliminated by the establishment of orthodoxy both theologically and musically. This process disadvantaged women.

2a Public/Private

It is important to identify the space in which various ritual practices were carried out at this time. In Judaism, certain rituals were associated with the domestic sphere – like the separation of the dough, the lighting of the Sabbath candles, the Passover meal and the preparation of the dead for

burial. Teresa Berger challenges rational assumptions about Jewish women's
public role as well, claiming that, particularly in the Diaspora, women were
regularly present at public worship, functioned as synagogue leaders and
elders and were not separated from men during worship (Berger 1999 p. 29).
However Irit Shillor, speaking of Jewish women's music writes:

> Certain constraints have been made religiously explicit for Jewish women (which
> we can rebel against, ignore or struggle with) concerning singing in public. (Shillor
> 1993)

To chart the history of women in early Christian worship, the domestic
as well as the public sphere needs to be taken into account. When rituals
were carried out in the home it is likely that women had a greater hand
in controlling the music used. The story of Christianity, as we have seen
above, is one of moving from the domestic to the public sphere. Although
Roman women were allowed into the market place, to the shops and to
hear lectures, they were always 'chaperoned' by men or slaves. This was true
of aristocratic women. Poorer women were more evident in public spaces.

> When Christianity went public on a large scale in the fourth century, it entered a
> sphere where, in varying degrees in the larger culture women were marginalized. A
> public liturgy, therefore, almost inescapably entailed some measure of marginaliza-
> tion for women in Christian worship. (Berger 1999 p. 47)

As we have seen above, often it is certain categories of women that are
referred to as singing. Some religious women not only sang in their convents
but at least in the fourth century, sang the psalms in city churches. Marûtâ
of Maipherkat in the second half of the fourth century says:

> It is the will of the general synod that municipal churches should not be without this
> class of sisters. They shall have a diligent teacher and shall be instructed in reading
> and especially psalmody. This is decreed in the synod without anathema. (Quasten
> 1983 p. 79)

It is clear that women did not only sing but also held positions as cantors
as they did as lectors; indeed these two roles may have been interlinked as
the readings were possibly sung to a recitative like chant. Susan Ashcroft

Harvey draws attention to the office known as the Sons and Daughters of the Covenant, who were found throughout the Syrian orient, both in Persian and Roman territory. In the earliest sources they were an identified group in the wider church community who had taken vows of celibacy and simplicity and worked in the service of the priest and bishop. They were not separated out into monastic communities. She likens them to consecrated virgins elsewhere, like Cappadocia and Egypt, although their function and role is not entirely clear. They are:

> mandated in [the] canons to have the task of singing the psalms and especially the doctrinal hymns of the church ... Both the Sons and Daughters are enjoined to strict restraints in the Rabbula Canons, and these rulings may well indicate an increased effort to enclose women and to curtail their public activity ... Their liturgical role of psalmody and singing the madrashe grants them a more central function in the ritual life of the Christian community than that accorded to deaconesses or widows at this time. (Harvey 2000 pp. 233–4)

Particular groups of women were permitted in other places to sing in public worship, particularly women ascetics. But in the end both they and women religious were confined in their own spaces to sing, and singing women became banned in public worship. Cyril of Jerusalem encourages women to pray only silently in public worship by moving their lips without making a sound (Berger 1999 p. 60).

One place where women did dance and sing was cemeteries (see below). These spaces were redefined by Christianity, as the devotion to the graves and shrines of martyrs and saints increased in popularity. They became foci of Christian ritual and seem to be semi-public spaces:

> For women in the ancient world, the cemetery areas had always been a zone of 'low gravity', where their movements and choice of company were less subject to male scrutiny and the control of the family. (Brown 1981 p. 44)

Monica, mother of St Augustine, appears to have gone to the cemetery in North Africa with a basket of meal-cakes and bread and wine on memorial days. When she moved to Milan, she was prevented from doing this by a doorkeeper operating the instructions of Ambrose. This was part of a movement to exercise increasing control over women's worship in the area of its location. At the beginning of the fourth century a canon of the Synod of Elvira, held in Spain, runs: 'women are forbidden to spend the night in a cemetery since often under the pretext of prayer they secretly commit evil deeds' (Laeuchli 1972 p. 130).

These women may have been attached to the Circumcellion religious movement who were criticised as 'superstitious folk' by the Donatist writer Tyconius in about 380 CE for their visiting of the tombs of the martyrs (Frend 2002 p. 103). And so space once available for women is now closed to them. Teresa Berger (1999 p. 52) links this with a wider reaction to 'rival' ritual powers. These took two forms. One was women who attended ritual festivals other than Christian ones. Chrysostom, for example, criticised women in Antioch who attended a Jewish festival (possibly Rosh Hashanah) (Kraemer 1988 p. 31). The second is women's own ritual spheres of ritual power within the confines of Christianity. These spheres were often designated 'superstitious or magic' and I will deal with them below.

What is clear is that as worship moved from the sphere of the home to the public sphere, the liturgical space became gendered. Boundaries between the genders were increasingly enforced. The *Didascacalia Apostolorum (XII)* shows a community ordered from east to west, and hierarchically. The Bishop is seated at the east end. Then from east to west the ordering appears to have been: priests – lay men – women who were divided according to marital status i.e. young girls, married women, widows.

The *Testamentum Domini* suggests a separate entrance for women, and women worshipping separately. Widows and deaconesses were placed separately in the sanctuary for the Eucharist but were barred during menstruation (Berger 1999 p. 55 and also see below).

The way the space was divided varied and Chrysostom even mentions a dividing screen (Aston 1990 pp. 238–40). Berger sees three potential reasons for this development:

- A link with Jewish practice
- A link with such institutions as the theatre and circus which also had separate spaces for women
- A replication of Christian meal etiquette (Berger 1999 pp. 55–6)

Menstrual taboos played an important part in the regulation of liturgical space for women (Branham 2003). Dionysus a third-century student of Origen writes:

> Concerning women in their menstrual separation, whether it is right for them in such a condition to enter the house of God, I think it unnecessary even to inquire. For I think that they, being faithful and pious, would not dare in such a condition either to approach the holy table or touch the body and blood of Christ. (Branham 2003)

Although Gregory tried to open the space for menstruating women at the end of the sixth century, in 688 Theodore of Tarsus not only reversed this but also introduced a forty-day waiting period after childbirth, following Old Testament practice.

Liturgical functions were gradually withdrawn from women. In 367 CE the fourth canon of the Council of Laodicea said that 'it is not fitting for women to draw near the altar nor to touch things which have been classed as the duty of men.' This stopped women's singing activity and although Quasten sees this as a reaction to women's participation in heterodox communities (Quasten 1983 p. 85 ff), Berger disputes this and draws attention to the ritual power of women within Christianity in marginal rites. The Syrian *Testament of the Lord* (fifth century) would tolerate a female response in psalmody providing it was led by a male singer (Quasten 1983 p. 119).

Early Christian hymnody appears to have started in Syria (Werner 1959 p. 346). The role of hymnody is very complex and has to be seen in relation to psalmody. The sects like the Gnostics and the Marcionites both used hymns and also included women in positions of authority as prophetesses, lectresses, deaconesses and singers. Ephrem harnessed the power of the hymn, even using popular or heretical tunes and replacing the words. Paul of Samosata was attacked largely for writing new songs rather than using traditional hymns and to a lesser extent for getting these sung by women (Smith 1962 pp. 32–3).

Parallel to this story is the story of the development of boys' choirs. These were regularly found in pagan worship, where they were deeply praised as:

Perfectly delicate, not so deep as to be called masculine nor so fine as to be effeminate and lacking in power, but falling soft, mild and lovely on the ear. (Quasten
1983 pp. 87–92)

In Egeria's account of her visit to Jerusalem she refers not to singing by
children but to singing by boys. The Emperor Julian in an attempt to sup-
plant pagan music, offered prizes to boys who practised religious singing and sacred music. According to *The Testament of the Lord*, the boys
responded to the cantor with the virgins and responded antiphonally to
them and seemed to be replacing the role of the general congregation. The
canticles at vespers were sung only by boys, and the people responded with
the Alleluia. They were already replacing the cantor. This was linked to the
development of boy lectors. Both boy lectors and choristers came to be
educated in special schools. Ephrem refers to the boys singing psalms and
virgins songs in the Easter liturgy.

To summarise, I have shown how, as Christianity moved from the
domestic to the public sphere women's role was gradually reduced leaving
men and boys in control liturgically and musically.

2b Product/Process

The notion of the power of the Holy Spirit (following the Pentecost experience) ensured some measure of musical improvisation was present in early
liturgy. It is likely that there was a considerable degree of elaboration of
basic chants in the chanting and reading of the early Church. The subject
of the gift of tongues – glossolalia – is much debated in the early Church
and it would seem to have had musical expression (Smith 1962 p. 41).
There seems to have been a democratic freedom of people to sing from
their experience according to Tertullian.

Werner draws attention to the presence of improvisation in early
Christian liturgy, particularly in the development of the jubilus, from
Jewish psalmody and its use for alleluias which he links with apostolic

practice (Werner 1959pp. 168–9). He dates the loss of the improvisatory tradition from the time

> When the western Church attempted to systematize its songs according to the mis-understood teaching of Greek theorists, it was the melismatic type that suffered most. Forced into the Procrustean bed of the eight Church Tones, it was modified and mutilated. (Werner 1959 p. 352)

It is likely that improvised song was acceptable at mealtimes in the absence of knowledge of a hymn according to Tertullian. So there were examples of freer more improvisatory practice in early Christian practice. How far women were part of these is difficult to ascertain. However, the process of codification saw the systematic reduction of these elements.

3a Excitement/Relaxation

We do not know with any certainty the sound of the music. W.S. Smith refers to the likelihood of the nasal tone colour associated with Judaism (Smith 1962 p. 12). We see also how the Church Fathers struggled to keep worship decent and modest to combat the freer pagan traditions. This would indicate that the music was fairly controlled in terms of volume and speed. Indeed there are several recommendations of a high degree of silence. It is women who are associated with music of a more lively kind often associated with dancing and bodily gestures (see below), a tendency that had to be curbed.

3b Challenge/Nurture

In the Syriac church, women's voices were more clearly heard than in other traditions. Distinctive voices were given to biblical women. Susan Ashbrook Harvey shows how in Ephrem's *Hymns of the Nativity*, Mary the Mother of Jesus is given a distinctive voice. She shows how these hymns (and sermons) are different from extracanonical texts in that they are set clearly in the liturgical context with probably a didactic function. Many of the texts are anonymous. There were two forms: the madrashe which dealt with doctrinal matters. They included verses sung by a soloist, interspersed with a choral response or alternating with psalm texts in antiphonal singing (which, as we have seen, was much favoured in the early church in general). The Mimre were verse homilies chanted in a simple metre. A favourite form was the dialogue poem which gave the opportunity for two conflicting voices to be heard, as in the hymn of Abraham and Sarah disputing over Isaac's sacrifice or the dialogue between Satan and the Sinful Woman. In the first Sarah wrestles with Abraham's determination to sacrifice Isaac. In the latter Satan provides the normative voice while the Sinful Woman replies in tune with her steadfast faith in Christ. The voices represent the traditional position of male opposition to women's Wisdom.

In a character sketch of Mary in another hymn, God warns Gabriel:

> Do not stand up to [Mary] or argue,
> For she is stronger than you in argument;
> Do not speak too many words to her,
> For she is stronger than you in her replies ...
> If she starts to question you closely,
> Disclose to her the mystery, and then be off. (Brock 1994 pp. 135–40)

These hymns are great testaments to women's strength and integrity and by rediscovering them and reconstructing them in performance we bring to the fore what Lucy Winkett (2010) highlights in her prophetic book *Our Sound is our Wound*:

> There are so many wonderful stories in the Gospels that are brought alive by imagining the scene from the woman's point of view and listening for her voice not only of protest against exclusion but hearing too the humour and energy of these first-century women ... we hear women speak with passion, insight, anger and not a little irony, and it opens our minds, changes our perspective and enriches our experience of God. (Winkett 2010)

In these hymns, there was a brief setting of the context at the opening and a closing doxology. It is likely that they were sung antiphonally by a female and male choir, probably the Sons and Daughters of the Covenant or by choirs of women. What is remarkable here, in a tradition that lasted from the fourth to the sixth century, is that they

- Gave voices to women silent in the scriptures, not found in Greek and Roman traditions
- Used the dialogic device to give women a voice
- Had the hymns sung by women's voices in civic churches in the village, town and city

These gave women two voices, one rhetorical in words placed in the mouths of women who were silenced in the canonical Scriptures and one performative in terms of women's choirs (Harvey 2001 pp. 105–9).

> So too did liturgical celebration establish a ritual space in which participants could speak and act in terms unlike those that governed their daily lives ... Ritual practices granted each member of the community a necessary place and purpose; they validate each person's contribution as worthy. Such a sacred order challenged the social order as it existed, and made possible other kinds of configurations. Women's voices could proclaim – and indeed embody –such possibilities. Yet the liturgy offered a 'bounded freedom'. ... Liturgy allowed a situation of social and cultural critique, wherein women's voices and their good works could be upheld as morally and theologically worthy. At the same time it negotiated the impact of that critique ... Women's ritual voices and women's rhetorical voices could offer a view of ... [the] Kingdom. (Harvey 2001 pp. 129–30)

There is an interesting record of female religious communicating their feelings about the Emperor Julian in song. In a convent a nun called Publia is recorded by Theodoret of Cyrus as follows:

> She had a choir of virgins who were praiseworthy for their lifelong virginity, and with them she ceaselessly worshiped God the creator and preserver of all things. At the time when the Emperor died they sang more loudly than usual, for they considered the evildoer contemptible and ridiculous. They sang those songs most often which mocked the weakness of idols, and they said with David: 'The idols of the pagans are silver and gold, the work of human hands. Those who make them are like them, and so are all who trust in them.' (Quasten 1983 p. 80)

So here we can see evidence of women's writing and performing in the area of hymnody, at least some of which was protected and preserved by church authorities.

4a Rational/Intuitive

The association of music with magic practices and its perception as having a power of its own is clearly part of cultic practices surrounding the early Christians. The Greek poet Menander writes:

> No god, O woman, saves one man on account of another, for if a man could bring a god to do what a mere mortal willed simply by playing the cymbal, then he would be more powerful than the god. (Quasten 1983 p. 2)

Such a prohibition clearly indicates that this was part of the pagan rituals of the day. It is interesting that it is addressed to a woman, implying that it is directed at women's traditions. The link between women, 'magic' (or I would rather use the word intuitive) pagan ritual practices was not to serve the cause of women well in the early years of Christianity.

The initiation dances of the groups of women Maenads clearly included women playing tambourines and cymbals. Quasten notes the cathartic power of music here, linking it with the purifying character of the fire carried around the initiate at these ceremonies. Plutarch said that anyone who consults the oracle is 'surrounded by tunes'. Here it was heard as a purifier facilitating the perception of the god.

Music clearly played an important part in prophetic inspiration in pagan practices, along with honey, fasting, dancing and intoxicating infusions. In this context, Quasten questions the role of the female flautist in *The Acts of St Thomas* who has been seen as part of this prophetic, ecstatic tradition. He claims that her power was simply that she could understand the Hebrew which the Apostle spoke. In the light of female roles in mystic practices, this may or may not be an accurate interpretation (Quasten 1983 p. 40).

One interesting sphere that is often called 'superstitious' concerns ritual practices of women at the fringes of the Christian liturgy. They were often around the menarche, love, marriage, fertility, birth and the lives of children. They were regularly attacked for using 'magic':

> It is important to find other ways of describing this female ritual power than by labeling it 'magic'. At a time when the public liturgical realm successively marginalized women, women's ritual activities not surprisingly became located elsewhere, usually at the margins of the liturgical realm. This ritual 'margins-become-centre' for women must be interpreted in relation to 'public-worship-become-a problem' for women at this time. One possible reinterpretation is to see this as a conflict between rival systems of ritual activity and power: the one centered around public acts of worship and under the control of ecclesiastical authorities, the other largely in the hands of ordinary people and located at the fringes of the liturgy or in the private sphere. (Berger 1999 p. 52)

The records of this area are scanty. In general there are oblique references in writers such as Chrysostom's references to a baby-naming ritual. Many concerned reproduction in some way (Aubert 1989 pp. 421–49), and included curses as well as more benign prayers. The Church clearly saw these as threats to its own power.

Werner associates the songs associated with these rituals with a failure in musical construction. He compares what he calls a Gnostic-magic incantation with a Gregorian chant:

> The magical pieces show no discernible rhythm nor metre and convey, in general, a rather amorphous, not to say, chaotic impression. (Werner 1959 p. 353)

Such writing in the tradition of patriarchal musicology shows the valuing of the shaping and forming that characterises the more rational approach to construction we examined in Chapter 1. The free flowing figures which can, as he remarks, 'exert a strong magic appeal' (Werner 1959 p. 352) may well have been completely suited to the context of these rituals and the mood needed for them. In commenting on the hymn/dance in the *Acts of St John*, again he shows his love of order over chaos:

> The tenor of the hymn is Gnostic ... From a purely literary point of view, the hymn appears rather primitive, for the only artistic device applied is the principle of response and a repeated antithesis of active and passive expressions, with no discernible trace of metre or organized rhythm. (Werner 1959 pp. 209–10)

Here a male musicologist supports the values of the dominant patriarchy by commending order and structure rather than the more free-flowing character and structure of pieces that have a more intuitive origin.

4b Embodied/Disembodied

We have already seen the mind/body/sprit split opening up in the early Church as dancing is increasingly marginalised and finally banned. Dancing is often associated with women in the Old Testament. The place of dancing in early rituals seems to be indicated in the apocryphal *Acts of St John* where dancing is affirmed by Jesus (in a hymn which may have been the one sung at the Last Supper) in such lines as 'Grace danceth. I would pipe; dance ye all. Amen' (Werner 1959 p. 209). This hymn in one tradition was sung by Jesus at the last Supper, standing in the middle of a circle of the Apostles, all solemnly dancing, the apostles responding to Jesus with 'Amen' (Smith 1962 p. 40).

Chrysostom's most vehement attack on dancing was reserved for wedding ceremonies:

> If then, someone asks, since neither maidens nor married women may dance, who may dance? No one. What need is there of dancing? Dances take place in the pagan mysteries, but in ours there is silence and decency, modesty and peacefulness. A great mystery is being celebrated. Out with the harlots, out with the unclean! How much of a mystery is it? Two come together and form one. When the bride enters why is there no dancing, why no cymbals, but rather profound silence and calm? Rather when they come together, making not a lifeless image or the image of an earthly creature but the image of God himself, why do you introduce such a pagan uproar, disturbing those present and filling their souls with shame and confusion ... Tell me, do you celebrate the mystery of Christ and invite the devil?... Where flutists are, there Christ is not; but even if he should enter he firsts casts them out and only then works wonders. What can be so disagreeable as such satanic pomp? (Chrysostom quoted in Quasten 1983 p. 132)

We have already seen how women's dancing was condemned by Basil of Caesarea and associated with the Church's problems with the pagan funeral ceremonies. When they apparently danced at martyrs' graves outside the city on Easter morning unveiled, he condemned them for dancing unveiled 'publicly', which means, before the eyes of men. Although women dancing in front of men were not unusual at the time, it was typically as entertainment in such venues as the brothel or the circus, where the dancers would be female slaves or prostitutes (Berger 1999 p. 50). Patriarch John III of Constantinople (d. 577) threatened excommunication to the women who visited family graves and played tambourines and danced (Quasten 1983 p. 86). The usual reason given for the prohibition concerns licentiousness, so this move was part of a wider movement within the early church denying sexuality within the context of worship and locating it quite firmly in the secular world which became increasingly separated from the religious world as it became more and more narrowly defined.

There are some indications of the use of instruments in early worship. Women clearly played them in Greek pagan practices as in Plutarch's account of a woman playing the lyre annually at the sacrificial feast of Bona Dea. On the pedestal in the Capitoline museum two women play flutes at the offering of incense in a ceremony to Artemis. One of them wears a mantle on her head. They surround two younger girls who are veiled. This is one of a number of portrayals of women flautists in Greek religious rituals. In the Roman tradition a women playing a lyre appears on an Etruscan ash coffer in the Vatican Museum portraying a sacrifice to Iphigenia.

The sound of cymbals and bells were seen as driving away demons and potentially evil spirits. And at the feasts of Saturnalia and Lupercalia horns were added. Christian women hung little bells round their children's necks and placed them round their wrists, following this practice. However, this was condemned by Chrysostom who claimed that only the Cross had this power (Quasten 1983 p. 16). This is but another example of the trend listed above where women's intuitive use of sound was suppressed.

In early Christian art women are depicted playing instruments, as in the third century sarcophagus in the Vatican museum where two women musicians are at the ends of the portrayal. The portrait of the deceased old woman is in the centre. The right hand woman is younger and is seated playing an instrument with a long fret board and four strings attached with pegs. The older woman on the left had a lute-like instrument and a club in her other hand. These images may be those of the deceased woman from different phases in her life (Quasten 1983 pp. 123–4), or may also reflect the role of instruments in the passing over of the soul at death, in which Christians may have taken on surrounding pagan beliefs. Gradually women's use of instruments became restricted – because of their association with paganism, mysticism, licentiousness, as we have already seen. Instruments were eventually forbidden to women. Jerome writes:

> Let the maid of God be, as it were, deaf towards instruments. Let her not know why the flute, the lyre, and the zither have been made. (Meyer 1917 p. 10 author's translation)

This move was, however, part of wider move towards the notion of spiritual sacrifice from the blood sacrifice of the pagans. This involved widening the mind/spirit/body split. The move to eliminate instrumental music from worship came initially from the Greek philosophers. Plato concluded that all instrumental music should be removed from the liturgy because music without words contained no more spirit in it, likening it to animal sounds.

Philodemus of Gadara (c. 100–28 BCE) in his treatise *On Music* called the view that music mediated religious ecstasy self-deceptive. He saw the noise of tambourines and cymbals as disturbing to the spirit. He found it significant that only women and effeminate men subscribed to this folly. Here is the association of femininity with the intuitive response to music that we saw in Chapter 1. He therefore attributed nothing of value to this music associating it with the sensation of pleasure. The Greek educated Jew, Philo also rejected instrumental music feasts on the grounds that it produces only personal pleasure. He saw this as paganism exploiting men's weakness. He emphasised the interiority of the religious experience and eventually ended up in a position of the ideal of the worship of silence. The notion of spiritual sacrifice (replacing blood sacrifices) developed and the hymn served this purpose well. It became an allegory for the life of the believer. Philo drew attention to the fact that the priest laid aside his flowing robe adorned with bells to go into the holiest of holies and drew from it that music and colour were not to be used in worship which must be spiritual. Neo-Platonism developed this trend, developing the notion of purely spiritual sacrifice, which spelled the rejection of music.

This trend put the Christians at odds with the Jewish traditions as well. Chrysostom regarded the instrumental music of the Jewish cult as God's concession to Jewish weakness. The instruments became simply allegories – so that the psaltery became the tongue and the cithara the mouth. Theodoret sees the liturgical music of Judaism as a syncretism with Egyptian traditions made in their exile in Egypt, referring to Miriam's timbrel as an Egyptian instrument, locating the trumpet in Egyptian military music and sistrum in the cult of Isis. Herodotus does indeed report that women sang the praises of Osiris and the dancing to beating drums, flute playing and singing by groups of men and women formed part of the festival of Diana at Bubastis. Thus the persecution of these sensuous traditions fuelled the growing anti-Semitism in the early Church as it differentiated itself from Jewish practices (Quasten 1983 pp. 62–5).

Smith, summarising the use of instruments in the early Church, identifies the following issues:

- Drawing on New Testament sources it is likely that the harp and lyre were in use but only for accompanying song.
- References to instrumental accompaniment appear by the middle of the second century.
- There was a great variety of approaches 'from cordial approval, to mere mention, to a grudging toleration, to a spiritualisation, to the severest condemnation' (sometimes in the writings of the same person).
- There are many reasons for the criticism, including the association with pagan cults, the use of them in theatre and circus, the sensuousness of the experience, the spiritual nature of worship, the concept of 'speaking with one voice', the need to distinguish themselves from Jewish practices.
- Their use was only to support the voice, if at all. (Smith 1962 pp. 53–4)

The Church Fathers debated the role of music, particularly its dangers. In an era where liturgical song was clearly developing, Chrysostom saw it only as a divine concession to human weakness. Augustine also wrestled with the sensual nature of music and its association with pleasure. The final solution is seen in about 400 CE when in the *Canons of Basil* we read:

> Those who sing psalms at the altar shall not sing with pleasure but with wisdom; they shall sing nothing but psalms.

Elaborate psalm settings came under threat and Isidore of Pelusium wrote against the singing of women because it produced not feelings of contrition but arousal of passion; despite this, there is evidence of organs in the early Church.

So, to summarise, by the end of this period an ascetic theological position separated wisdom from joy, body from spirit and human beings from adding any more creative expression to the liturgy musically. This did not serve women well.

Summary

The end of the first period of Christianity came in 325 CE when Constantine adopted the Christian religion as the official religion of the Roman Empire. This led to the establishment of a uniform orthodoxy in place of the diversity of practice in the early Church. The ideas of the dominating group at the time (unfortunately for women) became the new orthodoxy. This was the ascetic group who believed in the evilness of the body. As women were associated with sex and the body, this spelled the end of any power they had in the early Church. Motherhood was now degraded in contrast to celibacy. The natural woman was condemned and homosexual love (common in the ancient Greek Empire) became exalted and reflected in the construct of the love between the three male persons in the Trinity. Funeral rites were transferred from the home to the Church and in 392 CE the celebration of rituals in the home was discontinued. This curtailed women's liturgical authority at a stroke. Heretical sects like the Marcionites who included women scholars and liturgists were persecuted mercilessly. Gnosticism was a made a heresy.

Men started to write the hymns for women to sing, thus setting up the pattern of putting words into women's mouths about women's intimate functions, such as childbirth, marriage and death (a custom still present today in the debates on such issues as abortion). As the body became regarded as sinful, dancing was banned. Eventually choirs of women and girls were forbidden. From a situation in which many diverse practices including some led by women, patriarchy had finally taken it in hand and suppressed and marginalised it. It would, however, be possible to read these numerous texts, in the way recommended by Elisabeth Schüssler Fiorenza (2000) for other writings of the period, so that the numerous prohibitions prove how prevalent and resilient these traditions were. We have certainly established this in relation to the funeral rites. It is the way that subjugated ways of knowing always behave and are, or rather are not, reported in the malestream tradition.

CHAPTER 3

Vignette Two – Ecologising Music: Hildegard of Bingen

Story

> I am Hildegard.
> I know the cost of keeping silent.
> And I know the cost of speaking out.
> Hear my story.

Perhaps you know me as Hildegard of Bingen. It was several miles from Bingen that I was born, in the Nahe Valley in Germany, in the year of Our Lord one thousand and ninety-eight. Do you know the Rhineland? It is the most beautiful place – rich and green, moist and fruitful. The rolling hills stretch as far as the eye can see, crowned with lush forests pierced here and there with rocky crags and tall watchtowers. Below, the deep valleys are dotted with neat villages and tidy fields that yield ample sustenance for all humankind and their beasts. On the southern slopes, the carefully tended vineyards ripple like green waves lapping the skirts of the hills. And through it all flows the mighty river Rhine bringing life and greenness to the land, moisture to the air, and the means of movement and transport to all who live there. They call it now, I believe, the Fatherland, but to me it will always be Mother.

For the earth is our mother. She is mother of all that is natural, all that is human. She is the mother of us all, for she contains within herself the seeds of all. The earth of humankind contains all moistness, all verdancy, all germinating power. It is fruitful in so many ways. All creation comes from it. Yet it contains not only the basic raw material of humankind, but also the substance of the incarnation of God's Son.

Being the tenth child, I was tithed to God, and sent at the age of eight to live with Jutta, a holy anchoress, who lived in a small house attached to the abbey of St Disibod. From Jutta I learned so much: of everyday things, of the ever-present, all-encircling love of God (we are embraced by Him), and of the Holy Spirit which flows like sap through our souls, bringing growth and fruitfulness. From my earliest childhood God revealed Himself to me in many vivid ways: sometimes in words, sometimes images, sometimes music, sometimes all three, but always He showed himself in the splendour of the natural world. And I learned to see also the evil in the world – the injustice, the corruption of state and church, the sloth and carelessness of priests, the violation of the natural world and the denial of the giftedness of all creation. And I knew anger as well as joy. I looked and listened, I saw and I heard, but I kept silent ...

Yet ever within me grew the pressure to speak out. But how could I, a woman, make my voice heard? Who would listen to me? Who would believe my words, not learned by rote from any human tutor? How could my words in any way be useful? I consulted my superiors and my spiritual director – people I was accustomed to respect and obey. They told me firmly it was not my place to speak out, my role was to tend the daily needs of my community and to pray ever faithfully – but silently. Eventually I became ill both physically and mentally. How could I then have recognised within me the burning torment spoken of by the prophets of the Old Testament, when the Word of God burns in the heart and aches in the bones? It was not out of stubbornness, but out of supposed humility that I refused to speak, and I felt myself pressed down by the whip of God into a bed of sickness ...

But behold in the forty-third year of my life's course, I was taken up in a vision. In great fear and trembling I beheld a great radiance, and in it was formed a voice and the voice spoke to me, saying:

'O frail human being, ash of ash, corruption of corruption, tell and write what you see and hear.' And so I rose up and set my hand to writing and behold, great power and strength were given me and I no longer felt beaten down. The words poured out of me in a torrent, a great overflowing of God's Word, His Spirit, His Dhabar. And contrary to all my previous fears and timidity, I *was* heard. I began to set down my many visions in my first book which I called *Scivias – Knowing the Ways*. It was to take me ten years to complete. People came to me from far and wide asking for spiritual advice and I entered into correspondence with many of the great folk of my day – rulers, nobles, leaders of religious communities – among them the Emperor Barbarossa and Bernard of Clairvaux. The Holy Father heard of me and when he came to a Papal Council in Trier, sent a commission to investigate me. They found me competent and authentic, and he wrote, commending and encouraging my writing.

By this time Jutta had died and I had been elected leader – abbess, you might say – of our small community of women. We had grown in numbers and more were coming every year, yet we were still crammed into Jutta's tiny house. The monks of St Disibod had expanded too, taking up all the available land for their farms and buildings and they would not yield us an extra inch of space. At first I became anxious, then angry. Abbot Kuno was implacable. Can you imagine the endless committee meetings, the pleadings, the arguments, the counter-arguments and the endless frustration of not being heard? Eventually, we just packed our things and left, taking our dowries with us, without waiting for the men's permission.

After much hardship we began to build a new house near Bingen which I dedicated to my dear St Rupert. I myself supervised the building, making sure that all was spacious and comfortable. We even had piped water. Perhaps I remembered all those cold winter mornings, and the journeys to the well and the breaking of ice on the washing trough. But more, I think I was concerned because I do not think our Creator God delights in our bodily discomfort, especially when it is self-inflicted. It has been said that the body is at war with the soul, but how can this be? He made us as whole beings and our souls can only find expression through the actions of our bodies. For I am persuaded that when the body and the soul act together in proper agreement, they receive the highest award of mutual joy.

In the years that followed, my sisters and I at St Rupertsberg found new ways to worship God – in poetry, music and drama, sometimes wearing colourful robes and golden crowns – not, I may say, always with ecclesiastical approval! I continued to write and to set down in words and pictures the many visions in which God had become known to me, I wrote many books on a variety of subjects, including medicine and natural history as theology and the lives of the saints. My vast correspondence continued. When in my sixties I began to travel the length and breadth of Germany and I, a woman, preached from the pulpits of the great cathedrals and abbeys. And ever I spoke of God's justice ever I exhorted the leaders of the church and state to excise corruption and to work for the peace and harmony of all creation.

And in it and through it and round it was always the music for music expresses most deeply the soul's yearning to sing praises to its Creator, and echoes most clearly the harmony of heaven ...

But in the last year of my life the music was silenced. We were placed under an interdict by the Archbishop and forbidden to sing the office or to receive communion. It was a time of great grief and heavy sadness. We had buried in our cemetery a young man who had been excommunicated as a revolutionary and we refused to yield up his body. He confessed before he died and received absolution and his bones were entitled to rest in hallowed ground. I myself, though I was old and ill, went to the cemetery and removed all traces of the grave that it might not be violated, for I fear the justice of God more that justice of men. Instructed in a vision, I wrote to the Archbishop, asking him to lift the interdict and reminding him that those who silence music in this life can have no fellowship with the praise of the angels in heaven. The interdict was lifted and the music goes on.

But the words and songs I uttered came from no human voice; they were given to me in visions. God moves where He wills, and not to the glory of any earthly creature. But I am ever in fear and trembling and I ever doubt my own capacities. But I lift my hands to God, that He may carry me as a feather, without power or strength of its own is carried on the breath of the wind.

I died in the year eleven-hundred-and-seventy-nine, but I do not think death silenced me. Some of you, today, may hear my voice. I was eighty-one years old and so had kept silent for half my life and I had spoken for half my life. Perhaps that is the right balance: taking in, receiving, and giving out. In and out – like breathing – like the breath of God.

— JEAN MOORE in Boyce-Tillman 2000b pp. 1–6

Materials

Hildegard wrote over seventy songs. The texts are in Latin. There are two main manuscripts – the Wiesbaden copy, the so-called Riesencodex and the one she gave to the monks at Dendermonde. They are monophonic chants – single lines of melody using the modes that characterise the Gregorian tradition and of varying degrees of complexity. The notation system uses neumes, which are essentially drawings of groups of notes similar to those used in the St Gall manuscript. It is the standard German Gregorian notation of the period. The notes are placed upon four or five staff lines. However, her use of the signs and in particular the sign called a quilisma is not identical with other medieval usage, so we cannot always be sure of their meaning. The neumes indicate the pitch of the notes but there is no rhythmic indication. This is possibly because the rhythm is dictated by the words. It is a very subtle style reflecting the fluidity of poetic rhythms. No notational system could capture its ever-changing patterns satisfactorily. As we see below, she treated the modes in her own distinctive way.

There are no performance indications or any sign of any accompanying instruments. The relationship between the various liturgical forms conforms to contemporary practice. So the hymns are the least melismatic pieces with the words set with only one or two pitches to each syllable; the antiphons and responsories are the most complex. These sometimes have a wide range like *O vos angeli*. We cannot be sure at what pitch the pieces would have been sung or whether they were sung by a single singer or divided between singers with different ranges.

No instrumental parts are suggested but recordings often include accompaniments of varying degrees of complexity and using a variety of instruments very few of which would have been contemporary with Hildegard. These are sometimes voices, sometimes instrumental, based on her references to instruments in her writing. Gothic Voices conducted by Christopher Page in their measured calm interpretation of the pieces use instrumental drones regularly. These are also commonly used on the more ecstatic performances of Sequentia (*Canticles of Ecstasy* and *Voice of the Blood*) directed by Barbara Thornton. Here they are often performed on the hurdy-gurdy (which is very effective if perhaps anachronistic). The Anonymous Four in their recording *11,000 Virgins* use a mixture of drones and unaccompanied singing. The nuns of the Abtei St Hildegard sing unaccompanied, with reverberation in their resonant acoustic creating a kind of harmony.

Expression

The music was given as part of visions and she refused to revise them in any way. Although difficult to read and sometimes strikingly unusual the verbal 'text' of the visions present a powerful way of accessing truth. This valuing is reflected in other aspects of her life and work. Her trust in the

visionary experience as the main source of her theology shows her clear
trust in the intuitive and the non-verbal. She is able both to trust the intuitive visionary experience and to interpret it in words. Her visions are not
a private, inward-looking spirituality but the source of a life focussed on
issues of truth and justice. In the Middle Ages there was a greater trust
of the visual image as a source of truth. There were a number of women
visionaries; indeed it was the only way a woman could claim authority in
the Middle Ages. She could not claim it from a position like Archbishop.

Her visionary experiences started at three years old and continued
into old age. The still pictures that we have today that were painted by her
community under her supervision, cannot recapture dramatic moving
images which were filled with colour, sound and movement. From *Vitae
Hildegardis* comes the following account which starts with the way in
which she conceived them relating to issues of justice:

> And in the third year of my life I saw so great a brightness that my soul trembled;
> yet because of my infant condition I could express nothing of it. But in my eighth
> year I was offered to God, given over to a spiritual way of life, and till my fifteenth I
> saw many things, speaking of a number of them in a simple way, so that those who
> heard me wondered from where they might have come or from whom they might be.

> Then I too grew amazed at myself, that whenever I saw these things deep in my soul I
> still retained outer sight, and that I heard this said of no other human being ... Then,
> seized with great fear, I did not dare reveal it to anyone; yet nonetheless, speaking
> or composing, I used to make many affirmations about future events, and when I
> was fully perfumed by this vision I would say many things that were unfathomable
> (aliena) to those who listened. (Bowie and Davies 1990 pp. 63–5)

After her oblation to the Abbey she told only 'a highborn nun', Jutta, who
told a monk, probably Volmar who acted as her secretary. She received
the vision in:

> 'an unknown language yet to be heard, not in the ordinary human form of expres-
> sion'. From this it was dictated to Volmar in a mixture of German and Latin whose
> task it was to be 'a file, to eagerly smooth this speech so it receives the right sound
> for human ears.' (Nash 1997 p. xix)

The structure of the words mirror the feel of the visions, in piling image upon image in a cumulative way which moves them from the dogmatic statements of faith of other writers towards a discursive exploration of various themes. As these accumulate, the songs acquire a great power based on the varied repetition of small themes, both verbal and musical (see *O cruor sanguinis* below). Her song texts glitter with vivid images which have been criticised in dictionaries of hymnography for their lack of structure. She took traditional subjects and reworked them in vivid ways. She was not working in her native language but the associations of the images that she piles up have a dreamlike quality that would have excited the analyst Jung. Her *Hymn to the Spirit (O ignis spiritus)* is an example of this with image after image invented to portray the Spirit:

1. O fiery Spirit, our comforter!
   Life of the life of all that is created,
   Holy are you in giving life to all

2. Strengthening Spirit, you are holy in anointing the seriously broken,
   Holy in cleansing weeping, infected wounds.

3. O breathing place of holiness,
   O fire of love,
   O sweet flavour in the breast
   And infusion in the heart of beautiful perfumes of goodness.

4. O most pure flowing fountain,
   In which it becomes clear
   That God has brought together the strangers
   And is seeking the lost.

5. O close-fitting garment of life
   And hope of gathering all members together.
   And, O sword belt of truth,
   Please save the blessed.

6. Defend those who are imprisoned by the enemy,
   And dissolve the binding chains
   Of those whom the divine power would save.

7. O most reliable path,
   That finds its way through every place;
   In the most high hills,
   And in the flat plains,
   And in all the deep abysses,
   You bring all together and unite all.

8. From you the clouds stream out,
   The air flows,
   The stones take their character,
   The waters lead out their small streams
   And the earth releases its freshness. (Boyce-Tillman 2000b pp. 176–80)

The texts have multiple meanings held together by the power of her intuition not by her grasp of the formal strophic constructions familiar in the works of her contemporaries, Bernard of Clairvaux and Peter Abelard. Her texts cannot be read in a linear fashion because of their multi-layered multiple meanings.

This expressive style of writing is sometimes linked with a musical and verbal exuberance. There is a dramatic quality about her work with a regular use of wider leaps and triadic patterns that were unusual in medieval music. One of her favourite opening gestures is a leap of a fifth used as a springboard for a leap of a seventh or octave from the starting note as in the opening of *O virtus Sapientiae* (see Figure 4).

Medieval European music uses the Church modes based on ancient Greek practice. A piece usually stays within the chosen mode for the duration of an entire piece. Hildegard uses all the modes and seems to associate a particular character with each. The Dorian mode has an exalted feeling, while the Phrygian mode has a sense of timelessness. She challenges prevailing practice by changing modes in a piece. She ends *The Hymn to the Spirit (O ignis spiritus)* in a different mode from the one in which she starts, by the introduction of a Bb, thus challenging the musical tradition. Some scholars see it as changing hexachords rather than changes of modes akin to the much later device of modulation; but it is out of keeping with the usage of her day. The words and music are conceived as a unity and therefore are closely related. Hildegard clearly favoured and prioritised the expressive elements of music.

Her dramatic writing would seem to demand a vibrant vocal style allied to her concept of viriditas – vibrant, greening power. We have no stylistic indications which must be developed by each performer for her/himself. Here the text is the ultimate guide because of the unitive nature of the inspiration. It is similar to oral traditions with a measure of creativity needed on the part of the performer. Contemporary performances of her work sometimes do not reflect such expressive writing in the chosen singing style. Having worked on her dramatic play with music, *Ordo Virtutum*, I decided that a similar dramatic element underpins all her music. There is a lack of inhibition about her music that calls forth a similar performance style. Hildegard writes in praise of a sweet clear, ringing tone (dulcissima, clara, sonans) and in a letter to Elisabeth of Schoenau she compared her own voice to a trumpet resounding by the breath of God.

Construction

The visionary experiences are central to an understanding of the way Hildegard's music is constructed. They demonstrate how much she values intuitive knowing and the non-verbal. The result of this is that the music is of an improvisatory character. Compared with the works of her male contemporaries like Adam St Victoire, her works are free form rhapsodic pieces, lacking the concern from symmetric construction of phrases and verses. This gives her work a flowing, unfolding quality close to a musical meditation. The words use conjunctions to give them a quality of inter-connectedness. The antiphon *O cruor sanguinis* is a continuous sentence building in intensity:

> O wound flowing with blood
> That cries aloud to the highest,
> When all elemental force
> Are themselves entangled
> And crying with lamenting voice
> Bringing terror,

Because this is the blood of creation itself touching them,
Anoint us
So that our wounds may be healed. (Boyce-Tillman, 2000b p. 38)

The music flows similarly. She draws on quite a small bank of motifs which she reworks in various forms in each individual piece. This is not unlike the techniques of traditions that are based on improvisation. The works were thus conceived in a different way from pieces in the European canon (see Chapter 1). It therefore requires a more cyclical way of perception, one of returning to certain ideas and motifs rather than of a steady linear progress from one end of a score to the other. The music is perceived as rotating around a central axis rather than a linear development of ideas. This form of Construction means that her pieces do have a certain musical stability which is based not on the crafting of blocks of sound into regular strophes, but on motivic repetition and variation.

Her longest, most complex piece is the music drama *Ordo Virtutum* (*The Play of the Powers*) which may have been written for her novices for the celebrations at the consecration of the new buildings on the Rupertsberg. It is certainly in keeping with the way the parts for the Virtues are written, each having a short solo part and then singing in the chorus. The central character is the human Soul. The heavenly powers in the form of the Virtues (who are all female) confront the lower world symbolised by the Devil. He is the only man with a significant part in the piece, making the work strikingly different from later examples of the operatic genre. He only speaks showing that he is not connected with God. There is a chorus of Patriarchs and Prophets but they only sing an opening chorus and do not appear again. At the beginning the Virtues give the Soul the pure robes of faith and she aspires to be one of them. But before she can be fully integrated with them, the Devil appears and attracts her attention. The Soul struggles with her calling to heavenly things but in the end decides that it is too difficult and casts off the robe of faith to follow the Devil, who promises her honour in the eyes of the world. The Virtues lament her loss and the apparent victory of the Devil. He replies with insults but he is unable to hurt them. They gather together. Each Virtue introduces herself with her character carefully drawn. The other Virtues affirm the singer. For example, Victory organising the Virtues for their final onslaught on the Devil reaches some of the highest notes. The soul returns bruised and battered by her experience with the Devil in the world. She cries out for help from the Virtues and they comfort her and clothe her again in the robe of faith. The Devil's plans have been defeated. He makes one last appeal but the soul rejects him once and for all. The Virtues are victorious and fall upon the Devil and bind him up in a dramatic scene that resembles Michael and the Angels' victory in the Book of Revelation. The gendering of the Devil as male and the Virtues as female subverts the Church's traditional characterisation of women as sinful.

As a mystical play, the drama is quite statuesque, the interest lying primarily in the way in which the allegorical themes are developed in the music. The piece is 'through-composed' which means that there are no passages that recur exactly although the music is constructed from a number of small melodic motifs as described above. The text and melody are closely bound together and there are clear examples of word-painting as in the running melisma when the soul sings of running from the Devil. It is difficult to grasp the dramatic quality in audio-recordings. The DVD produced by Vox Animae beautifully set in an ancient Abbey is a fine introduction to it.

Values

It is impossible to understand Hildegard's music without locating it within its liturgical context. All her pieces were intended for liturgical use and even *Ordo Virtutum*, the morality play with music, may have been associated with the office being placed at the end of Matins or Vespers. The placing in the liturgical year is, however, not always clear with particular days or offices seldom specified. They all use forms like antiphons, hymns and responsories that would have been part of the regular offices or the celebration of the Mass. Hymns would probably have been sung by the whole congregation. In the Middle Ages it was more common to add to the bank of available liturgical material especially for the celebration of particular local saints like Hildegard's antiphons for St Rupert and St Disibod. It was also not uncommon to revisit traditional themes as Hildegard did in the pieces concerning the Virgin Mary and the Holy Spirit in particular. Her works include 1 Alleluia, 1 Kyrie and 7 sequences for use with the Mass. For the Office she wrote 43 antiphons for use with psalms, 18 responsories, 3 hymns and 4 devotional songs.

Her collection of songs is entitled *Symphonia armonie celestium revelationum (The Symphony of the Harmony of Heavenly Revelations)*. It was primarily an oral tradition (see below on musical literacy in the Middle Ages). Some material may therefore have been lost, as were later women's songs like those of the beguine Mechtild of Hackeborn, the so-called Flemish nightingale. The pieces have the character of having being created for particular festivals with no grand scheme in mind, following the themes that she loved and considered underrepresented in terms of the music of the Church. From the addition of the psalm tones in the margins of one of the manuscripts, it looks as though some of the songs may have had an independent life before being linked (somewhat uneasily) with the psalm tones. It is likely that the *Symphony* was not conceived as a grand cycle but was an ordering by Hildegard of diverse material created in different occasions. The Dendermonde manuscript, almost certainly ordered under Hildegard's supervision, places the hymns to the Virgin Mary in the middle of the Trinity. The Riesencodex places them later at the head of the saints.

Hers was an inclusive view of music. It was central to being human. It was not for a select few but intended as an essential part of the life of all human beings. Her nuns would have been selected for their religious vocation not for their musical gifts. Their musical skills would have undoubtedly increased in Hildegard's convent, but the sound of contemporary highly selective choirs may not bear any relationship to the sounds of Hildegard's convent.

In her day, music was valued in the curriculum. It was a higher order subject being included in the Quadrivium. Astronomy, geometry and mathematics were the other subjects included. However, the study of the Quadrivium was only open to aristocratic boys, because women were not considered capable of abstract thinking. Hildegard, therefore, would not have had access to this. Her musical education consisted of being immersed in liturgical music from an early age. It is unlikely that she wrote down her own music and it is possible that Volmar her secretary, was also not musically literate. Musical scribes in the Middle Ages charged a high price for their services to cover their specialist skill and the cost of the materials for the manuscript. It is likely that a wealthy patron paid for her pieces to be written down near the end of her life giving a more public face to her pieces. This was unusual for a woman composer. The material would have been held in the memory of the people at the convent.[1]

She is one of the earliest notated women composers in Europe. She was preceded by Hrotswitha, a tenth-century German Benedictine nun from Gandersheim who wrote poetry, drama and music; and Kassia, a Byzantine nun in the early ninth century who wrote about 49 liturgical compositions. It is unlikely that Hildegard would have been aware of her female composer predecessors. It is not by accident that the main stream of women composers runs through the convents. These all women communities gave women a freedom from the round of childbearing and an authority unavailable anywhere else in medieval society. In her *Alleluia* Hildegard prays that her own closed up womb will give birth like that of the Virgin Mary. It was in the 77 hymns and *The Play of the Powers* that her wish was realised.

Spirituality

For Hildegard music was central to her theology of the cosmos. Her high view of creation saw that God had arranged all things in consideration of everything else. She saw music as playing a very significant part in this unity:

---

1   The ability to memorise is in inverse ratio to the ability to read. In an age where literacy is limited the memory is correspondingly more retentive. Anyone who has listened to the song repertoire of a class of five-year-olds with limited reading skills will have experienced this.

In music you can hear the sound of burning passion in a virgin's breast. You can hear a twig coming into bud. You can hear the brightness of the spiritual light shining from heaven. You can hear the depth of thought of the prophets. You can hear the wisdom of the apostles spreading across the world. You can hear the blood pouring from the wounds of the martyrs. You can hear the innermost movements of a heart steeped in holiness. You can hear a young girl's joy at the beauty of God's earth. In music creation echoes back to its creator its joy and exultation; it offers thanks for its very existence. You can also hear in music the harmony between people who once were enemies and now are friends. Music expresses the unity of the world as God first made it, and the unity which is restored through repentance and reconciliation. (Van der Weyer 1997 p. 79)

She sees music as flowing between human beings and God:

Music is the echo of the glory and beauty of heaven. And in echoing that glory and beauty, it carries human praise back to heaven. (Van der Weyer 1997 p. 79)

Music plays a significant part in the redemptive plan of God:

Musical harmony softens hard hearts. It brings in them the moisture of reconciliation, and it invokes the Holy Spirit. When different voices sing in unity, they symbolise the simple tenderness of mutual love. When different voices blend in song, they symbolise the blending of thoughts and feelings which is the highest pleasure human beings can know. Let the sweet sound of music enter your breast, and let it speak to your heart. It will drive out all darkness, and spread spiritual light to every part of you. (Van der Weyer 1997 p. 80)

So music for her was imbued with expressive and symbolic significance. She wrote in a letter

Just as the body of Jesus Christ was born of the purity of the Virgin Mary through the operation of the Holy Spirit so, too, the canticle of praise, reflecting celestial harmony, is rooted in the Church through the Holy Spirit. The body is the vestment of the spirit, which has a living voice, and so it is proper for the body, in harmony with the soul, to use its voice to sing praises to God. (Baird and Radd 1994 p. 79)

Margot Fassler commenting on this passage sees the significance of music thus:

Hildegard defined the rendering of communal song as an incarnational act, basic to the creative regeneration of life that takes place within the monastic community. Singing was central to her definition of what it meant to be a nun. (Fassler 1998 p. 149)

In her vision of the Choirs of Angels, her vision of the global power of music takes shape and links singing with her theology of the Virtues, the feminine figures who underpin her Wisdom theology. Her theology includes instruments. The sound of stringed instruments calls forth compassionate and remorseful tears; they are associated with laments. The harp and psaltery are particularly blessed. She uses them as a metaphor for the soul's relationship to God. We need to rest in the hands of our creator like a harp in the hands of harpist. The flute signifies the mystical union of the soul with God, the goal of all mystical activity. The trumpet is associated with reason. So in music she sees reason and emotion brought together for the purposes of right action:

You who know, love and adore God, with simple and pure devotion
Praise him with the sound of a trumpet – that is, with the faculty of reason ...
And praise him with the lyre of profound emotion ...
And with the harp of softness and gentleness ...
And praise him with the timbrel of mortification ...
And with the dance of exultation ...
And praise him with the strings of repentance ...
And the flute of divine protection ...
Praise him too on high-sounding cymbals – by loud and joyful declarations.
Praise him also with cymbals of true joy – by statements of praise
Let every spirit who wills to believe in God and honour him, praise the Lord, Him who is Lord of all. (Van der Weyer 1997 p. 81)

She saw music as an important way of reconciling the dualism between body and soul, because it is by nature an embodied art. It is a high expression of the unity between body and soul, writing:

The words of a hymn represent the body, while the melody represents the soul. Words represent humanity, and melody represents divinity. Thus in a beautiful hymn, in which words and melody are perfectly matched, body and soul, humanity and divinity, are brought into unity. (Van der Weyer 1997 p. 79)

She works her theology of music out most carefully in the significant letter she wrote to the prelates of Mainz when she had been banned from singing the Office (Baird and Radd 1994 p. 79). She uses this theology to try to persuade the prelates to lift their ban on her singing (Baird and Radd 1994 pp. 79–80).

In her theology of the overall cosmic plan of salvation, she constructed her own theology of music giving each of the five tones a meaning, linking the first tone with Abel, the second with Noah, the third with Moses and the fourth with the incarnation of Jesus and concluding:

> The fifth tone will be completed when all error and mockery is at an end and then all men will know and see that no one can do anything against the Lord. In this way, in the five tones sent by God, the Old and New Testaments will be fulfilled and the marvellous number of mankind completed. And after these five tones a time of light will be given to the Son of God so he will be known clearly … afterwards the divinity in him will be manifest, for as long as he wants. (Baird and Radd 1994 p. 79)

Pozzi Escot (1990) develops these ideas forward by analysing the Construction of her music in the light of the numerology of the cosmos, seeing the construction of Hildegard's music intimately connected with the wider cosmos.

Hildegard's view of spirituality is one in which the division in everyday living are resolved in a transcendent relationality. Accounts of many people's experience of her music are often filled with this luminous liminal cosmic connection.

Summary

Music was central to Hildegard's concept of harmonious living. Her own music given as part of her visions, summarises all her thinking. We cannot fully understand the dramatic nature of these manifestations of the Divine will that she received. Although received *individually* from God the visions were worked out in community probably with both Richardis of Stade and

Volmar. Her relationship to the *community* is central and in her theology this community equates to the whole of the cosmos. Her visions are no isolated phenomenon but in the context of a Divine cosmic scheme no arts for art's sake either. She therefore has a vision of music which is very *integrated*, reflecting the medieval frame of a strong overarching metanarrative for the whole of life. We have no indication of her relationship to the vernacular traditions of her day. But there was an influx of influences from the East at her time and it is possible that her problematic use of the quilisma reflected some sound from this tradition. This is, however, purely, speculative.

Her visions were received in a very inner way. They were a *private* experience and her story shows the dilemma of making them public and the problems that this caused for her. However, a vision tells her halfway through her life that this is God's intention for her and eventually they become *public* works shared and sung by her community in performances that were remarked on by visitors to the convent.

Her *process* is very evident in the product, leading music critics of some generations to condemn then as untutored and unstructured. This is due to the oracy of her method of creation. It is unlikely that she was literate musically and all of these songs would have been held in the memory of her and her nuns and only written down towards the end of her life. We therefore have a magnificent example of the complexity possible within an oral tradition.

We have no indication about the speed used for her performances and therefore how *excited or relaxed* they appeared. In *Ordo Virtutum* there are dramatic elements that lead contemporary performers to use a variety of speeds to delineate the character of both individual singers and the dramatic action itself. Certainly many people receiving her music today see it as a form of relaxation but it is impossible to say whether it was viewed as such in her own day.

She had a strong sense of the *nurturing* role of music within her theological scheme. On the other hand her visions were given to her to *challenge* the surrounding society and by her divergence from the contemporary use of the modes and also exploration of gender in Christian theology in *The Play of the Powers* she showed how to use the medium to challenge and subvert.

Hers was essentially an *intuitive* approach to music based in her visionary experiences. She writes about the necessity for 'wit and wisdom' but
she approaches the creative process intuitively and refuses to allow the
more 'rational' approaches of refining the pieces to be carried out on these
essentially intuitive creations.

She struggles with the *soul/body split* in much of her writings and does
encourage dancing in her convent and the adornment of the body. In line
with her cosmic theology she treated the dualisms that characterised her age
as being in continual relationship. Oppositions such as dark/light, good/
evil and body/soul were revisited by Hildegard. For her, the negative was
always in relationship with the positive. This runs through all her writing
and is typified by the following quotations:

> Human beings fly with two wings; the right wing is the knowledge of good and
> the left is the knowledge of evil. The knowledge of evil *serves the good* insofar as the
> good is sharpened and highlighted through the knowledge of evil; and so through
> this knowledge human beings become wise in all things. (Letter from Hildegard to
> Wibert quoted in Fox, 1987. p. 350)

This clearly relates to the figure of Wisdom with three flying wings as
discussed earlier. Hildegard represents in the history of women's liturgical music a connected, visionary, collaborative, improvisatory, integrative,
committed and authoritative voice.

CHAPTER 4

Vignette Three – Encloistering the Angels: The Renaissance Nun Composers

Story

And the organist is Prospera Corona and the *Maestra di Capella* is Suor Laura Benzona; and every feast-day they sing the Magnificat, and various antiphons. The former plays the organ, and the organist accompanies their singing ...

Asked, she responded: I have the organist's duty of singing and playing ... In my cell I sing sometimes with keyboard accompaniment ... and I sing only sacred motets, and I know how to intabulate them, and sometimes I sing with the nuns in my cell to rehearse what is to be sung.

In polyphony I sing only sacred pieces; I never sang with Suor Paola Giustina except in church, and in the refectory or the washing room, and outside church sometimes with Suor Laura Bezona, Suor Prospera Corona, and Suor Claudia Sulpitia ... I heard some *canti alla bergamasca* were found in Suor Paola Giustina ['s cell], but I don't know how to speak Bergamasque.

I know a little polyphony ... Sometimes I help sing in church, and sometimes they rehearse in the room of Suor Laura, the *Maestra di capella* – and I never sang in the garden ... Sometimes they sang the sacred poems from the *Tesauro della Sapientia* that Messer Father Paolo gave me, and those pieces were sung by the above-mentioned Suor Prospera Corona, the organist, and Suor Laura, and Suor Prospera Vittoria and other musicians.

— ACCOUNT OF THE BISHOPS' VISITOR TO THE HUMILIATE OF
S. MARIA MADDALENA AL CERCHIO in Kendrick 1996 p. 55

Introduction

The process of enclosing women in convents on the one hand put them firmly in the control of the patriarchal structures of the Church but on the other gave them an all-female space in which to operate that was protected from the wider society. The vow of chastity also protected them from the regular round of child-bearing and rearing that would have characterised the lives of their secular sisters. The previous chapter has told us something of a conventual tradition in the hands of a remarkable German musician in the twelfth century. This chapter is a wider overview of the characteristics of music-making in these conventual traditions from 1550 to approximately 1700, the time around the Tridentine 'reforms'.[1] There is still a great deal of work to be done in this area and the scholarship available at the time of writing is limited.

This chapter will concentrate on Italian convents in the cities of Siena and Milan. In the 250 years of European history between Hildegard and these nun composers/performers the musical style of Europe had changed from the monophonic[2] chants of Hildegard to the complex polyphony[3] of the Renaissance. This period itself saw a further change – the 'invention' of opera around 1600 and the beginning of the dominance of harmony (or the chord) replacing the complex interweaving of melodies that made up Renaissance contrapuntal textures.[4] Women musicians are as involved in these changes as their male counterparts. But the Darwinian evolutionist approach to musical history (see Chapter 1), concentrating on the marking of stylistic changes and those who embraced novelty, has meant the denying of the great diversity of the period; it saw the so called *stile antico*

---

1   The Council of Trent (the adjective is Tridentine) attempted to reform the Roman Catholic Church in the light of the Protestant secession.
2   Single line chants with no accompaniment.
3   Many tunes moving together.
4   This saw the invention of the monody, a single line of melody with a chordal accompaniment played by a bass instrument playing the bass line and a chordal (often keyboard) instrument playing the chords. The combination of the instruments was called the basso continuo.

existing confidently alongside the operatic monodies of male composers like Monteverdi. This has meant the marginalisation of sacred music as representing the outmoded *stile antico*. Added to this was also the often unquestioned belief that the requirements of the Council of Trent – that music should be 'clear in declamation and simplistic in technique' (Kendrick 1996 p. 7) – were followed to the letter by religious composers. The result of this is that Latin text music (liturgical and non-liturgical) has largely been ignored, and with it the music of the nun musicians.

This story is necessarily that of upper- and middle-class women in both of the cities. There was a distinction between houses for patrician women and those for more plebeian women.[5] There were none for the poor in Milan, although there were a few houses in Siena who took poor women.[6] But their status was different from that of aristocratic women. The interrelationship between the convents and the patrician world is complex and full of intrigue; but this very relationship protected many of the sisters from some of the rigour of the imposition of restrictions by presiding Bishops and Papal decree. The fact that the sisters were often aunts or sisters, for example, of the men in positions of authority gave them a degree of respect and independence.

This was a time when women played a significant part in music-making traditions in Northern Italy as a whole. In Venice, there was the tradition of the ospedali with their orchestras; and there were women singers at court in other Italian cities, to name but two examples. Robert Kendrick (1996 pp. 9–10) cites evidence for significant musical activity by nuns in the following Italian cities: Turin, Monferrato, Asti, Vercelli, Novara, Milan, Bergamo, Brescia, Verona, Vicenza, Padua, Venice, Genoa, Piacenza, Parma, Reggio Emilia, Modena, Ferrara, Bologna, Florence, Siena, Lucca, Rome, Macerata, Naples and Foggia. Gabriella Zarri[7] has also drawn attention

---

5   In general, it was the aristocratic houses music that featured in travellers' accounts of excellence. They tended to have more resources with double choirs, for example.

6   It was from one of these, the Convertite designed for reformed prostitutes, that the mystic Vannini came.

7   Zarri (1990) *La Sante vive: per una tipologia della santità feminile tra '400 e '500* Turin; referred to in Kendrick 1996 p. 2.

to a whole range of women in religious roles such as 'court prophetesses, holy widows, tertiaries and women designated beata' who played significant parts in Italian cities at this time; and there was a great increase in choir nuns from 1550 onwards. They have all been 'written out of history'. Kendrick (1996) cites a huge rise in scholarship in this area, drawing attention to how the Renaissance has been represented as an area of decline for women's non-domestic activities, when, in fact, there is more evidence of their activity than that in male monasteries or cathedrals.

The process of enclosure involved a dowry being given to the convent in question – one that was often smaller than that required by marriage. Some of the sisters' enclosures, therefore, were the result of family financial circumstances rather than always a religious vocation, although there were injunctions to ensure that the woman had a real sense of vocation. There was the possibility of dowry reduction on request. Once in the convent, promising singers, like Sessa and Ceva in Milan, rose to fame very quickly and some nuns kept performing throughout their lives like the Milanese sisters, Rusca, Taverna and Quinzana. Many of the houses were situated right in the centre of Milan and Siena,[8] which enabled people to hear and see the nuns' music-making (see below).

The relationship between the cloister and the wider world was also more relaxed than we associate today with enclosure. After the Council of Trent, there were greater attempts to keep the nuns within the convent walls. From 1566 the 'walling off' process began and nuns had a legal status separate from the outside world; but as we shall see below this did not always work in practice. There was also to be an annual visitation by the bishop or his appointee followed by written recommendations and disciplinary statements. These give us one source of evidence for women's music making; but the reports of these visitations have a particular purpose, which is not to say what was going on, but what should go on. These accounts need to be balanced by the nuns' own accounts and those of travellers visiting the cities.

8   Many of the Siena houses had originally been outside the city but by the mid sixteenth century had been relocated inside the city walls (Reardon 2002 pp. 12–13).

Music was an important means of linking the world outside with that inside the convent walls. The sisters were often accomplished musicians before they entered the convent; the convents were also considered musical jewels in the ecclesiastical and civil crowns of the cities, although the bishops were not always happy about this. Music lessons and tuition clearly needed to be continued, and that often required the services of male instructors who would have to attend the convent on a regular basis. This offered opportunities to lay musicians that were not so readily available in the male-dominated world. It also gave opportunities for composers and arrangers for convent ensembles. There was also the possibility of performing music involving male voices and sometimes male instrumentalists, which also involved rehearsal as well as performance. This practice varied from place to place. There is no record of this in Milan as there is in Bologna and Siena.

There was also the phenomenon of the nun's participation in civic festivals:

> Of special concern were the *mascherate* plays [in Milan] performed by nuns as part of the carnival season, with their invariable connotation of female transvestism. A series of printed orders from vicars outlawing such theatre were predictable in their regularity as well as their apparent ineffectiveness. (Kendrick 1996 p. 81)

All of these phenomena made the nature of enclosure very different from the grilled portals that characterised later traditions, although we see here the beginning of the process.

Kendrick, in his definitive text *Celestial Sirens: Nuns and their music in early modern Milan* (1996), draws attention to the following themes that have led musicology to ignore this tradition and calls on the use of more ethnomusicological methodologies to examine:

- Music's relationship to rapture and ecstasy
- The strongly oral character of some repertories
- The musical definition of sacred space
- Claustral music in the public ritual life of the city
- 'Insider' versus 'outsider' accounts of music-making
- Status, role-playing and authority in the regulation of female monastic musicians
- Currents in Seicento epistemology that differentiated between the perceptual or experiential capacities of men and women (Kendrick 1996 p. 81)

This introduction has set out the environmental and cultural context of the nun's music-making. The rest of the chapter will look at the nature of their music using the analytical frame set out in Chapter 1.

Materials

In both cities, the nuns' patrician families supplied the musical needs of the sisters in terms of their instruments and lessons and in some cases printed music. It is likely that there was a less clear relationship between the printed and performed pitch than would be standard today, particularly because written music was expensive and difficult to come by. In Milan, four-part works were transposed to enable the nuns to sing all four parts. Indeed in the preface from a 1662 set of *Madrigale, e canzoni spirituali e morali*, Pompeo Natali describes how some of the continuo parts are transposed up a fifth to allow for nuns to sing them. In Siena, there was more of a tendency to turn to lay musicians to help and these people also served as teachers. In the middle of this period there was quite a relaxed attitude to this practice (Reardon 2002 p. 36). They were also expected to provide music suited to their abilities as musical performers. Colleen Reardon (2002), in her significant text *Concord within Sacred Walls: Nuns and Music in Siena 1575–1700*, sets out a scenario in which the lay musician composed the work and nun maestra did the copying and teaching and initial rehearsals. The lay musician would then fine tune the ensemble. Then the performance involved the maestra conducting the group in the chiesa interiore[9] and liaising with the lay musician in the chiesa esteriore (Reardon 2002 p. 42).

Some convents had organs, but other instruments were also available, as in this description of the translation of the saints' relics and the consecration of a new shrine:

---

9   The internal church – the chiesa interiore – was separated from the outer church – the chiesa esteriore – by a dividing wall.

> [We] entered the church ... with bells, the organs, trumpets, drums sounding ... Arriving at the main altar, the relics were deposited ... as the nuns sang the litanies with organ accompaniment. (Kendrick 1996 p. 163)

At the beginning of the period Bishop Carlo Borromeo of Milan had questioned the nuns having organs at all and also the need to have male music teachers to teach them. He was advised that to remove the organs would cause a storm and that certain regulations should be in force that would allow certain male organists of proven upright character to teach in the outer parlour with the nun following the instruction on a clavichord in the inner parlour. His most punitive order was when a male musician outstayed his *licenza* to practise in this way. The result was to remove the nun's veil for three months, relieve her of her organist's duties, remove her harpsichord from her room and require her to eat off the floor of the refectory. It is not known whether any penance was demanded of the male teacher!

Other criticisms approved the organ and condemned other instruments:

> Most Reverend Mother ... Setting fires, shooting mortars and archebuses, playing trumpets, and similar things, are actions totally foreign to nuns' traditions and piety, and these are expressly forbidden ... Music is to be made only by nuns, with no instruments other than organ and regal, and for two choirs only; nor should any nun sing solo, and the pieces should be sacred and serious, far from worldliness. (Kendrick 1996 p. 14)

Here this condemnation is linked with the dancing at St Chiara in Milan during the carnival. In Siena, Ascanio I Piccolomini tried to take away the lutes and citterns from the sisters at the Convertite convent. Possibly this was a punishment for their refusal to take the full enclosure or out of concern about the musical reputation of the ex-prostitute Vannini. It would seem that the decree was never enforced and that by the mid-seventeenth century lute and theorbo playing was well established in many of the Sienese houses.

So the nuns had considerable resources in terms of tuition and a variety of instruments that they retained, despite instructions to the contrary. It is clear from the difficulty of the works written for them that many of the nuns had considerable vocal skill, in particular.

Expression

Some of the texts set were linked with the Office. Others, for pieces like motets and laude, were chosen by the composers. These were carefully considered, and embodied the spirituality both of the nuns and the secular world. The texts set were often concerning the women of the Bible like Mary Magdalene and Mary the Virgin and female saints. Here, as we saw in the songs of the Syrian women in Chapter 2, we see women elaborating the stories of women as Lucy Winkett (2010) describes under the heading of The Sound of Lament in the contemporary world:

> An artist told me in conversation that he had visited a convent and talked with one of the sisters there about what Mary, mother of Jesus, would have done on the evening of Good Friday. They imagined together that she would have gone to visit the mother of Judas. He painted this scene: two women, two uncomforted mothers, sitting talking together about their terrible, terrible day. (Winkett 2010)

The nuns would have been schooled in the *Song of Songs*, the breviary, and medieval devotional writings like those of Bonaventure, and they made personalised journals of spiritual devotion. These were seen as projected into the world by means of the music and debates about appropriate texts reflected the concern of the nuns to get the spirituality right. A popular text, referred to in the opening story, was the *Tesauro della Sapientia (Treasury of Wisdom)* which included *laude* (devotional songs) by a Bolognese nun and concentrated on the role of the soul as Christ's bride. In terms of inclusivity, there are examples of nuns changing the gendered language of the office book into sisters from brothers (Kendrick 1996 p. 42).

Claudia Rusca (c. 1593–1676) was in the convent of S. Caterina in Milan and flourished under the period of Bishop Frederigo Borromeo's encouragement. She left two *canzoni francesi*, the first surviving examples of instrumental music by a named woman in Europe. Her *Sacri concerti 1–5* included, in addition to these pieces, small scale sacred concertos, Vesper psalms and eight-voice motets. The themes of Rusca's book reworked the Bishop's views on spirituality in terms of music. Two other Milanese nun composers, Cozzolani and Badalla, were in the vanguard of a trend in the century to experiment with liturgical texts in the 1660s. There was also a move away from scriptural and liturgical texts as the century progressed.

This was a time when the Expressive characteristics of music in the wider world were much debated and there was a more clear relationship between musical gestures and certain moods or motifs than we are familiar with today. The relationship between the nuns' use of these techniques which were developing and evolving at this time was subtle and complex.[10] There were, associated with them, rules or traditions of performance that concentrated on the affect, the expressive elements. The origins of the monodic style lay in its relation to the delivery of speech and the ability of music to highlight its expressive elements.

Official decrees tried to prevent nuns using secular music, but it is clear that these were not always followed out. Visitation notes were critical of finding music using non-Latin texts in the cell of the singer Bascape, as we have seen in the story at the beginning of the chapter. She claims to have found them amongst a gift from her family.

There are a number of musical plays written for Sienese convents where secular elements were present. Six survive from Sienese convents, three of them written by men. The music has not survived. They were often based on Bible stories or lives of the saints, and, although primarily intended for the nuns' own entertainment, it is clear that members of the public did see them. One of them, Benvenuto Flori's *L'evangelica parabola*, at least has a subject that was considered appropriate for nuns to sing. Drawing on the parable of the wise and foolish virgins he uses the story as the basis for a music drama about the separation of the sacred and profane. The music for the foolish virgins uses secular forms to great effect, and only in the last act do the wise virgins have music of the interest that characterises the profane scenes. It is not known what the nuns

---

10   I would recommend readers interested in this to examine Kendrick's book (1996) in detail. It is dealt with on pp. 23–4 and many following pages.

thought of the play, but Colleen Reardon suggests that they may have been glad to have the opportunity to perform musical forms otherwise not be available to them. It may have been written for a nun's clothing, a time when elaborate music was performed, or it might have formed part of the Carnival which was characterised by the overturning of the established order (Reardon 2002 pp. 87–97).

To summarise, the nuns had a ready supply of texts associated with female figures that appealed to their chosen role as Brides of Christ. They used the developing expressive style to project their spirituality into the wider society and despite restraining orders they did have some opportunities to perform secular pieces.

Construction

The range of music sung in the convents varied from plainchant to elaborate pieces written for festivals and special occasions, as with the nuns of St Maria degli angeli in Milan on May 17th 1592. They celebrated the installation of a fountain by processing through the gardens weeping tears of joy and singing a *Te Deum* (Reardon 2002 p. 30).

As we have seen, this period saw a change from the polyphonic Renaissance style to the more chordal basis of the Baroque style using the basso continuo. This is evident in the music written for and by the nuns. The nuns in Milan were important in the development of new musical genres, in two areas. The first area is in the pieces that were written specially for them and the second in the role played by two remarkable nun composers in the development of the new style – like the high voice duet in the early seventeenth century, the solo motet in the middle of the century and the *cantata morale e spirituale* in the 1660s.

Two Milanese nun composers played a significant part in the stylistic developments of the period. Chiara Margarita Cozzolani[11] was born in 1602 from a wealthy background to a family with many links with the monastic tradition. She was nurtured as a composer in the convent having being professed aged 17 or 18. She later became an abbess. She embraced in her *Concerti Sacri* the new Lombard style and in her collections of 1650 she used this for large scale pieces. In these she fused the new arioso style with the older style of the eight-voice settings for Vespers. She embraced the new use of dissonance and chromaticism for expressive purposes, producing a new original style that has not found its way into the traditional textbooks outlining the development of the musical canon.[12] She developed the dialogue form of the motet which consisted of a dialogue expressed musically between allegorical figures like angels, Biblical characters (such as Mary or Christ) or historical saints. The form fitted in with Bishop Frederigo Borromeo's theology which emphasised the potential communication between human beings and God. Kendrick challenges the idea that these were merely a staging point towards the development of the oratorio, arguing for their acceptance as expressive pieces in their own right (Kendrick 1996 p. 323). Cozzolani's works in this genre include an extended, complex dialogue between the soul and its guardian angel entitled *O mi domini*. It deals with the soul's progress from a life of sin to recognition of God's acceptance. (It is interesting to compare this with Hildegard's *Ordo Virtutum* discussed in Chapter 3.) The soul's initial statement is a dramatic monody. The angel is given a similar harmonic basis but includes more leaps; eventually the angel has an arioso in triple time. The next dialogue is a shortened form of this one. She uses an ascending chromatic bass line to represent the angel's advice to the soul, while the soul's response moves from low to high. The angel reassures the soul in an arioso and the soul's response leads to an arioso too. There is a florid statement by the angel and

11   There is now an exciting project started in the year 2000 recording Cozzolani's compositions. See <http://www.cozzolani.com/>.
12   The notion of the musical canon was explored in Chapter 1. It is the body of works that are considered by contemporary historians, musicologists and concert planners to be central to the development of stylistic developments in music in Europe.

then a closing passage where both sing together in triple and duple time. This ending was a characteristic of the form representing the resolution of the dialogue. Even in this short description we can see a skilled composer able to put together a large scale structure to express this allegorical drama.

Her dialogue motets of 1642 contain indications that they may have been staged as well. There is a long dialogue on Mary Magdalene, which includes themes beloved of her community, who identified with the lamenting Magdalene. It uses melodic differentiation for the characters and a powerful use of musical rhetoric to create a fine musical representation of the Christian optimism of the time. She develops the solo motet in her *Concertati Sacri* and her *Scherzi*. In these, her grasp of internal formal structures strengthens. She uses extended melismas, transposable phrases and complex internal references by modifying small musical ideas to shape her pieces. Her style reaches its climax *In quis mihi det calicem bibere* which is a long extended meditative piece on Jesus' suffering, linking it with that of the martyrs. She died in the late 1670s. It has taken Robert Kendrick's work to restore her to the position that she clearly occupied in her own day.[13]

A second nun composer is Rosa Giacinta Badalla (c. 1662–c. 1710). She has her publication of *Mottetti a voce solo* at 20 in 1684. Her work shows the greater codification of the form. Within this, she demonstrates her originality in terms of melody related to the expressiveness of the texts; these include Eucharistic subjects and pieces for other Christian feasts and metrical pieces in honour of St Radegunda (her convent dedication). Her single authored publication was alone of its kind between 1675 and 1695. However, as we have seen above with other women composers, this has found no mention in the literature associated with the canon of Western musical masterpieces. Indeed, some of it has been downright inaccurate. Remarks like those of Denis Stevens about nuns singing in unison simply served to perpetuate a lie which had no foundation in the truth (Stevens 1980) and served to deny women's musical achievements.

---

13   This is a situation common in the story of women composers in Europe. Hildegard
      of Bingen (see Chapter 3) and Clara Schumann are but two examples.

Travellers' accounts refer largely to the work of performers and not composers, indicating the priority given to performance within this tradition. Many pieces were dedicated to accomplished nun performers and composed for them; and in Milan these women religious were important in the development of the high voice duet which in other cities like Ferrara and Mantua was more associated with court circles. The technical achievements of the women performers were considerable. The Sienese composer, Alessandro Della Caia, composed his *Sacred Lamentations and Motets* for one voice with basso continuo specifically for the Sienese nuns. They were complex pieces offering a vehicle for display for the most distinguished singers.

Periodically, particularly in Siena, Bishops tried to discourage complex music. Bishop Camillo Borghesi, for example, tried to limit the number of times lay musicians came in to perform with the nuns. This regularly happened at such events as a nun's clothing, when the Sienese nuns would be able to celebrate with ensembles including male musicians and tenor and bass voices. He believed that the overly frequent concerts were distracting women from their pursuit of purity of heart (Reardon 2002 p. 23).

To summarise, nun composers showed themselves well able to handle the musical forms of their day. As performers, nuns were also able to handle complex music. They experienced a wide range of styles and textures in the breadth of music performed in the convents.

Values

At this time the prevailing Value systems were controlled largely by the presiding bishop and this resulted in regionally differing practices even within Northern Italy. More work in this area needs to be done to explore this variety in greater depth than is currently understood. In Milan, the 1570s saw the attempts at reform made by Bishop Carlo Borromeo. However, with the advent of Frederigo Borromeo, the tide started flowing in ways

that favoured women's spirituality; there was a general increase in devotion and a feminisation of spirituality. Women's music-making flourished
but ecclesiastical appointments in the 1660s led to more troubled times.

In terms of the relationship between the *individual and the community*,
the traditions were rooted in the community of the convent. In Milan and
Siena many houses had traditions and there was no concentration of music
in particular houses unlike the situation in Ferrara or Modena.

This was a time when the solo song was coming into prominence
and, as we have seen above, was taken up both by the nun composers and
people writing for them. The seventeenth century saw a new emphasis on
individual performance and solo singing. This led to increased competition between singers. There was a move to keep the nuns anonymous in
their performances, but this clearly was unsuccessful because of the dedi-
cations in compositions owned by them. There were many injunctions to
humility and nuns' musical achievements varied in their reception by the
ecclesiastical hierarchy. There is an example of a nun musician in a Bologna
convent who damaged herself physically to prevent herself getting too vain
over her instrumental playing, and another who refused to sing, 'applying
herself to prayer alone'. Colleen Reardon suggests that these instances are
examples of the Bishop's general disapproval of women's music-making in
that city (Reardon 2002 p. 104).

There is evidence of admirers flocking to the chiesa esteriore to see their
favourite singers, and indeed of visits to the parlours and the transvestite
carnival theatre. It is clear that within some houses there were jealousies
and rivalries within this context. However, what these accounts show is
that there was real interaction between the religious houses and the surrounding community.

The division between sacred and secular was less well-established
than traditional history has led us to believe. Not only have we seen how
secular styles were used by the nun composers to project religious texts
with expressive power but also the role the convents played in the so-called
secular life of the city shows how Catholicism was the shared belief system
of the wider society and sacred and secular interacted powerfully within
the life of the city.

In terms of *unity and diversity*, the Council of Trent had traditionally been portrayed as a drive to uniformity and as a bastion against the
rise of Protestantism in Northern Europe; but scholarship has revised this
opinion and looked more carefully at how diverse ways (O'Malley 1991)
were suggested to renew local churches and encourage a vibrant spirituality. But variety was a subject of debate, and how much was allowed was
dependent on the Bishop or his representative in charge at any given time.
So in Siena, Ascanio I Piccolomini took a much lighter handed approach
to enclosure between 1578 and 1588, but, when the nuns started to travel
outside of Siena, begging or working in the harvest fields he took a tougher
line. But, in general, Bishops were wary of invoking the wrath of the nuns,
who, in Siena, would write to The Sacred Congregration in Rome if regulations displeased them.

On the one hand, the ritual space the women occupied was seen as
transcendent, especially in the chiesa interiori (see above). On the other,
in Milan, it was subject to varying degrees of control and regulation by
various bishops:

> But perhaps the contradiction is only apparent: if nuns' musical liturgy was indeed
> the most important, most 'heavenly' form of organized prayer in the city ... then it
> had to be carried out correctly. In this respect (as in many others), the disputes over
> monastic polyphony came down to differing views between nuns (along with their
> families) and the hierarchy concerning what was appropriate – that is – different
> views of piety and its musical expression. (Kendrick 1996 p. 417)

The amount of control exercised (both in Milan and Bologna) was in general, more evident in houses of lower-class women (the so-called plebeian
houses) than those of aristocratic women.

At this time, both the Roman and the Ambrosian musical rites were
in use for the liturgy – the Ambrosian more often in the more plebeian
houses. The inseparability of the liturgy from the music of the liturgy is
clear in all the liturgical disputes of the time.

The division of *public and private* was the subject of much dispute at
this time. It was a time of debates about the nature of enclosure and the
relation between the nuns and the wider society. The decrees of the Bishops
and their visitors attempted in varying degrees to control the inner private

life of the convent. The classical Lombard architectural shape in female convents was that of an exterior church (chiesa esteriore) for the public separated by a wall from the interior church for the nuns themselves (the chiesa interiore), as identified in the introduction to this chapter. The parlours (parlatorio) in Milan were also supposed to be divided into a section for visitors and an interior one for the nuns separated by a grill. Carlo Borromeo, Bishop of Milan, set down a rule in 1577 that this was to be a small window, suitable only for speaking, but what is clear from contemporary accounts is that the rule was largely ignored.

What is clear again is that the truth must be read between the lines of the various orders that were issued to the nuns, particularly against the use of two choirs or the use of the music in the *parlatori*. The fact that so many injunctions needed to be written indicates the likelihood that they were seldom obeyed. None of the constraints lasted long because of the interlinking of the patrician families with the religious houses. There are no similar restraining rules issued in respect of male monastic houses. The Milanese nuns, Bascape and Taverna, had public opportunities for performance all their lives. It was music that enabled the nuns to project their lives into the city after the restraining orders of the Tridentine decrees.

Links between public music making and the vow of chastity were an ecclesiastical problem. Archbishop Alessandro Petrucci in Siena pointed out how music could be a sinful force if not rightly used, linking it with 'distractions':

> He therefore required nuns to secure permission from the archbishop any time they wished to have music performed in their external churches. He also forbade nuns to perform in their parlors and ordered that they refrain from singing secular tunes at all times. He commanded that convents with a tradition for performing music have a *maestra del canto* and an appropriate rehearsal space situated in such a way that the constant practice of musicians would not disturb other members of the monastic community. Musical performance was permitted only at divine rites; the music was to be serious and solemn, as it was sacrilege to sing of divine things with secular music. Apart from the services, the nuns were not permitted to sing or play either for lay or ecclesiastical persons in the churches or elsewhere, except when the archbishop came to visit ... He found polyphony of little use to young women at this stage in their careers, and thus he recommended that their musical experiences be restricted to learning plainchant. (Reardon 2002 pp. 23–4)

But the appointment of Ascanio II Piccolomini saw a greater freedom from intrusion than before and a relaxing of the rules that allowed lay musicians in convents. With the fall of Siena to the Grand Duchy of Tuscany, music was seen as an important way of asserting Sienese identity. The elaborate music for the festivals of the Christian year made the religious women of the city central to the maintenance of a distinct identity and an area out of the control of the Tuscan authorities. They also represented, as in Milan, the presiding spirituality of the city; and the lay community valued the opportunity to teach in the convents, play with the sisters and borrow their relics for processions (Reardon 2002 p. 29).

The excellence of the nun's polyphonic singing is referred to in many travellers' accounts of the period. In a period of economic crisis in Lombardy, the nuns' polyphony was considered a status-maintaining activity by the civic authorities:

> Indeed, in terms of the classical anthropological categories, the women of this study [the nuns of the early modern period in Milan] transformed themselves from an unmarked status (anonymity, death to the world) by means of their polyphony into marked beings (individual fame, supernatural mediation). They were not only the most famous musicians, but also the most famous women of the early modern city. (Kendrick 1996 p. 416)

It is clear that the musical events in the convents in Siena were a significant part of local entertainment. The following are always mentioned in scribes' description of monastic rites:

- superb decorations
- the number of choirs involved
- the crush of the public
- the universal satisfaction at the event

> Then, as now, the grandiose and the spectacular were undeniably enticing, and the crowds came not only to hear but sometimes to see the nuns' performances. Tridentine decrees were clearly meant to prevent such occurrences, but in these cases nuns, archbishops, and citizens were clearly obeying the precepts of Trent to the letter and not one whit further: the nuns did not exit the convent, nor did the public enter the enclosed spaces, but there was no decree concerning the city walls that happened to offer a good vantage point for a procession inside a cloister. (Reardon 2002 p. 48)

In terms of *product and process*, what is clear for the publications was that the nun composers were able to turn out musical products for wider dissemination. Although publication was more difficult for women, Badalla and Cozzolani were published, even though other women, like Quinzana, were not. Like so much else in the lives of these women musicians, it seemed to depend on the attitude of the Bishop in power at the time.

Kendrick also draws attention to the oral nature of some of the repertory in use. It is possible, for example, that nuns improvised discant parts for liturgical chants. In a Sienese antiphonary comes the indication that in the Palm Sunday procession the nuns embellished the plainchant with dramatic gestures (were these musical or purely gestural?) that turned the procession into a piece of theatre (Reardon 2002 p. 31). There is also reference to improvisation in relation to the mystics.

In terms of the rhythm of *excitement and relaxation*, we cannot be sure of the public (chiesa esteriore) or the private (chiesa interiore) repertoire but there was a notion of what was suitable for nuns to be singing, an aspect not present in the literature concerning male monasteries. We have already seen above how certain instruments were considered by the authorities (not by the nuns themselves!) as appropriate like organs and that they sang expressively a range of music.

In terms of *challenge and nurture*, there were conflicts between the nuns and their bishops. Frequent conflicts between nuns and the curia in Milan led to the banning of singing at St Marta for a period in the mid-century and also at St Radegunda later on. Sometimes these conflicts were provoked by the actions of the nun's themselves (as we have seen with Hildegard in Chapter 3). In other times and places they were encouraged by the authorities. It was the musical sisters' ability to manage polyphony that symbolised their status in the civic world. In the late sixteenth century the flourishing of polyphony accompanied an upsurge of devotion that was focussed on the convents, especially under Bishop Frederigo Borromeo in Milan. This included the redecoration of many of the churches, like the new altarpiece by Simone Peterzano in the chiesa esteriore of the convent of St Radegunda in Milan in about 1585. He appears to have wanted to recreate the role of the nuns as intercessors for the wider community and the providers of its main spiritual nourishment. Here they were seen as representing a foretaste of the angelic choirs of heaven and encouraging music-making was a way of preparing nuns for their life in heaven.

Accounts of visitors attending Sienese convents show that the music was regarded as much more than a frill and time filler. When Berenice Della Caia visited St Maria degli Angeli, the nuns sang a madrigal that included instruments and 'lovely sinfonias,' through which they managed to convey their compliments to their visitor, her husband and the pope. After this:

> They went to the refectory where an abundant lunch had been prepared with various refreshments and pastries and diverse fruits with all sorts of exquisite chilled wines. While the women were satisfying their appetite and thirst, their ears were gracing in ariette and concerted music on various instruments. (Reardon 2002 pp. 43–4)

Here music is linked with the process of nourishing the guests. Carol Walker Bynum (1987) in her study *Holy Feast and Holy Fast: The Meaning of Food in Medieval Religious Women* shows how women exercised power and leverage in the wider society through their control of food. Here it is clear that their music-making was linked with this function. The account clearly sees the food as satisfying physical hunger and the music spiritual and emotional hunger. A similar link is seen is their participation in the civic processions on Low Sunday when they lent their relics and provided music. This was particularly marked when the relic was returned, at which point the bells were rung, the organ played and spiritual compositions performed. In one procession a group of girls were dressed as angels to sing and the body was ceremonially 'lost' before being 'found' and returned to the convent with a polyphonic mass. Such events cemented the relationship between the surrounding community and the nuns. Their command of a combination of sets, music, gesture and choreography was developed in the theatrical events that they put on, often in the presence of lay visitors. In these nuns were required to sing and dance (Reardon 2002 pp. 45–7).

In the area of the *rational and the intuitive* there was a feminisation of ecstasy in the writings of Bishop Frederigo Borromeo in Milan. In his treatise on female mysticism he postulates a difference between men's and women's mysticism:

> The treatise considered that women were more prone to both true and false (even diabolical) ecstasy than were men, and enumerated the pastoral lessons to be learned from this fact; in this sense, it marked a change from the long tradition of Christian possession literature largely undifferentiated by gender. (Kendrick 1996 p. 157)

He drew examples from women singing in ecstasy during the office, citing the singer Vannini who became enraptured after improvising on the lute. She appears to have been improvising, producing otherworldly music never before heard. During the ecstasy she would wear a hat shielding her eyes, drawing attention to the fact that ecstasy did not need bodily sensations.

> When she came out of ecstasy, she sometimes sang so much better than usual, and all who heard her marvelled as at something never before heard, and she used to say, 'Don't be so astonished, for I learned this manner of singing in heaven. There, the saints sing in such a manner and continuously praise God. It is in imitation of such saints that our songs should be composed, and not out of vanity, from which may God preserve you.' (Reardon 2002 p. 106)

Suor Maria Francesca Piccolomini also was renowned for her ecstasies. In this she appears to become united with the Madonna of the Manger, in contrast to the usual notion of being united with Christ. The Virgin produces miraculous cures of various ailments some of which were preventing her from playing the theorbo which she needed to accompany the religious songs in the convent Ognissanti. In another vision, she finds her own voice. It is not clear whether this was her singing voice or simply a way of speaking out and overcoming the 'invisibility' of the cloistered nuns. In the stories of both women the fact that they were required to play and sing by their spiritual experiences manages effectively to get round the problem if they were accused of vanity. The source of their inspiration is not human (Reardon 2002 pp. 111–22). We have already seen a similar phenomenon in the visions of Hildegard in Chapter 3.

In terms of the relationship between *mind, body and spirit*, according to Bishop Frederigo Borromeo in Milan, women best embodied the natural goodness of creation; and there is no linking to sexuality in any of the literature except that of 'obsessed' prelates (Kendrick 1996 pp. 426–7). Carol Walker Bynum (1987) examines the identification of women with the Real Presence of Christ at the Eucharist in the food symbol and the sufferings and Passion of Christ. She shows how they used the erotic imagery of the Song of Songs to cement their identity as brides of Christ. Texts on these issues were favourites of the Milanese nun composers. In contemporary writings, parallels were drawn between virginity and the Holy Spirit (the indwellings for the Holy Spirit) and attention drawn to efficacy of the nuns' harmony to dispel evil spirits and attract heavenly power.

Undoubtedly the spirituality of the nuns' life was projected onto the city by means of music often in the polyphonic settings. So, during Frederigo Borromeo's time as Bishop of Milan, the city would have been part of nuns' clothing ceremonies, Holy Week meditations and Marian devotion, all through the means of the music. The moment of profession was marked by ceremonies that involved gesture and bodily acts such as hair cutting and the putting on of the nun's robes. This moment was often marked by an elaborate composition rather than the chant that was used in the rest of the ceremony. The music symbolised her becoming the bride of Christ. There were disputes about whether the habit could be exchanged for costumes in the theatrical pieces in the convents in Siena. Bishop Alessandro Petrucci allowed sacred dramas and costumes being put on over the habits. However, it is doubtful whether these edicts were fully observed.

Many of the sisters did practise ascetic habits like self-flagellation as part of their spirituality. So there is a certain ambivalence as towards their attitudes to the body. On the one hand, they used them effectively to produce celestial music and indeed gestures associated with dramas. They provided nourishment for others in the form of food and music, but privately these same bodies would be beaten into spiritual submission.

To summarise, we can see in the value systems underpinning the musical traditions of these women composers a developing of solo singing accompanied by warnings against excessive vanity (keeping them rooted in their communities). Despite the Council of Trent there was undoubtedly a variety of practices musically. The process of enclosure was being worked out during the period and is an area where the definition of women's private and public spaces was being, sometimes acrimoniously, worked out. However, the nuns proved remarkable resourceful at keeping themselves within the public life of the city to which travellers' accounts bear witness. They were able to use improvisation in worship as well as notate and publish

their works; but it is likely that a great deal of transmission in the convents
was done orally. Although certain styles and instruments were sometimes
deemed unsuitable for nuns, in general this advice was ignored. Music
was seen very much as part of women's nourishing functions and linked
with their embodiment. There are examples of women musicians whose
music was influenced by their ecstatic experiences and some of these, in
particular, practised ascetic acts of self-harm in the interest of spirituality.

Spirituality

Music was central to the nuns' spirituality (as in Hildegard's high theology
of music that we examined in Chapter 3) and their most important act after
the Eucharist. It had clear purposes within their own lives of experiencing the Divine. Through it, they experienced divine love, nourished their
identification with the angels and experienced a rapturous union with God.
They saw music itself as a path to spiritual perfection[14] (which today we
might identify as liminality).

The themes that the nuns enjoyed expressing in their music involved
what are regarded as 'feminine' elements in spirituality. Caroline Walker
Bynum sees some themes as favourite ones with women mystics like the
Double Intercession (Bynum 1987). This theology sees both the wounds
of Christ and the milk of the Virgin as assisting the bodily salvation and
nourishment of Christians. It is a theme of two of Cozzolani's motets.
Female figures play an important in the spirituality of the nuns' music
with the Virgin and Mary Magdalene playing significant roles along with
the female figures like St Radegund.

The convents were regarded as sacred spaces for the whole community. Certainly accounts of travellers regularly refer to 'heavenly' music
and it is clear that their experience of it included a large measure of pious

---

14   Suor Maria Crocefissa quoted in Kendrick 1996 p. 429.

devotion and wonder and awe. They perceived the cloistered musical space as the Heavenly Jerusalem. The Sienese composer, Alessandro Della Caia's *Sacred Lamentations and Motets*, drew heavily on the image of the heavenly Jerusalem where the woes of the world are escaped – a reference to the perceived status of the life in the convent walls accepted by nuns and surrounding culture alike. Here nuns are cast in the role of angels (Reardon 2002 p. 191). 'If this is the convent of S. Maria degli Angeli, then it must be inhabited by many angels from paradise' said an Archbishop on a visit. But not only were the nuns cast in the role of angels by the surrounding community, they were also able to summon up the angels for those communities. From the S Abbondio chronicle comes an account of a time when the lay community entered the chiesa interiore and a little boy saw angels crowning one of the nuns who was singing (Reardon 2002 pp. 48–9).

For the nun musicians, spirituality was the starting point and the life blood of their music-making. They lived in a spiritual climate where a number of 'feminine' elements were in favour both with their superiors and in the wider society. Cast in the role of inhabitants of the New Jerusalem, this status enabled them to reach a standard of music making unrivalled in the history of music and attested to by contemporary accounts, but often ignored by traditional histories of European music. They were capable through music-making of elevating themselves and their listeners to a heavenly sphere. Their faith permeated their understanding of the function of music and enabled them to experience the Divine through it.

Summary

Here we see clearly the controversies surrounding the process of enclosure. On the one hand women are subject to the changing whims of local bishops, on the other they have a freedom in the enclosure unparalleled in the wider society musically. This was a time when female creativity flourished, giving the lie to the idea that the Renaissance diminished women's power.[15] Travellers clearly went to Milan to be inspired by the renowned performances of the nuns. The accounts that have been preserved, like those of Rosa Badalla, show them developing the ideas of the day and being acclaimed for their representation of these ideas. These were encapsulated in the music of the nun composers, like Cozzolani, who also pushed the boundaries of the musical forms of the day. In the lives of these nun musicians, their gender, class and vocation fused to give them considerable musical opportunities. These were recognised by the civic authorities for whom they fulfilled the dual role of providing the spiritual dimension to the civic life and maintaining the prestige of the city. They meanwhile used music to project their ideas into the wider community (despite admonitions to stay in the clausura) and to achieve a significant identity in their culture because of their gender and their musical command.

They had available a rich variety of musical materials and were able to use them effectively in the expressive style of the day to enhance the spirituality of their texts. They were able to handle both simple and complex forms effectively as performers and to a certain extent as composers. Their Value systems show how individuality was held in a community context, how they could embrace diversity and control their private space effectively despite attempted intrusions into it. Their view of music as nurture and intercessory gave them an important role in the surrounding community. They also used dramatic elements in their music. Of the five areas of the musical experience outlined in Chapter 1, spirituality was paramount and served to permeate all the other four domains of musical experience.

It is interesting to reflect how these circumstances came together to produce this flourishing of a female musical tradition. The enclosure of women gave them a safe place in which to work and in which they could often ignore the regulations suggested by the enforcement of the demands of enclosure. They were, in general, able to receive musical tuition and to perform publicly protected by their vow of chastity. The array of female saints, and Marian devotion gave them a raft of spirituality that was clearly

---

15   S. Cusick referred to them as 'spiritually eccentric' in the review of *The Crannied Wall, JAMS 47* (1994), p. 348 quoted in Kendrick 1996 p. 426.

feminine and to which they could relate as brides of Christ. The surrounding culture found in them a representation of its idealised spirituality which entertained as well as nourished. Meanwhile, all these elements were being systematically removed from their Protestant sisters in northern Europe, where there are no such flourishing of women's religious musical traditions; and women outside convent worlds are apparently more restrained by the patriarchal societal structures such as the family than in the clausura.

CHAPTER 5

Vignette Four – Radicalising the Vision: Ann Lee and the Shakers

Story

There is very little left to reveal Ann Lee's life. There are no portraits of her. We know of a room or two where she stayed, some scraps of fabric from her dress, a chair in which she is said to have sat ... Ann Lee Standerin was of the working class, born in an English factory city. Her husband and father were both blacksmiths. Her brothers thought it was all right to beat her when they didn't like what she preached. Ann worked in textile mills and was illiterate. The only writing we have from her hand is the X she put by her name on her marriage license. Although Ann could be persuasive when she spoke, as her converts later testified, her power was expressed most forcefully in other ways – in her gaze, her demeanor, the way her body shook when she was filled with spiritual zeal. She was known to call herself 'Ann the Word.'... How different Ann Lee was. In a world that taught women to be obedient and to 'keep within compass' and whose church and state made obedience the only acceptable course of behavior, Ann Lee violated the laws of men and convention. She was a separated woman who took back her maiden name after her husband left her. She was the acknowledged leader and spokeswoman of her small group, which included men. She preached in public and went into churches to interrupt services. She was arrested, imprisoned, and physically and verbally abused for what she preached. Her behavior was not socially acceptable. Her opponents called her a witch or a whore, while her followers believed her to be a saint of the Christ spirit incarnate in a woman, but no one could have called her a 'lady.'... We remember Ann Lee for herself and for the Shaker world that she helped to bring into being. It is a privilege to remember her, this bold, uncomfortable unconventional woman.

— SPRIGG 1990 in Campion pp. xi–xiv

Introduction

Ann Lee lived 1736–84. Nardi Reeder Campion in her influential book *Mother Ann Lee, Morning Star of the Shakers* states:

> Ann Lee has never been recognized as one of the first – if not *the* first – women in this country to possess power and to use it for the liberation of other women. Consider these verifiable facts: Born in the eighteenth century when nearly all women were the possessions of men, a deeply religious Ann Lee spread her faith by daring to be an evangelist. She preached in the streets, since no woman could set foot in a pulpit, and was thrown into jail for it. In the grim mill town of Manchester, England, she led evangelical services of worship that included public confession of sin, speaking in tongues, ecstatic dancing – and went to jail for it. After marriage, she defied convention by using her own name instead of her husband's. Most importantly she founded a religious order, which became The United Society of Believers in Christ's Second Appearing – the Shakers.
>
> To escape British tyranny, Mother Ann took her small band of disciples on a perilous fifty-nine-day voyage across the ocean to an unknown land called America. In the wilderness of upstate New York, She and her followers carved out the first Shaker settlement. During the American Revolution, Mother Ann, a dedicated pacifist, stood unequivocally for nonresistance, quoting Jesus; 'Love your enemies, bless them that curse you, do good to them that hate you, and pray for them which despitefully use you, and persecute you.' Again she was sent to prison.
>
> Later she trekked by carriage and sleigh through New England, enduring unbelievable hardships and persecution in order to attract new members to the Society of Believers. This Society, ruled by *both* women and men, was based on a conviction that God had to be *both* male and female. To generations of followers, she became the female Christ. Clearly Mother Ann Lee was a morning star, not just for the Shakers, but for the independence of women in the New World. (Campion 1990 pp. xvi–xvii)

Her life was built on her faith in Jesus Christ. She had a mystical vision in which her soul broke through to God'; from this she thought herself to be the second coming of Christ in the body of a woman.

She was brought up in poverty. She was an introspective mystic and became taken up with the nature of sin. Acutely doubtful about her own salvation, she was an emotional visionary. She 'caught' the faith of a group of 'shaking Quakers' in Manchester in 1758 led by James and Jane Wardley.

She was given a leading role on this movement which believed in the imminent Second Coming of Jesus and the destruction of the world. She was forced by her father into a marriage with the blacksmith Abraham Stanley. At that time a woman's existence was seen to be subsumed into that of her husband on marriage; but there is no record that Ann ever took her husband's name. The death of her four children led her to a complete nervous breakdown. *A Summary View of the Millennial Church*, a Shaker history describes it thus:

> The convictions of her youth often returned upon her with great force ... She sought deliverance from the bondage of sin, and gave herself no rest, day or night, but often spent whole nights in laboring and crying to God for deliverance from sins. (Campion 1990 pp. 3–4)

Following this experience, she developed a notion of a God angry at carnal relationships. Somewhat reluctantly her husband agreed to a vow of celibacy. In 1772 she was imprisoned for preaching her ideas on celibacy. During her time in prison she was 'anointed' by the Spirit and came out as 'Ann the Word', Bride of the Lamb and convinced that confession, followed by the renunciation of carnal relationships, was the way to salvation. She was regularly in trouble with the authorities for such actions as disturbing the worship in a Manchester church.

In search of religious tolerance, she and eight members of the order (including Ann's husband and father) sailed to America in 1774. On the ship the group celebrated their worship in their own distinctive style – singing, shouting and dancing and Ann preached against the sins of the crew. Their services were stopped but allowed to resume when the prayers of the group saved the unseaworthy ship from being wrecked in a storm.

They got employment in New York. Here her husband deserted her for another woman. In 1776 a community was established in the wilderness at Niskeyuna near Albany, New York. They worked hard to make the area habitable. Mother Ann established good relations with the neighboring Native Americans – the Mahicans who had a reputation for ferocity. The gift of tongues enabled her to converse with their chief and such was the relationship between the two communities that representatives from the Mahicans came to her funeral. After a slow start in their evangelisation they were helped by a New Light Baptist revival in New Lebanon whose converts found their small colony a community manifesting the spirit-infused characteristics of the early church:

- Men and women living a life of celibacy
- Common ownership of goods
- The prizing of work and industry
- Speaking and singing in tongues
- Joyful worshipping rituals
- The preaching of a Christ leading followers to everlasting life.

Both Ann and the elders were imprisoned for treason and pacifism. This drew publicity to the order, and a two-year mission produced communities in Massachusetts, Connecticut and New York. Mother Ann died in 1784.

The communities were organised in family groups governed by two elders and two eldresses responsible for the spiritual well-being of their charges. An order of deacons and deaconesses looked after temporal matters and trustees cared for the property. Newcomers were welcomed into a form of novitiate and children joined a children's order. The government was quite centralised and harmonised by the common worship and statutes. Father Joseph Meacham developed Ann's essentially simple belief system into forms of governance and belief. People entering the order started in a gathering family or type of novitiate and only gradually moved towards giving up their property and full commitment to the community. Women were in equal positions of leadership in line with Mother Ann's own position as a messianic leader. She said:

> The order of nature requires a man and a woman to produce offspring ... He is the Father and she is the Mother; and all the children, both male and female, must be subject to their parents ... but when the man is gone, the right of government belongs to the woman. So it is with the family of Christ. (Campion 1990 p. 75)

Mother Ann foresaw the spread of Shakerism. It did spread to make the communities in various parts of New York State, Massachusetts, Connecticut, Maine, Florida, New Hampshire, Ohio, Kentucky and Indiana. The peak of membership was 6,000 in 1845. They held in common between them more than one hundred thousand acres of land.

Materials

Shaker music can be divided into songs, tunes and dances although they were conceived in the tradition as being inseparable in the life of praise and worship. There was a tradition from early on in the movement of wordless tunes. Both in Manchester and on their boat trip to the North America they had no songs to express their new faith. They deliberately abandoned the music of the world that they had left behind including religious music of other traditions, marching songs (which had words of a carnal nature), ballads and hunting songs. Their early music consisted of intoned psalms, singing in tongues, songs with meaningless syllables such as 'do-do-diddle-o' and cries of such words as Hallelujah.

However, there was also a clear strand of song creation. Meetings involving song and dance often lasted late into the night. The three 'witnesses' – Mother Ann Lee, Father William Lee and Father James Whittaker – often created what they called 'solemn songs'. Mother Ann Lee was also portrayed in visitors' accounts as humming 'in a melodious voice' (Andrews 1962 p. 9). Valentine Rathbun (who joined the movement for a brief while) writes in 1760 in his *Some brief hints of a religious scheme*:

> Some will be singing, each one his own tune; some without words, in an Indian tone, some jig tunes, some tunes of their own making, in an unknown mutter, which they call new tongues ... (Quoted in Andrews 1962 p. 86)

No instruments were used in the early movement. Until 1870 instrumental music was banned as 'worldly', 'superfluous' and 'inferior to vocal music'. These were attitudes probably drawn from their Quaker origins; there was also a strand that saw instruments as encouraging pride on the part of performers and as inimical to the spirit of community. Instruments were imitated in the wordless songs; in 1843 Macdonald describes a procession to the holy foundation in Wisdom's valley:

> Each one made a sound with the mouth, to please him or herself, and at the same time, went through the motions playing some particular instrument, such as the Clarionet, French Horn, Trombone, Bass Drum, etc. and such a noise was made

that I felt as if I had got amongst a parcel of Lunatics. It appeared to me much more
of a Burlesque Overture, than I had heard performed by Chrystys Ministrels on the
Cow Bells. (Quoted in Andrews 1962 p. 86)

Later, instruments were introduced. In 1870 a cabinet organ was purchased
at Canterbury and two years later a piano. Musical instruction was based
on these instruments, the use of which gradually spread to other communities. The organ then appeared more regularly in worship:

After the first song, Brother Delmer, read from the Bible, and then another song was
sung. Sister Della sat at the organ during the Bible readings. (Carr 1995 pp. 14–15)

In the early movement there was little musical instruction and the first
organised instruction appears to have started in the second quarter of the
nineteenth century. The early songs were single line melodies with harmonies only appearing gradually. The withdrawal of the ban on instruments
coincided with the development of singing in parts.

There had been the gradual development of music instruction started
by Seth Wells. Here 'singing meetings' were gradually developed between
1820 and 1825, as times when music leaders (both men and women) were
able to learn the material. Two inventions were used to help in the process
– the tone-ometer which was a one-string monochord for giving pitch and
a speediometer, a bullet attached to a string to set the speed. Initially, they
used the 'same round-note manner of tune writing and the same tune forms
used in non-Shaker circles' (Andrews 1962 p. 87). However, inspired by
Mother Ann, in the Harvard community the use of letters was developed
in the interest of simplification.

Many of the rituals took place in the meeting houses. These were bare
of furniture except for movable benches. Blue, a virgin colour, was used
for doors, window frames and pegboards on the walls. The outside of the
meeting house was painted white, symbolic of purity. White and blue
characterised the colour of clothes as well. In the meeting house men and
women were separated. They often faced each other in lines retreating and
advancing and circling but not touching. Around 1818 the ranks and files
became more flexible with a group of singers in the middle of the room.

There were some outdoor rituals like the mountain meetings instituted in 1842 which were held on a selected high place and included many rituals and a feast. Other rituals involved movement around all the community buildings, like *The Midnight Cry* which was instituted in 1842 following a spiritual visitation by Wisdom. Two mediums carrying lamps led six male and six female leaders through every room carrying lighted lamps, which took all of two weeks.

To summarise, the musical materials used were essentially simple at the start. They became more complex, involving instruments and notated books of hymns and songs later. In the interests of simplicity, a notation system based on letters was developed. The meeting house was the main context for worship, but rituals could take place outside or in the other community areas.

Expression

Their stress on simplicity meant that their worship was often filled with 'a curious primitivism and child-like innocence' (Andrews 1962 p. 8). Their furniture, life style, clothing and language were deliberately plain and simple. It is encapsulated in their most famous song:

> Tis the gift to be simple, tis the gift to be free,
> Tis the gift to come down where we ought to be,
> And when we find ourselves in the place just right
> 'Twill be in the valley of love and delight.
> When true simplicity is gained,
> To bow and to bend we shan't be ashamed,
> To turn, turn will be our delight
> Till by turning, turning we come round right.[1]

---

1   Written and composed in 1848 by Elder Joseph Brackett.

The process of singing and dancing was central to their worship. Members composed tunes, dances, marches (which were given special titles such as *Comforting March*, *Sweet March to Heaven* and *Purity March*), ring dances and songs but the stress was always on appropriateness for the community. It is interesting to note the prevalence of titles indicating the expressive feel of the dances; some of these were very marked such as the 'sacred' marches that represented the progress of the soul to heaven. The songs had to reflect the common aspirations of the group and the tempo was prescribed for certain parts of the service. The musical form and expression were like the furniture shapes – freedom contained in a simple form. The songs were interpreted with as much emotion as appropriate to its place in the ritual. This would include ornamentation, triumphant shouting and trembling on notes like a vibrato. The tradition was very contextual, with the context influencing the performance style.

Passion was very much valued in the movement. From the Wardleys' meetings, Mother Ann learned impassioned preaching and also the practice of public confession because of its cleansing properties. The high point of the meetings was the expression of feelings which took many forms. It started with walking and moved through various forms of movement and music including shouting, dancing and shaking. Sometimes these would be done in trancelike states. There was a strong sense from the start of the movement of singing in the spirit. Valentin Rathbun reports that the singing was preceded by a violent shaking of the head from side to side. (Rathbun, Valentine (1781), *Some brief hints, of a Religious Scheme, Taught and Propagated by a Number of Europeans, living in a place called Nisqueunia in the State of New York*, quoted in Andrews 1962 p. 85)

Mother Ann regarded dancing as an important way of sublimating the sexual feelings in the context of a celibate community. In contrast to the surrounding society who saw dance as exciting sexual desire she saw it as an important way of releasing pent up feelings and anxiety. Public confession was also an important part of worship as a means of freeing the believer from sin when followed by appropriate work.

Some of the rituals had a highly dramatic character. An example of this was the warring songs designed to drive out the devil which could be accompanied by these gestures:

The movement involved drawing the right knee nearly to the chin, placing the arm in position of the sportsman, then straightening themselves with a jerk, and a stamp of the foot, accompanied by a quick bursting yelp, in imitation of a gun. (Andrews 1962 p. 38)

In another ritual called *Gift of Holy Mother Wisdom* the inspired members placed a golden band inscribed with Wisdom's name on other members' heads.

Many of the dances were characterised by clapping, stamping, bowing, bending and shaking their fingers as if to get rid of sin:

Who will bow and bend like a willow,
Who will turn and twist and reel
In the gale of simple freedom,
From the bower of union flowing?

Who will drink the wine of power,
Dropping down like a shower?
Pride and bondage all forgetting,
Mother's wine is freely working.

Oh ho! I will have it,
I will bow and bend to get it,
I'll be reeling, turning, twisting,
Shake out all the starch and stiff'ning! (Campion 1990 p. 19)

Some people watching the dancing were surprised by the animalistic type movements within it, identifying postures like kangaroos, penguins, or dancing dogs (Greeley 1838 p. 537).[2] In line with the integration of body and soul, the worshipping dancers were beautifully dressed. The artist-author Benson-Lossing describes the sisters as dressed:

in spotless white, with neat lawn caps, pure white kerchiefs over their marine blue prunella; the brethren in their pantaloons of blue linen, vests of deeper blue and white cotton shirts. (Quoted in Andrews 1962 p. 156)

2   This is similar to indigenous traditions where dance traditions demonstrate their connectedness with the natural world.

The ring dances for example, later developed into having four concentric circles symbolising the four spiritual cycles of Shaker theology:

- The lion period from Adam to Abraham
- The calf period from Abraham to Jesus
- The human face period from Jesus to Mother Ann
- The flying eagle period (the outer, biggest circle), the time of the millennial church, Shakerism

In 1853, Walt Whitman saw this wheel dance and was told that the singing represented 'the harmony and perfection to which all tend and there is God.'[3] The French traveller, Mme Therese Blanc interpreted the symbolism of the dances she saw:

> The movement of their hands-stretched forth to receive blessings or to offer to one's neighbor in prayer the grace he seeks – seems of very noble symbolism. And their feet barely touch earth in the rapid processional accompanied by hymns to tunes sometimes very lively, at others remarkable for the repeated returns [of] the same note, as in oriental music.[4]

Some visitors were surprised by the joy expressed in the liturgy, because they often expected a solemn service. Lieut-Col Maxwell in 1840 wrote of a meeting in Enfield:

> If the Shakers' doctrine be the true one, our system of kneeling and praying ought immediately to give place to singing merry songs and dancing Scottish reels … I never beheld the double-shuffle, the cut the buckle, and the Highland fling in greater perfection.[5]

---

3   Holloway, Emory (1930), *Walt Whitman's Visit to the Shakers*, Colophon Part 13. quoted in Andrews 1962, p. 152.

4   Bentzon, Th (Mme Therese Blanc) (1898), *Choses et gens d'Amerique* pp. 86–7 Paris. An account of the Alfred community at Maine translated by John Alden in the public library of Springfield, MA, quoted in Andrews, Edward D. (1962 but first published 1940) p. 157.

5   Maxwell, A.M.K. (1841), *A run through the United States during the autumn of 1840*. *Vol 1* London pp. 90–1 quoted in Andrews, Edward D. (1962 but first published 1940) p. 85.

The mountain rituals included the rite of drinking spiritual wine which made all participants 'merry' and included singing the 'fool' song:

> Come, come,
> Who will be a fool,
> I will be a fool. (Andrews 1962 p. 34)

During this, people would behave as foolishly as possible, including imitating animals.

To summarise, the expression of emotion was central to Shaker services. This was done through dance, song and confession. There was a freedom of expression that involved movements and sounds that appeared strange to visitors from the outside world. It included laughter and joy. Symbolic meanings underpinned much of the ritual including the songs and dances.

Construction

The Shaker worship pattern consisted of waiting in silence like the Quakers, each family having before the service had a half hour period of 'retiring time' to prepare. From this they marched to the meeting house in double file led by the elders. The men and women entered by different doors. The presiding elder gave the signal to start, usually with a devotional hymn, at which point the benches were removed. Then there was a sermon designed also for the public who were present. When the meeting was under way marches and dance songs were 'laboured', often ceremonially. The meeting might work up to a high point of emotion (see below under Values).

The earliest song was a brief verse sung at a meeting in Turtle Creek, Ohio in 1805:

With him in praises we'll advance
And join the virgins in the dance. (Andrews 1962 p. 12)

In 1806 hymns composed 'in the spirit of the work' were being circulated. These included wordless tunes but were later dropped or words provided.

It is clear that improvisation formed an important part of the tradition at the beginning. This grew from the freedom of the early Shakers who sang, danced, shook, shouted, whirled and laughed as the spirit moved them. The original Shaker dances were not organised. An early account of a Manchester meeting ran:

> After assembling together and sitting a while in silent meditation, they were taken with a mighty trembling ... at other times they were affected ... with a mighty shaking; and were occasionally exercised in singing, shouting or walking the floor, under the influence of spiritual signs, shoving each other about, – or swiftly passing and repassing each other, like clouds agitated by a mighty wind.[6]

These so-called 'exercises' or 'labouring' were designed to shake off the desires of the flesh. There was a strong desire to get rid of pride and self by means of mortification. The motivation for bowing, shaking, speaking in tongues, confessing faults was to 'debase' and 'simplify'. They were aware of how strange these would appear to outsiders and despite the apparent confusion, the believers themselves were aware of an inner order and harmony. Here is an account of what historians entitled the 'back' manner of worship:

> As the singing and dancing progress, the Worshippers become more zealous, then frantic with excitement – until nothing but what the 'World' would call disorder and confusion reigns. As the excitement increases, all order is forgotten, all unison of parts repudiated, each sings his own tune, each dances his own dance, or leaps, shouts, and exults with exceeding great joy – the more gifted of the Females engage in a kind of whirling motion, which they reform with seemingly incredible velocity with their hands being extended horizontally and their dresses blown out like a balloon all around their persons by the centrifugal force occasioned by the rapidity of

---

6   Anon. (1810), *The testimony of Christ's appearing* p. xxv Albany, quoted in Andrews, Edward D. (1962 but first published 1940) p. 143.

their motion. After performing Fifty to one Thousand revolutions each, they either swoon away and fall into the arms of their Friends, or suddenly come to stand, with apparently little or no dizziness produced. Sometimes the Worshippers engage in a race round the Room, with a sweeping motion of the Hands and Arms, intended to present the act of sweeping the Devil out of the Room. (Andrews 1962 p. 156)

The presence of improvisation and freedom in the form is clear here. The form of whirling dancing is interesting to compare with such traditions from other faiths like the Whirling Dervishes from the Sufi tradition. Here, however, it appears to be a women's tradition.

The songs fell into various types – 'gift' songs, ritual songs, 'vision' songs, greeting and farewell songs, dance songs, songs in unknown tongues, 'Indian' and 'negro' songs, songs of humility, hymns and anthems. Here is an example of a song designed for whirling from 1844. The verse was repeated with a wordless tune between:

Figure Five: Turning Song

Here is an example of a vision song probably from 1838 given in an unknown tongue. It is described as 'learned in a vision by one of the sisters at Groveland (N.Y.) while visiting the moon.' Sometimes this type of song was followed in the worship meeting by an interpretation:

Figure Six: From The Moon

The early songs were usually simple single line melodies easily learned. This 'welcome' song shows the warmth and simplicity of this style:

Figure Seven: A Mince Pie or a Pudding

The forms were often simple and repetitive although some were more carefully shaped like this marching tune:

Figure Eight: Marching Tune

The rhythms were sometimes more complex than this. The Shakers divided metre into three modes which they called even, triple and compound. Here is an example of a solemn 'noted' song in a 5/4 metre:

Figure Nine: Solemn Song

The 'anthems' given from 1840 onwards, were like long prose poems with no rhymes and no fixed metrical pattern. The music was free-flowing with changes of mode and some were very mystical in character.[7]

The songs and dances were often received by visionaries in trancelike states and sometimes new forms were given in this way, like the three new dances given between 1837 and 1847. These included:

- *Check*, devised for the young people and possibly relating to the Virginia reel step,
- *Walking the Narrow path*, a solemn march in which one foot was placed immediately in front of the other and a marching pattern that involved a sort of shuttling movement with lines moving in and out of one another.

---

7   There is a parallel here to some of Hildegard's pieces (see Chapter 4).

Initially there were songs without dance and dances without song, like this early shuffling tune from the early 1790s in a slow 3/4 time which was intoned or hummed or sung to wordless syllables:

Figure Ten: Shuffling Song

As the order developed, worship became more ordered and singing words and dancing were brought together.

The earliest Shaker songs were composed by a few people and many of tunes were borrowed from secular and religious sources. Some were printed but others were remembered and retained orally. As the number of hymns and songs proliferated, the process of 'retaining' and 'conveying' the hymns became increasingly difficult. People like Abram Whitney, Seth Y. Wells and Isaac Youngs began to encourage and develop an understanding of musical notation.

However, the process of shaping and forming tunes did not develop in the way it did in other hymn traditions. The form was often free, and there are influences from American religious folksong evident. Music critics have described them as rambling, little more than note-sequences and lacking in consistency in the metre, especially in the free-flowing pieces called 'anthems'. But, from a different point of view, they can be seen as representing a type of musical freedom. Edward Andrews gives four potential reasons for their failure to embrace the more common formal principles:

- The songs are the products of individuals
- Such productions were not subjected to that *zersingen* process which comes from wide and general singing over long periods of time[8]
- The ritualistic function of many of the songs
- The unusual demands of the texts themselves to which the tunes had to yield (Andrews 1962 p. 90)

As the worship became more formal, three and four part harmony began to appear in songs. These mostly date from after 1870, although there are some examples before that for such combinations as 'treble, tenor and base' or 'tenor, alto, air and base'. This latter designation appears to be similar to the designations used in the English gallery choir tradition.

In an increasingly 'set' approach to the form of the liturgy, dances became codified from the first improvised movements. The 'squared order shuffle' was first taught by Father Joseph Meacham from a vision of angels in 1785. The services became more solemn, but Mother Lucy Wright believed in a more joyful ministry and in 1805 and 1806 the Kentucky revival also made the services more lively again. By the 1830s the dances were showing signs of being intricate and carefully rehearsed. Lieutenant E.T.Coke writes of a performance event in 1832:

> There was such a scene of marching and counter-marching, slow step, quick step, and double quick step, advancing and retiring, forming open column and close column, perpendicular lines and oblique lines, that it was sufficient to puzzle and confound the clearest head of the lookers on.[9]

There is no doubt that the freer elements in the early Shaker traditions gradually became more fixed as the tradition grew older. Emerson in his essay, *Goethe or the Writer used*, cites the Quakers and the Shakers as examples of the movement of rituals towards spiritless form:

---

8   This was not possible because of the practice of living in family units which meant that some of the 'received' songs may never have been sung in the wider community.
9   Coke, E.T. (1833), *A subaltern's Furlough Vol 1*, New York p. 199 Quoted in Andrews 1962 p. 152.

The fiery reformer embodies the aspiration in some rite or covenant, and he and his friends cleave to the form and lose the aspiration. The Quaker has established Quakerism and the Shaker has established his monastery and dance; and although each prates of spirit, there is no spirit, but repetition, which is anti-spiritual. (Quoted in Andrews 1962 p. 157)

To summarise, the origins of the movement saw a considerable degree of improvisation and reliance on intuitive methods for constructing songs, tunes and dances. The apparent confusion was seen as ordered by participants. The development of notation meant tunes were retained and became more shaped; nonetheless they developed in different ways from other hymn traditions. Dances also became codified and more intricate. Some critics saw this as signifying the loss of the earlier freedom of the Spirit.

Values

Mother Ann saw that all the problems of society were interconnected and saw the problem as one of human relationships. Community was central to her thinking. She laid stress on all being members one of the other and said that there was no such thing as individual salvation. Despite the fact that the sexes were kept separate in worship there was a strong sense of being bound together:

We love to dance, we love to sing,
We love to taste the living spring,
We love to feel our union flow
While round, and round, and round we go. (Campion 1990 p. 66)

She challenged dominant views of beauty, centering her ideas on a simple functionality. Describing Shaker style, Charles Nordhoff says that 'it seeks only the useful and cares nothing for grace and beauty, and carefully avoids ornament'.[10]

10   Nordhoff, Charles (1875) *Communistic Societies in the United States* quoted in
       Campion pp. 153–4.

Ralph Emerson in his *Journals* writes that the Shakers showed that 'not merely that successful communism is subjectively possible, but that this nation is free enough it let it grow' (Campion 1990 p. 156).

Mother Ann was an early leader in the Peace movement, being imprisoned for her pacifism. She saw the answer in a radical shift in value systems which she could do in her new community. Ralph Emerson saw them as pioneer socialists in challenging the dominant culture:

> This immensely brave visionary woman, Mother Ann Lee established a Shaker society where, for a time, men and women were able to escape from the chains of competition, materialism, sexism, and self-gratification. (Campion 1990 p. xviii)

I Ier answer to being able to live by the Value systems subjugated by her society was to found a community separated from the dominant culture which could present a challenge to the dominant values.[11] She described herself as turning the world upside down. Many feared her as a threat to the fabric of society in her rejection of clerical leadership, formal liturgies and creeds, sacraments, her pacifism, her refusal to take oaths, her hostility to marriage, her insistence on communal living and her insistence that women should preach, teach and prophesy. She saw clearly the struggle that women would have if they were to gain full equality and release from the oppression of contemporary society. The result of this was that accusations were levied against her of witchcraft. In Poughkeepsie, an attempt was made to set fire to the house in which she worshipped. In the Massachusetts village of Petersham, she was called a 'virago' – a woman containing masculine qualities. She was kidnapped by several local men and brutalised by them. She returned to her community singing for joy. There are many examples of Shakers who when attacked and persecuted sang songs during their victimisation as a way of keeping true to their divine calling.

We have seen how Shaker songs are characterised by taking a variety of forms. Mother Ann established excellent relations with the neighboring Native American people, the Mahicans, who attended her funeral. Shakerism drew on this tradition through the idea of the visitations of spirits.

---

11   There were many other examples of such separatist/socialistic/utopian religious communities that emerged in America during or around this period. Ann Lee could be seen as a product of a particular historical moment.

There was a category called 'racial' songs given in visions; these drew
on many different traditions, including Eskimos [Inuit], Abyssinians,
Hottentots and Chinese. This one is in the Native American tradition. It
also ends with a 'shout':

Figure Eleven: Mother's Love

Mother Ann encouraged the inward journey in her followers. She had found
the Christ Spirit within herself and realised that her community also needed
to find the God within to claim their power. She saw music and dance
as playing an important part of this. There was a great balance between
the internal spiritual life and the lively extraverted elements of the public
worship. In these, all were invited to play a part in a non-hierarchical way.

In terms of freedom and spontaneity, there was, as we have seen, a considerable amount of improvisation in Shaker worship but this spontaneity
gradually tended to disappear. Freedom was central to Mother Ann Lee's
thinking. Her experience of release from prison was encapsulated in a song:

> We're children of the free woman,
> We're free'd from the bondage of sin and death,
> If we have any bands a-binding in us
> We must break them and break them
> And burn them up. (Campion 1990 p. 32)

Although she encouraged free improvisation in worship, she was concerned
with order because she believed it to be of God. But this order she saw as
coming from within and not from without. She asked people first of all
to establish order within their own selves.

As we have seen above, excitement was an important part of Shaker worship. In fact, one might say that the expressive curve of a gradual rise to a peak of excitement accompanied by free improvisation defined the shape of Shaker worship. Some contemporaries accused her community of taking alcohol to achieve excitement. It is difficult to know whether the 'highs' of Shaker worship did include taking wine or were the result of their religious ecstasy. There was a category of songs called 'drinking songs' which concerned the gift of spiritual wine which produced symptoms of spiritual intoxication. This one from the Mary Hazard Hymnal of 1847 has a tune with a similarity to *Yankee Doodle*:

Figure Twelve: Drink ye of Mother's Wine

It was during times of high emotion, often known as 'awakenings' or 'revivals', that the rituals were likely to reach a frenzy and the control of the ritual would disappear. This is an extract from a letter from Elder Archibald Meacham to the elders in the east from West Union County Indiana territory April 23rd 1815. He describes how the worship began with solemn songs, but how the singing was 'entirely drounded by Diferent Exercises':

> The sound is like mighty thunderings, Some a Stamping with all their mighty and Roaring out against the nasty stinking beast ... Others turning with great Power and warring against the flesh, and at the same time a number Speaking with new tongues with Such majestic Signs and motions that it makes the powers of Darkness tremble ... (Quoted in Andrews 1962 p. 154)

An account of meeting in 1820 shows a Shaker 'high' getting out of control when an opening march turned into quick dancing of a promiscuous kind. An elder instructed the brothers and sisters to 'shake off the flesh':

> A faint staggering seized the members, which, by degrees turned into a heavy shaking. Every position of which the human frame is susceptible, was to be seen – One leaping up, turning around; another flying around the room in the swift dance, and all engaged with their whole strength in every manner of action.[12]

Mother Ann was an intuitive mystic. She had received visionary experiences from her childhood. During her time in prison in 1770, she received the visions that shaped Shakerism:

> The most astonishing visions and divine manifestations were presented to her in so clear and striking a manner, that the whole spiritual world seemed displayed before her.[13]

During her ecstatic experiences she felt a strong current of energy flow through her spine. This swept away all emotion and she felt a great sense of release from all her sins and a feeling of being in peace and harmony with everything.

The receiving of the songs and dances on the part of members of the community was often part of a visionary experience but later more 'rational' processes were used to refine what had been given in the initial vision:

> The *elements* of the song were undoubtedly produced by the visionist – though we can be fairly certain that in many cases the piece was reshaped, improved, titled and properly notated by another, a deliberate and experienced hand ...
>
> It is unlikely that a worshipper who spontaneously sang a 'song' in the excitement of worship would be able to remember it afterwards ... If the visionist had the ability, especially a knowledge of music, to make the record herself or himself, no

---

12   Haskett, William J. (1828), *Shakerism Unmasked or The history of the Shakers*, Pittsfield pp. 190–2 quoted in Andrews 1962 p. 155.

13   Green, Calvin and Wells, Seth Y. (1823) *A Summary View of the Millennial Church of the United Society of Believers (commonly called Shakers)*, Albany, NY: Packard and van Benthuysen, quoted in Campion 1990 p. 24.

assistance was required; but in many cases the gifts were recorded by versifiers like Mary Hazzard, Henry deWitt ... The completed tune-and-text was built up into acceptable form from the unorganized elements of the original inspirational experience. (Andrews 1962 p. 46)

In the 1840s, many Shakers became vehicles for messages from Mother Ann, other early leaders, the heavenly Father, the Holy Mother Wisdom, angels, saints and so on. These included vision songs, which often contained prophesies, warnings and promises. The gift songs were addressed to people in recognition of their spiritual gifts. In these messages it was the tune that was often considered most important. The 'gift' of a song might take place at any time like splitting wood or cutting apples.

Mother Ann believed in the keeping together of body, mind and spirit. Ann's motto was: Put your hands to work and your hearts to God. The pattern of the Shaker day saw a carefully balanced pattern or work and prayer. She saw work as a form of worship. Work brought the community closer to God in her theology. Work songs accompanied their manual labour:

Sweep, sweep and cleanse your floor,
Mother's standing at the door,
She'll give us good and precious wheat,
With which there is no chaff or cheat. (Campion 1990 p. 68)

Cleanliness was very important to her, declaring that there was no dirt in heaven. This was carried out both spiritually – clearing evil spirits – and materially, sweeping floors, clearing cobwebs, burning rubbish etc. In this 'sweeping' song from Elder Abraham Perkins the rhythm of the work clearly dictates the rhythmic pattern of the song:

Low,—low! Low,—low! In this pret-ty path I will go. For here Mo-therleads me and I know it is right. I will sweep as I go I will sweep as I go, For this Mo-ther bids me and it is my de-light, And the sword I will wield, and the sword I will wield. For Mo-ther bids me so. And I will hold, And I will hold, For this is my work while here be - low.

Figure Thirteen: Sweep as I Go

Within the rituals, body and soul were held together through the medium of sung dances and the combination of preaching and movement. Mother Ann was criticised for her use of dancing in worship but she drew her authority from Biblical stories like David and Goliath, in which David danced energetically before the Ark of the Lord.

One of the main differences between the Shakers and the Puritans was the attitude to joyful self-expression as we have seen under Expression above

> while the Puritans valued thought and suppressed feeling, the Shakers exalted feeling, so long as it was not sexual in nature. (Campion 1990 p. 65)

Mother Ann solved the problem of the relationship between body, mind and spirit by her vow of celibacy. She was convinced that sex was the reason for humanity's separation from God. She saw the answer to bringing about a new era of spirituality in a life of celibacy. This characterised the life of the Shaker movement, although she did not think that the call to celibacy was for everyone. She believed that as people dedicated their lives to God all lust would fade away. This was the process of transformation that Mother Ann saw as an ongoing in people's lives. She advocated tenderness and compassionate caring to take the place of sex.[14] After her death, the separation of the sexes became encapsulated in more petty rules and regulations.

After the decline of the movement, however, it was for their material things that they were remembered while their spirituality was regarded as eccentric and difficult to grasp. They were renowned for their trading, cultivation, furniture making and mechanical arts. They were great innovators; they were the first to dry seeds and sell them in packets, to invent a four wheel wagon, to air-condition beehives, to weave leaf bonnets on a loom, to produce herbs and manuals on cultivation, to make a permanent press and water repellent fabrics. They invented the flat broom, a static electricity generator, a pill dryer, a peanut sheller, a sleeve ironer, a revolving oven, a threshing machine, a turbine water wheel, a spindle bender, a pea sheller, a potato peeler, an apple parer, a bread cutter, a reel for widening yarn, a circular saw, to name some. Some say there are forty inventions (Campion 1990 p. 152).

To summarise, Mother Ann challenged the Values of the surrounding society by stressing notions of the individual's relationship to the community, embracing a diversity of styles, setting up a balance of public and private in the lives of her followers, including excited elements in the worship, seeking to nurture her followers spiritually, establishing a life style that sees the spiritual and the material inextricable intertwined.

Spirituality

Mother Ann saw singing as a way of accessing Divine power. When imprisoned the Shakers used songs to maintain their spiritual identity. So, when James Whittaker was being beaten by an angry crowd, William Lee composed a wordless tune that is now known as *Father William's Love Song*.

---

14   This is similar concepts in Elizabeth Stuart's thinking on female friendships in *Just Good Friends* (1996).

His voice was 'melodious and powerful' (Andrews 1962 p. 118). After Father William died as a result of wounds defending her, Mother Ann was approaching death herself; but she sang:

> I know how to pray,
> I know how to be thankful,
> For God has blessed me
> With a broken heart. (Campion 1990 p. 144)

The Shaker belief system included the doctrine of a dual Deity – a masculine and feminine Godhead – the 'Eternal Two' who embraced fatherhood and motherhood. In the Wardleys' meetings Ann learned that Christ represented the male principle but the female principle was yet to come. Ann came to regard herself as that principle. Her charisma included all the powers the early Christians were reputed to possess. This realisation did not put Ann out of touch with her real identity in the world, but rather empowered her to carry out her mission more effectively. The Shakers did not worship either Jesus or Mother Ann. Rather they were regarded as elders of the Millennial Church. Mother Ann writes:

> It is true. I am the embodiment of the Christ spirit. But you, too, can experience that in-dwelling presence, if you will forsake the world and the flesh and let yourself be imbued by his consuming love. (Campion 1990 p. 89)

This notion of a feminine aspect in the Divine was particularly remarkable in an age in which women's roles were clearly defined as wives, child bearers and home makers. In law at that time, women were still the property of their husbands. The early hymns were rousing songs that embodied these doctrines as some of the titles indicate:

- The Son and Daughter
- The heavenly Bridegroom and Bride
- Resolution against a carnal nature
- The believer's faith
- The Tree of Life

Mother Ann stressed that it was by their fruits that true believers would be known. The seven principles underpinning the Church were:

- Duty to God
- Duty to human beings
- Separation from the world
- Practical peace
- Simplicity of language
- Right use of property
- The virgin life

She saw certain virtues emerging from their beliefs, such as:

- A singleness of purpose which fuelled their crafts and their worship
- Faith
- Hope
- Honesty
- Continence
- Innocence
- Simplicity
- Meekness
- Humility
- Prudence
- Patience
- Thankfulness
- Charity[15]

Shakerism is often regarded as a millennial church, but when confronted by people fearful of the end of the world, Mother Ann told them over and over again that she was only concerned with the end of worldliness not of the world. The Second Coming was seen to be here and now. So confident were they in God that funerals were gloriously joyful affairs. The soul was seen as being transferred from the body to a fusion of earthly and heavenly spheres (Campion 1990 p. 145).

15   This is based on the list in Andrews (1962) p. 6.

As already seen above, there was a strong sense of being in touch with a spiritual world of angels, saints and most significantly, the founders of the tradition, like Mother Ann. They believed that the souls of the dead wandered around in touch with human beings as they moved towards regeneration. Through attunement with the dead, heavenly songs, melodies and messages could be received. This has led to some likening Shakerism to spiritualism.

The movement was based on a powerful faith in a God with male and female aspects. There is also a powerful belief in a spirit world that can be freely contacted and provide inspiration for ritual practices like songs and dances. There is great stress on faith being manifest in action. Thomas Merton writes of the Shakers:

> After their departure these innocent people, came to be regretted, loved and ideal- ized. Too late, people ... recognized their extraordinary importance of the spiritual phenomenon that had blossomed out in their midst ... The Shakers remain as wit- nesses to the fact that only humility keeps a man[sic] in communion with truth, and, first of all, with his own inner truth. This one must know without knowing it, as they did. (Campion 1990 p. 160)

To summarise, the spirituality of music in this tradition involved high degrees of relationality – within the Divine, between the immanent and the transcendent, between human beings. As such, it was an important source of accessing Divine Power.

Summary

The Shakers were a distinctive movement founded by a woman, who was determined to challenge the Value systems of the prevailing culture. Mother Lee embraced the subjugated values of her age, and she and her follow- ers were regularly persecuted for embracing them. It included a belief in a male and female aspect to God, the equality of women and men and the need for communal ownership. Women had an equal role with men in shaping the tradition. In worshipping situations, this was reflected in a non-hierarchical structure in which it was possible for all to be inspired by spirits and receive messages of various kinds; some of these messages were received as dances and songs. The form of Shaker worship allowed for a considerable degree of freedom and included improvisational elements in gesture and song, which made them appear strange to visitors from the outside world. The song structures tended to be freer and have a variety of melodic structures, some apparently drawn from different musical traditions through the medium of spirits who came from other continents and relating with other cultures like the Native American.

The development of Shaker traditions demonstrates clearly how the embracing of subjugated value systems in association with a spirituality that includes male and female elements has significant effects on the materials being used, the expressive character (which is much wider than the worship in other traditions of the day) and the methods of Construction. As the movement expanded, the liturgy became more formalised and the elements became more fixed. The dominant value systems became more apparent in the increase in complexity, the use of instruments, the decline in freer and more spontaneous elements and the greater emphasis on the imposition of order.

CHAPTER 6

Vignette Five – Hymns or hers: Hymnody Past and Present

Story

As a pastoral theologian, I am concerned to write texts that give voice to the passions that dwell at the deep heart of faith and questioning, [like] the pain and bafflement of a family watching a loved one struggling with Alzheimer's ...

— BRINGLE 2002 p. 6

... The first set of texts that I did was for a little volume called *A Prayer Book for Remembering the Women* ... a collection of morning and evening prayers on the themes of God as Holy Wisdom, God as Birthing Mother and Creative Life-giver, Women Apostles and Prophets, and Women as Anointers. Normally ... I start with a piece of music, and then I just play the piece of music until words start taking shape for that piece of music. And then, as words begin to take shape, then I realise the subject matter, and go off and do biblical research ...

Craft is important, but, for the most part, the words sort of come as a gift. I've found frequently that if I start working on a hymn before I go to sleep at night, I'll wake up in the morning and the rest of it will be finished off. One of the things I like about writing hymns is that they can be very simple structures that use strategic repetition ...

I use inclusive language and feminine images for God ... One of my most recent texts has God as Mother Hen, Mother Bear, Mother Eagle. I use Sophia language. In some texts, I have ... an asterisk that gives an alternative for people who are not yet comfortable ... I wrote just fairly recently a little hymn/chant for candle-light vigils to protest the United States' invasion of Iraq ... When people are gathered in prayer vigil, ... they don't need to learn a lot of words ...

Many people seem to be moving toward kind of sacro-pop music, and praise courses, and I find some of them quite appealing. I just don't want a steady diet of it. Just as I don't want to drink Coolade for every beverage, but every once in a while it tastes pleasant. So I think music that's singable, and that's accessible to people, a balance of things that people have some kind of history with because I still think there are sort of deep roots in us from texts that many of us sang as children that we don't get from singing a new hymn. I think [we need] openness to differences, musical differences, differences in style and rhythm, instrumental accompaniment, but I think that has to be used fairly sparingly with most congregations simply because they don't move as fast as a professional musician would ...

... What's so very engaging about this particular art form or craft, is the synergy between text and tune ... The text would be the embodiment and the humanness, and the music is far more celestial, in my judgement, than the text.

— BRINGLE 2003

Introduction

That interview with an American hymn writer echoes many of the themes that will run through this chapter on hymnody:

- Inclusive language
- The heritage of the past
- The interlocking of craft and inspiration (the rational and the intuitive)
- The biblical roots
- The theological synergy of text and tune
- The embracing of diversity

In the Victorian period there were a number of women hymn writers who found considerable acceptance for their theological ideas when expressed in the form of the hymn: Fanny Crosby, Charlotte Elliott and Frances Alexander are a few of the considerable number who still find a place in contemporary hymnbooks.

The advent of feminist theology gave women (and some men) hymn writers another impetus to get their voices heard in this form. The hymn has been a valuable medium for dissemination of the insights of feminist theologians in the UK since the 1980s. At the same time, there was the foundation of a number of such groups as Women in Theology and Catholic Women's Network. Feminist theologians such as Mary Grey in books like *Redeeming the Dream* (1989b) and *The Wisdom of Fools* (1993) have had a profound impact on my work in this area. These ideas are filtering slowly through into hymnbooks.

Celebrating Women (Ward, Wild and Morley 1995 based on a publication in 1986) included more hymns and songs but without the printed music. Single author publications, like those by Miriam Therese Winter's *WomanPrayer, WomanSong* (1987) and my own *In Praise of All-encircling Love I and II* (1994a and 1996a) also started to become available; authors like Kathy Galloway (1993) included hymns in their collections of poems. Publishers are now issuing collections by women writers. Books of alternative liturgies like *Human Rites* (Ward and Wild 1995a), and Catholic Women's Network's *Making Liturgy: Creating Rituals for Life* (McEwan et al. 2001) include some material by women but usually without music.

Reflecting Praise (1993), a hymnbook celebrating the work of women past and present, as well as men who use 'softer', feminine or inclusive images for God, was the first collection concentrating on women's contribution to hymnody with both words and music. It was initiated by Women in Theology as a vision of the two editors, Janet Wootton and June Boyce-Tillman. We trawled through an immense amount of material, grading and selecting until we had about a hundred hymns. We became aware how much excellent material had not found its way into mainstream collections, which selected more on the grounds of who held positions of power rather than any merit. The Introduction summarised the editorial policy:

> There exists a great wealth of women's creativity as composers and poets from every generation. Much of this is only now being rediscovered, as women reclaim their own history ... Preference has been given to pieces that have women as author, translator, composer, or arranger, or which tell the stories of women ... All hymns use inclusive language for humans. A number use female or inclusive images when referring to God,

> many exploring new or newly reclaimed images ... Most exciting of all, new writers
> continue to spring up in the field of inclusive language, broadening its scope, and
> introducing the idea to wider audiences. (Boyce-Tillman and Wootton 1993 p. iv)

It included material from the past as well as material from a variety of
Christian traditions and other faith traditions. It included black spirituals and a variety of idioms and accompaniments. In this, we had resisted
attempts to make us provide piano accompaniments and guitar chords
for all pieces, on the grounds that this would iron out cultural difference.

In the US, collections like *Canticles and Gathering Prayers* (Mossi
and Toolan 1996) started to appear, drawing on the themes of liberation
and feminist theology, ecotheology, the ecumenism following Vatican II
and lay leadership of worship. The mainstream churches in the US have
been quicker to respond than those in the UK, except for collections like
Peculiar Honours (Wootton, Watson et al. 1997). The American Episcopal
Church produced a supplement in 1997 in response to a resolution that said:

> The Standing Committee on Church Music be directed to continue preparing sup-
> plements to *The Hymnal 1982* which provide this Church with additional service
> music, inclusive language hymnody, additional texts in languages other than English
> ... (Episcopal Standing Committee on Church Music 1997 Preface)

It also suggests the use of a cantor:

> Someone with musical ability and who may introduce an antiphon or chant the
> psalm. A cantor may be anyone in the church who has a strong and pleasant voice,
> and who can learn to sing the designated parts. (Episcopal Standing Committee on
> Church Music 1997 Publisher's note)

This supplement contains the promised variety with black spirituals,
alongside Latin hymns and Shirley Erena Murray's *Give thanks for Life*.
The embracing of inclusive language, however, does not necessarily mean
that more women writers are represented and there are few women this
collection.

Published in the US, *Voices Found* (Thomas et al. 2003) *is* a collection hymns with similar aims to *Reflecting Praise*. Its origins, however, are
very different. It originates in the Women's Liturgical Music Project run

by Lisa Neufeld Thomas. It grew from the Lady Chapel Singers founded in 1997 at St Mark's Episcopal Church, Philadelphia, a group of women who wanted to worship with an inclusive language liturgy that had recently been approved by the Bishop. She began to look for materials, especially music and texts by women, finding almost nothing in the Hymnal 1982 of The Episcopal Church and so the vision of a Hymnal Supplement that would focus totally on the gifts of women was born. Lisa laid great stress on the fact that she tried to keep the committees representative of a variety of traditions, including conservatives, charismatic Spanish Americans, African Americans, and a Native American woman bishop. The collection was to include texts and music that were by, for or about women, and could be accompanied by keyboard or with flexible accompaniment, indicating sensitivity to the needs of small parishes that do not have large musical resources. They looked for a wide range of cultural and ethnic representation. The collection included a hymn from the notebook for Anna Magdalena Bach translated in the tradition of the Winkworth sisters. It included historical material from the eighth century onwards. They made the same decision as Janet and I had done, that anonymous pieces could be included on the ground that in the process of aural transmission women had played a part. The collection is designed to be very mainstream and as uncontroversial as possible, concentrating on subjects such as women saints, women in scripture, and creative imagery for God and avoiding areas like debates on sexuality. Lisa is loath to identify herself with American feminism, an attitude shared by members of the singers: 'I don't want to become identified with a really radical approach. I think that it puts women off' (Thomas 2003).

There is music composed by women and some associated with dance, including *The Song of Miriam*, which was written by Debbie Friedman, a Jewish composer. The book represents the dilemma of hymnody that the collection will not be radical enough for some groups and too radical for others. The result can be that such collections suit nobody's purpose. They are too radical for the mainstream and too orthodox for the women's groups themselves, many of whom prefer simpler chants to the denser theological statements of the traditional hymn.

This raises the complexity of the issue of women's musical contribution to liturgy. It is not only a question of texts but also of the style of the tune (although this chapter will concentrate mainly on texts). Theorists like Lacan saw the maleness of the phenomenon of language. Nowhere has this been truer than in the language of hymnody, where the lexicon has been assertively male. As Janet Wootton writes:

> For all of my childhood and early adult years, I sang hymns and said prayers that made no reference to my own identity. The only reference to my gender was in the introduction to the children's address, which was to 'boys and girls' and the occasional hymn which used the non-gender-specific 'children'. Once again, pre-pubescent females were all right, but mature women were hidden, excluded by the language. (Wootton 2000 p. 30)

Brian Wren expresses this clearly in his seminal text *What Language can I borrow?* (1989). This chapter will look at these themes under the headings explored in Chapter 1. It will include material from interviews with contemporary hymn writers mostly carried out early in the millennium. It will concentrate on the Value systems embraced by these hymnwriters.

1a Individual/Community

Singing has always been an important way of building community. Carl Daw (2003), the president of the American hymn society, sees singing as at the heart of liturgy and close to the heart of Christ. He sees some hymns as representing a sort of 'collective individualism', drawing attention to the dangers of the worship song which 'has a kind of emotional release in it that doesn't lead anywhere else' and does not draw the singer in to the worshipping community.

The issue of inclusive community involves the somewhat contentious issue of inclusive language. Denise Dijk sees these developments as arising from:

The changed self-awareness of women ... [It] also originates from a change in our experience of language ... In the field of women, language and liturgy, many women nowadays appear to experience words like 'man', 'brother', 'son', and 'him' exactly and not inclusively. They experience these words as referring to male persons only, while they can be experienced inclusively. If our experience of language has become more exact, words like 'seed', 'brotherhood' and 'he' will be experienced differently in comparison with former days ... This has implications for the ways in which women as well as men experience the liturgy, and particularly for the encounter with God. (Dijk 1997 p. 1)

She sees this as having two results:

- God is seen as masculine
- 'The naming of God with masculine words limits and restricts God more than it did in the past' (Dijk 1997 p. 1)

Marjorie Procter-Smith identifies how words are capable of suggesting and legitimating sexual violence. She problematises the Lord's Prayer in this respect in its asking for forgiveness in relation to our own capacity to forgive, which does not leave space for righteous anger. Here she is joined by the hymn writer, Ruth Duck (1993), who sees the virtual impossibility of a uniform liturgical language about guilt in situations involving sexual abuse (which may well be most worshipping situations). Procter-Smith helpfully suggests four strategies of resistance and survival:

- Praying between the lines – struggling to include certain voices in liturgy like those of Lesbians
- Appropriation and reinterpretation – which involves ridiculing the androcentrism of the text
- Juxtaposition – subverting the text by inserting references to women like Sarah alongside Abraham in the Magnificat
- Refusing to say certain prayers [in this context, certain hymns] – so remaining silent (Procter-Smith 1995 pp. 31–54)

She helpfully defines a number of linguistic possibilities:

- Non-sexist language – employing gender-neutrality with such terms as God of compassion rather than Father (Here she identifies the problem of denying gender as an important element of identity in what becomes a genderless world.)
- Inclusive language – in which both genders are named equally and gender naming of God uses male and female images like 'Mother, father God'
- Emancipatory language – a language encouraging resistance to existing power-relations (Procter-Smith 1995 pp. 63–71)

As we can see, the issues are very complex. The least contentious aspect of it concerns inclusive language for human beings. The third person pronoun 'he' has traditionally been used as an inclusive pronoun, as has the generic term 'man'. Organisations like *The Association for Inclusive Language* have shown that the use of these terms was confused and that women were disadvantaged by the use of these terms which were sometimes used as inclusive and at other times as exclusive of women. Feminist writers have therefore, pushed hard for inclusive descriptors of people. This involves

- finding non-male descriptors for people – like human rather than man
- avoiding the third person singular pronoun 'he' and using the third person plural 'they'

Feminist writers writing materials for women's gatherings are producing material addressed only to women. Marsie Silvestro (see Chapter 8) has produced many examples like:

> Refrain: We are weaving a revolution, many women, many threads
> And through our cultures and with our spirit
> A healing power will rise from earth. (Silvestro 1993b)

As we shall see later with the area of gender images for God, these are not strictly speaking inclusive; they simply replace male with female. Inclusive descriptors are gender-neutral. But we have had such a long period in which hymns like *Rise up O men of God!* have held their place, that maybe there is a case for a similar period when female descriptors are used to rebalance this.

This highlights the problem of what to do with a past which was not inclusive – either in language or in other ways. The hymns of the past clearly reflect the value systems of the past. Changing the past is difficult, because of the metrical constraints of hymnody. It is well illustrated by lines from Cardinal Newman's hymn *Praise to the holiest in the height*:

> The double agony in man
> For man should undergo.

The metre will clearly not take a version that might run:

> The double agony for human beings
> For human beings should undergo.

What is interesting here is that it is not only an issue of language but also an issue of the underlying theology. It is a theology of sacrifice and substitution which has been challenged by many feminist theologians. The theology itself – not just the language – was a male construct.

Luther's hymn *A safe stronghold our God is still* presents a different problem. Here the wife is clearly regarded as a chattel to the man:

> And though they take our life,
> Goods, honour, children, wife
> Yet is their profit small.

This has been changed in *Hymns and Songs*, to –

> And though before our eyes
> All that we dearly prize
> They seize beyond recall,
> Yet is their profit small.

Other hymns are still presented in many collections in their original form. *Who would true valour see/Let him come hither* is a case in point. It could easily be changed to, 'Let them come hither'; or people could be given the option of what pronoun they use.[1] Contemporary writers, like Brian Wren, do rewrite their material often with dramatic effect as in his *Lord Jesus if I love and serve my neighbour* where he rewrote the second verse:

---

1   Service sheet of St James', Piccadilly, London, Jan 16th 2005.

> When I have met my sister's need with kindness
> And prayed that she might waken from despair
> Open my heart, if, crying now for justice,
> She struggles for the changes that I fear.

The Unitarian/Universalist hymnbook (1993) contains many fine examples of how the past can be reworked. The fine prophetic hymn *Turn back, O Man* becomes *Turn back, turn back*. The final verse of *Now Thank we all our God* is simply omitted. In *O Little town of Bethlehem*, 'the blessings of his love' becomes 'the gift that is our own' (Unitarian/Universalist Hymnbook Resources Commission 1993 No 247). However, the changing of more familiar material can cause much more uproar in a traditional congregation than the writing of new material with inclusive language. Carl Daw (2003) makes the distinction:

> And so, we always have to make a distinction between the hymn as we encounter it and the hymn as we have experienced it, because they may not be the same at all … It's absolutely essential, first of all, that all language for people be inclusive … [But] there are places where I would want to reserve historic texts because I wouldn't want to muck about with them …

The possible solutions are:

- Leave the text as it is, and regard it simply as an historical statement
- Make the changes if they are minor
- In the case of favourite hymns, revise them into what is essentially a new text.

Latin and Greek hymns can benefit from retranslation. *Reflecting Praise* includes a number of retranslations of Greek and Latin hymns, like Janet Wootton's retranslation of *Veni Creator* which also includes the wonderful description of the Spirit as 'kaleidoscope of seven-fold light' (Boyce-Tillman and Wootton 1993 p. 33). In this role, Janet is in a strong tradition of women translators like Elizabeth Lee Smith and Catherine Winkworth. Catherine and her sister were significant figures in the development of women's education particularly in Bristol where she founded Clifton High School for Girls, in the nineteenth century. It is through Catherine's translations that we had the hymns of the early Protestant reformers in English, like this translation of Johann Scheffler:

> O Love who formedst me to wear
> The image of thy godhead here;
> Who soughtest me with tender care
> Through all my wand'rings wild and drear,
> O Love, I give myself to thee,
> Thine ever, only thine to be.
> (Boyce-Tillman and Wootton 1993 p. 25)

She believed passionately in congregational singing. In her preface to *Lyra Germanica* she wrote:

> The singing of hymns forms a much larger and more important part of public worship in the German reformed Churches than in our own services. It is the mode by which the whole congregation is enabled to bear its part in the worship of God.[2]

In extending the notion of an inclusive community, there is clearly a need for a reconnection with the natural world especially the image of the earth which has been traditionally marginalised by the Church. This had led to the rediscovery of the Celtic traditions. Betty Wendelborn draws on a favourite image of the ancestry of the earth:

> Grandmother earth,
> Holy be your name. (Boyce-Tillman and Wootton 1993 p. 56)

Carolyn McDade from North America has produced many songs concerned with ecotheology, some of them part of a large project involving women's choirs in the US and Canada:

> Spirit of Earth and Wind
> Spirit of life within
> May we be true in passing

---

2   Winkworth, Catherine (1855), *Lyra Germanica* 1st ser. Quoted in Wootton 2003 p. 127.

We are the land we sing
We are the prayer we bring
To these wide miles of morning. (McDade 1999)

In Doug Constable's hymn written for the 25th anniversary of the World Wildlife Fund, God is addressed as:

Warm God of seeds, all nature's source,
Womb of earth maker, and love's stirring pulse.
(Boyce-Tillman and Wootton 1993 p. 66)

Shirley Erena Murray's hymn hears the earth crying out:

I am your mother: do not neglect me!
Children protect me – I need your trust:
    My breath is your breath
    My death is your death,
Ashes to ashes, dust into dust. (Murray 1996 No 16)

My own thinking in this area led me to an exploration of the exclusive effect of the limited images of God to be found in our hymnbooks. In the end I saw it as breaking the second commandment against idolatry:

Finding God

1. A child once loved the story-
   Which angel voices tell –
   How once the King of Glory
   Came down on earth to dwell.

2. Now, Father God, I miss you –
   Your beard, your robes, your crown –
   But you have served us badly
   And let us humans down.

3. So easy to disprove you
   And doubt your truthfulness;
   For you were just an idol
   That kept Your power suppressed.

4. For You are deep within us –
   Revealed within our deeds,
   Incarnate in our living
   And not within our creeds.

5. No image cannot hold you;
   And, if to one we hold,
   We keep some from your loving
   And leave them in the cold.

6. Excluded groups are legion –
   Disabled, female, gay –
   Old Father of the heavens,
   Your picture moves away.

7. Life's processes reveal You –
   In prison, death and war,
   In people who are different,
   In gatherings of the poor.

8. For Godding means encounter,
   Gives dignity to all,
   Has every shape and no shape –
   In temple, tree and wall.

9. So we will go a-godding
   And birth You in our world;
   In sacrificial loving
   We find Your strength unfurled.[3]

The logical development of this is to have less hierarchical views of the Church including reworking the notion of the priesthood of all believers. Non-hierarchical approaches to structures require lay people to claim their authority, in particular their corporate authority as the body of Christ as in *The Wounds are human wounds*:

---

3   Boyce-Tillman, June, November 2012 (with apologies to Mrs Emily Huntington Miller) unpublished.

> In sharing grief and pain
> And joyful laughing love
> We are a priesthood here on earth
> Reflecting God above. (Boyce-Tillman 2006a p. 69)

Such texts reflect the values of truly inclusive community.

1b Unity/Diversity

This section will examine the notion of diversity of gender within God (as we saw explored by Mother Ann Lee in Chapter 5) as well the diversity of musical styles. There is a well-established theology of God as male reflected throughout the hymnody of the Church. Some contemporary women do not find it a problem (like Joy Webb in Chapter 7) and some men do. Contemporary writers in the evangelical tradition find the male images very acceptable; Graham Kendrick writes that the characteristics of true Christian worship falls under the headings:

- Worship the Father
- In Spirit
- In truth (Kendrick 2003 p. 92)

Other writers who take a Trinitarian approach, like Carl Daw, manage to treat the area traditionally associated with God the Father in inclusive ways with hymns like:

> God of wombing, God of Birth,
> God who formed us from the earth ...
> (Daw 1996 No 42)

There is a tradition of Marian hymns where Mary is very close to Divine and these can make her more use to contemporary women than the plaster images of traditional Roman Catholicism:

> Mary, our mother,
> Working and planning
> Making a home for
> Family and friends,
> Be with our working
> Be with our resting ...
> (Boyce-Tillman 2006a pp. 50–1)

Another possibility is to use non-gendered descriptors for God like friend, companion, and healer is one solution – the truly inclusive one. We find this in material from that past such as Margaret Cropper's (1886–1980):

> O Christ, whom we may know and love
> And follow to the end,
> We who are friends together come
> To thee our heavenly friend.
> (Boyce-Tillman and Wootton 1993 p. 76)

Dora Greenwell (1821–82), one of the Victorian hymn writers referred to earlier in this chapter, presents a deeply compassionate God in her wonderful hymn *And art thou come with us to dwell*:

> Each heart's deep instinct unconfessed;
> Each lowly wish, each daring claim,
> All, all that life has long repressed
> Unfolds undreading blight or blame.
> (Boyce-Tillman and Wootton 1993 p. 10)

Dorothy Gurney's (1858–1932) wedding hymn addresses God as:

> O perfect love, all human thought transcending
> (Boyce-Tillman and Wootton 1993 p. 75)

Sydney Carter frames a wonderful hymn about creativity around the image:

> The bell of creation is swinging for ever
> In all of the things that are coming to be ...
> (Boyce-Tillman and Wootton 1993 p. 65)

The use of feminine images for God is not, strictly speaking, inclusive and opinion is much divided here. Feminists see the use of the feminine images for God essential, while others see it as potentially as divisive as the older male language.

For example, Janet Wootton's hymn *Dear Mother God* starts:

> Dear Mother God, your wings are warm about us
> (Boyce-Tillman and Wootton 1993 p. 1)

Janet says that it has raised a storm when it has been used in some circles; but it is completely scriptural, based on the Eagle image from Deuteronomy. She comments on people's response to feminine images:

> There is something visceral in people's response, which even reference to Scripture and tradition will not allay. (Wootton 2003 p. 134)

Mel Bringle also uses feminine images from Biblical sources like:

> Held in the shelter of God's wing,
> Terrors of the night we need not fear ...
>
> Mother and midwife, cradling arms,
> Comfort when strength dries up like dust ...
> (Bringle 2002 p. 56)

There is also in *Reflecting Praise* Judith Driver's fine hymn, *My God is woman*:

> My God is woman:
> She is around me and in me;
> She is darkness and light;
> She creates and heals ...
> (Boyce-Tillman and Wootton 1993 p. 4)

I tried to establish a charismatic female figure like Dylan's Mr Tambourine Man in *The Tambourine Woman*, with its dancing Irish style tune and the chorus:

> We'll follow the tambourine woman
> And join in her tambourine song.
> We're riding a rainbow to heaven
> And dancing our journey along.
> (Boyce-Tillman and Wootton 1993 pp. 62–3)

Brian Wren's hymn moves to a genderless deity from a feminine pronoun:

> Who is She,
> Neither male or female,
> Maker of all things,
> Only glimpsed or hinted,
> Source of life and gender?
> (Boyce-Tillman and Wootton 1993 p. 8)

He also in Cambridge, Massachusetts sees the transformative power of feminine images of God as often underrated by churches. To illustrate this, he describes the effect of female imagery on a heterosexual male worshipper who then said how he had to review both his relationships with women and with his own mother:

> I've got a couple of texts where I decided I was going to write a hymn with female imagery for God, and just figure out how to do that in a non-sexist kind of way – non-stereotypical way, which was hard ... I took each stanza and tried to focus on some woman in my life, and write something about who God is through that person, and my mother was one stanza. – *The Holy Spirit Came to Me.* [Her verse is:]
>
> > *She fed and clothed me, worked and played, She showed me how to look and see the world and not to be afraid*

What he was demonstrating very clearly is a truly incarnational Wisdom theology where we find Christ in the people we meet.

We also see a move to include a greater variety of material in worship. Pat Michaels used material from orate traditions like *Sweet Honey on the Rock* in liturgy. In editing *Reflecting Praise*, Janet Wootton and I included material from a variety of Christian traditions and other faith traditions like this song from the Hindu tradition:

My mother you are and my father you are ...
My Wisdom you are and my wealth you are too
For you are everything to me, O my Lord.
(Boyce-Tillman and Wootton 1993 p. 5)

Denominational and even faith differences play little part in the worshipping communities of women.

To summarise, we see a move towards a greater diversity of images for God as people examine female images and metaphors in this area. There are few hymns that represent the goddess thinking within the thealogy[4] tradition and any female image needs introducing with caution to a mainstream congregation. There is also an embracing of a diversity of styles within a single collection.

2a Private/Public

The move of material – both by women and about women – from the private domain of the individual hymn writer's personal file to the semi-public space of women's worshipping groups (see Chapter 7) and then on to published collections is not easy. Published collections are often already filled with the well-loved offerings from the past and there is little room for new material at all, whatever it is about or whoever it may be by. Regular periodicals containing material for worship like *Worship Live* and *All the Year Round* in the UK have proved more accessible to women than the hard-covered hymnal. There is a real problem here:

> It is, perhaps in the area of hymn writing that the contribution of women has been most scandalously treated. Throughout the history of hymnody in the English speaking traditions – that is, the last 300 years – there have been many and prolific women writers. (Wootton 2000 p. 48)

---

4   Some writers prefer the word thealogy when they are talking about feminine images of God (Mantin 2002, Raphael 1999).

Hymn writing is an area where Protestant women have contributed a great deal to the genre in terms of words. The Rev James King's *Anglican Hymnody, being an account of the 325 standard hymns of the highest merit according to the verdict of the whole Anglican Church* published in 1885 purports to give an account of the best hymns in use at that time. He based this on surveying the chief hymnals in use at the time and it is a testimony to the Victorian women hymn writers referred in the introduction to this chapter that they are represented. However, the majority of writers are not only male but men who can boast a position of authority in the Church as clergy or in the Academy or both. The woman who came out with greatest number of well-known hymns are Charlotte Elliott with 6 hymns including *Just as I Am, O holy Saviour, friend unseen* and *O thou the contrite sinners' friend*. Next in the list is Cecil Frances Alexander with 4 hymns including *The roseate hues of early dawn, The brightness of the day* and *Jesus calls us o'er the tumult*. Sarah Flower finds a place in the first rank with *Nearer my God to thee*. Miss E. Cox features with her translation *Jesus lives!* and *Who are these like stars appearing* and there is also one of Catherine Winkworth's translations. Harriet Auber is represented with *Our blest Redeemer e'er he breathed* and Emma Toke with a hymn written for the SPCK. There is Anne Steele's *Father of Mercies in Thy word* and *Father whate'er of earthly bliss* and Anna Laetitia Barbauld's *Praise to God immortal Praise*.

We see here the strong tradition of women writing hymns for private devotion, epitomised by Charlotte Elliott. In this tradition is also the evangelical Frances Ridley Havergal (1836) famous for *Take my life and let it be* and Christina Rossetti with *Love came down at Christmas* and *In the Bleak Midwinter*, in which her verse about Mary breast-feeding Jesus is still often changed or omitted!

The Sunday School is represented by Cecil Frances Alexander, the vicar's wife fulfilling her accepted role and attempting to make the creeds accessible to children with such hymns as *All things bright and beautiful, There is a green hill* and *Once in Royal David's City*. In these texts we can see clear attempts to adapt the theology and shape the children to the prevailing Victorian social structures and mores.

Selah Publishing, a US publishing house that has produced a great deal of musical material to support liturgy, have brought out in the last 20 years three collections of women writers. Some of these like Rae E. Whitney (1995) are clearly very happy with male descriptors for God with titles like: *God bids us seek him*. But she provides useful hymns including stories of Jesus relationship with women like *Woman bent double*. There are gentler images for God like *God you loved us from creation*. She is quite comfortable with the descriptor *Lord* which is not acceptable in many more radical feminist circles, despite attempts to translate its meaning from a male leader to 'loaf giver'. Edith Sinclair Downing's hymns in her collection *A Season of Clear Shining* (1998) use inclusive language throughout. The collection embraces her concern for the action of God in Christ with passionate hymns written in the first person in the tradition of the Victorian women listed above:

> Holy One Who Breathes Me,
> Love That Never Leaves Me,
> Listener to my Soul
> When my heart is broken
> You hear words unspoken,
> You would make me whole.
> (Downing 1998 p. 37)

Justice is combined with this in hymns like *How can earth's wounds be healed?* Gracia Grindal is in the tradition of the translators. Her collection *We are one in Christ: Hymns, Paraphrases, and Translations by Gracia Grindal* (1996) includes translations of Lutheran hymns from the Czech that she did with the help of Sister Anita Smisek OP of St Wenceslaus Convent in Prague, including a version of the Stabat Mater entitled *Weeping Mother and Sorrow* and *Gladness are sister and brother*. Women's stories from the life of Jesus are there as in *At Jacob's well where Jesus sat*, poetic metrical psalms and hymns of private devotion:

> Give me faith, O God trust your Word
> When it is spoken to me.
> The troubles of the world rage all around
> And threaten to undo me ...
> (Grindal 1996 p. 78)

The language for God is not completely inclusive and her introduction lays great stress on the crafting of a hymn.

In being faithful to the spirit of the older text. I avoided the polemics of this age, at least in the poetry. (Grindal 1998 p. ix)

Such a position which she shares with other woman writers is a defence against the struggles of their more radical sisters and illustrates women's decisions to stay within the tradition.

Shirley Erena Murray's texts (Murray 1992) use inclusive language and place God's action firmly in the contemporary world:

Here in the busy city
Now let the Church be seen
When lesser gods are worshipped
In money and machine
Come and find the quiet centre
in the crowded life we lead. (Murray 1992)

Stories of women and issues of justice nestle alongside one another:

God weeps:
    At love withheld,
    At strength misused,
    At children's innocence abused,
            God weeps

God bleeds
    At anger's fist,
    At trust betrayed,
    At women battered and afraid
            God bleeds.
(Murray 1992)

If hymns *by* women are difficult to find, hymns *about* women are almost as difficult. Here we can look back to the hymns of the Syrian Orthodox women in the early Church described in Chapter 2. They dealt with the women of the Bible and contemporary writers mix these with the story of more recent women who have entered the struggle for justice. Elisabeth Cosnett commemorates the social reformer, Josephine Butler in:

For God's sake let us dare
To pray with Josephine ...

> She forced her age to face
> What most it feared to see
> The double standard at the base
> Of its prosperity.
> (Cosnett in Boyce-Tillman and Wootton 1993 p. 42)

Mel Bringle draws on our foremothers:

> Sisters in God's house,
> Bold to sing new songs,
> Marguerite, Umilta, Agnes,
> Julian, Clare, Macrina, Catherine;
> Mothers from our past.
> Daughters in one faith ...
> (Bringle 2002 p. 116)

I have written about Julian of Norwich with this ending which has not received the antagonism described by Janet Wootton in her use of Mother God:

> All shall be well in love enclosed
> The ring of fire will meet the rose
> In One who all our suffering knows,
> Sweet Mother Jesus, our repose.
> (Boyce-Tillman in Boyce-Tillman and Wootton 1993 p. 66)

The stories of Sarah, Miriam and Deborah have been overshadowed by the men in their stories and other figures like Hagar are as hidden behind these women in hymnody as in the Lectionary. Mary, the mother of Jesus, has few hymns in Protestant traditions except for Christmas carols and the women who are central to the resurrection narrative are curiously hidden. It does not help that many of these women in Scripture have no name. Brian Wren redresses some of the balance with his impressive hymn *Woman in the night* with its verses on woman at the well and woman in the house which continues:

> Nurtured to be meek
> Leave your second place

Listen, think and speak.
(Wren in Boyce-Tillman and Wootton 1993 p. 21)

This, for many women, rebalances the traditionally submissive position of Victorian writers like Charlotte Elliott. Many feminist groups find her *Just as I am* unacceptable because of its association with traditional positions allotted to women. Fred Pratt Green highlights the women at the tomb with his: *What tale is this the women bring?* with its chorus:

Hurry, hurry brothers, do not more delay
Maybe it is true what the women say.
(Pratt Green in Tillman and Percival 1980 p. 199)

Madeline Sue Martin brings together Mary the Mother of Jesus with the woman who anointed Jesus with the jar of nard in *A Prophet Woman Broke a jar* (Martin 1998 p. ix). Ruth Thomas retells the story of Miriam, starting with the jangling of her bangles and ending with the enigmatic verse:

What was Aaron thinking, tell me,
As Miriam danced
He as thinking if his people, O yes,
As Miriam danced.
(Thomas in Boyce-Tillman and Wootton 1993 p. 79)

The rediscovery of voices from the past has produced Kassia's (c.810–c.867) 50 hymns, about thirty of which are still used in the Eastern Orthodox tradition. She was a Byzantine abbess whose hymns continued the tradition found in Chapter 3 of giving biblical women voices. Most famous is her Song of Mary Magdalene in which Mary says:

Take my spring of tears
You who draw water from the clouds,
Bend to me, to the sighing of my heart.[5]

---

5   <http://muisc.acu.edu/www/iawm/pages/kassia.html>, accessed January 31st 2003.
    It is recorded on *Women as composers and performers of mediaeval chant* (1998) JARO
    4210–2.

Here are Mary's words from a hymn for the feast of the presentation of Jesus in the temple:

> 'How can I hold you as a child,
> you who hold everything together?'

> 'How do I bring you to the temple, who is beyond goodness?'[6]

To summarise, the journey of women's hymns from the private to the public is still complex and one hedged about with difficulties – many of which surround the changing roles and perceptions of women in the prevailing culture.

2b Product/Process

The music of women's worshipping groups is often orate in nature and there is a preference for material that can be taught and learned orally. In some of these collections there is material from more oral traditions and material that can be used as the basis for improvisation like Taizé chants. Many women have had a dilemma with this often because of their lack of music education. Bernice Johnson writes:

> You see, my singing relationship with music is oral. When I see a staff, I don't see music, I had never anticipated being intimately involved in moving my songs to appear in order to share them. However through the years, especially since working with Sweet Honey on the Rock, many people have asked if I would send them my songs and my harmony arrangements. I have for a long time considered myself a composer as well as singer and songleader. However, my method of transmission and teaching has always been oral. The process of developing this songbook has been one of expanding my horizons and reaching out to others in my music community who operate more comfortably from another language: musical notation. (Johnson Reagon 1986 Preface)

6   <http://www.roanoke.infi.net/~ddisse/kassia.html>, accessed 31st January 2003.

Some people, like Pat Michaels (2003), deliberately use material from orate traditions in general public worship. He introduced *Freedom is Coming* from South Africa:

> They didn't have to look at it. So, suddenly the people who didn't read music were leading ... The people who were sitting there trying to read it were following because they couldn't pick it up that quickly ... So it reversed everything.

The use of process words for God reflecting themes we have seen in Chapter 1 arose for Carl Daw (2003):

> I like the idea of using alternative language for God, other than 'Father', because I feel it's much too limiting to deal with only 'Father' language. On the other hand, I think it's very important that language about God not lose our sense of inter-relatedness, so that part of what was being countered in language – the traditional language of 'Father, Son and Holy Spirit' was that there was a connectedness among the Persons of the Trinity, and so I find it much more helpful to talk about God in terms of verbs rather than in nouns or pronouns ... God *does* something ...

There is a move in hymnody to more process views of God. Shirley Erena Murray wants to move from concentrating theologically on who God is to what God does:

> Life is a holy thing, life is a whole,
> Linking each creature and blessing us all,
> Making connections of body and soul
> 　　Let us care for your garden
> 　　And honour the earth.
> (Murray, New Zealand Hymnbook Trust 1993 No 54)

And I invented the verb 'a-godding':

> CHORUS *And we'll all go a-godding*
> *To bring the world to birth.*
> New life is calling;
> Help set it free.
> And we'll all go a-godding
> With a song of liberty. CHORUS

Hunger is calling,
Find food to share;
And we'll all go a-godding
To give out abundant care.
CHORUS (Boyce-Tillman 2006a p. 97)

So here we see the ideas of feminist theologians filtering into hymnody and also the rediscovering of orate, more improvisatory traditions. However, the ready availability of simpler chant-like material often means that women hymn writers' work is not well represented in the music of alternative liturgy groups who prefer chants that can be taught orally.

3a Excitement/Relaxation

The desire of women's worshipping groups to be distinctive has often resulted musically in an embracing of tunes with a more relaxing calming feel rather than what is perceived as the more militaristic, triumphalist, exciting sounds of large scale public worship. Some women's hymn texts (especially those from former periods) in established metres are strong like Priscilla Owens's (1829–99) *Will your anchor hold in the storms of life* set to the tune of the same name with its rousing chorus:

We have an anchor that keeps the soul
Steadfast and sure why the billows roll;
Fastened to the rock that cannot move,
Grounded firm and deep in the saviour's love.
(Owens in Boyce-Tillman and Wootton 1993 p. 56)

The most famous example is Julia Ward Howe's (1819–1910) *Mine eyes have seen the glory of the coming of the Lord* set to the tune of John Brown's Body, but it is often forgotten that later the author disowned this hymn with its militaristic overtones. Frances Jane Van Alstyne (1820–1915), writing under her maiden name of Fanny Crosby, has contributed powerful rousing hymns that many will associate with the excitement of the Billy Graham Crusades of the 1960s, like *Blessed Assurance* and *To God be the glory*.

As we have seen above there is an attempt to use softer more gentle images of God with tunes of that character. Very popular is the hymn from the Iona community concerning *A Touching Place*. Many of the softer gentler songs from this source are associated with the healing ministry. Colleen Fulmer's cassette (no date) is entitled *Her Wings unfurled: Original Songs of Challenge and Comfort calling forth Courage and Compassion* with the gentle theme song:

> You are fashioned in my image. You are woman radiant Glory.
> Spirit rising, wings unfurled: you are beauty for our world.

Mel Bringle's hymn is similarly gentle in character:

> Hold them in the Light of your ever-present love ...
>
> Hold them in the light, as they comfort aching hearts ...
>
> Hold them in the light, in their laughter and their tears ...
> (Bringle 2002 p. 60)

In her writing around the terrorist attacks of 9/11 she balances the violence with gentleness:

> When terror strikes through morning skies
> And fear-dazed minds grow numb,
> With interceding, prayerful sighs,
> O Healing Spirit, come.
> (Bringle 2002 p. 148)

Many of the singer/songwriters writing their own material use guitar accompaniments or the voices available on an electronic keyboard. Many have developed a distinctive feel which is quite gently powerful. Carolyn McDade's material is very distinctive in this way seen in the feel of this text drawing on her experience of working with the women in Nicaragua:

> Come with a love that loves so long
> Come live with a love
> Walk naked with open arms
> Among the people who leave the master's house.
> (McDade 1990 p. 10)

In her introductions Carolyn McDade distinguishes between songs that rally us and songs that call us to personal and communal reflection:

> songs which allow the landscape of our love and loyalty to shift and reform by contemplating it before the mists rise, before our minds become girdled in the knowledge the holders of knowledge have impressed upon us.' (McDade 1990 p. 7)

She talks about the feel of her songs:

> Give me the quiet song, slow and sustained, give me a sensual song that lets me derobe and runs its lover's hands across my body, its breath across my soul. (McDade 1990 p. 7)

Many women have moved towards guitars and keyboards as accompanying instruments, often because they work aurally (see Marsie Silvestro in Chapter 7). But some women still embrace the organ. Janet Wootton (2003), Minister of Union Chapel comments:

- I like the organ as an accompanying instrument, and being at Union Chapel has shown me what an organ, as opposed to a harmonium, can do ... An organ is no longer one instrument, but a whole variety. (I have a good, imaginative organist)... who will pull out all the stops on the last verse, and will go out of his way to find appropriate settings for particular verses ... and will, therefore, use the instrument to carry the ideas. On the other hand ... an unimaginative person who's been pressed into playing the organ and has never really liked it, and is a piano player – reluctant organist, is the term – who plays extremely slowly, and with no idea of the words ... it can be terrible – terribly damaging – but that's true of any instrument, I think.
- On the other hand, many of the tunes I select are not organ tunes, but guitar tunes or piano tunes, and I've heard some beautiful, lovely accompaniments and ... other instruments –
- I love unaccompanied singing. I was brought up singing campfire songs as a Girl Guide. – I think it is easily accessible, immediately enjoyable music ... I've written hymns to rounds. *By your shaping, by your wisdom and delight, we are crafted in your image*, which goes down well everywhere, because it's a very, very simple round tune.

Repetitive chants accompanied by drums generate more excitement in their emotional feel. The Taizé chanting tradition initiated by Jacques Berthier has achieved great popularity but women like Margaret Rizza (2004) are writing beautiful repetitive chants of a very nurturing character due to their almost complete lack of discord. Talking about her music, Margaret sees these as a part of her meditative practice and also being potentially part of other people's practice: 'my prayer is that this new collection leads us all to new awakenings of the eternal Spirit of Love deep within our being' (Rizza 2004).

She writes about how adaptable her collection is:

> *Awakening in Love* comprises chants and through-composed songs. Each setting includes choir parts, an accompaniment and separate instrument parts. There is great freedom of choice in singing these pieces; variety and experimentation are encouraged. The chants, especially, can be sung very simply or using diverse musical resources, but even the other compositions can be adapted according to available voices and instruments. (Rizza 2004)

Here we see a woman composer producing material that can be recontextualised in a variety of circumstances and to suit whatever feel the group needs. This notion of adaptability and response to situations is part of the Wisdom tradition as explored in Chapter 1.

So there is a preference amongst women in their group liturgies for more relaxed, meditative music although the drum is beginning to find some acceptance. In mainstream worship women are producing stronger hymns of a more energy-generating kind.

3b Challenge/Nurture

Many contemporary writers are concerned to balance justice and nurturing. Songs dealing with social justice rose to prominence in the UK with writers like Sydney Carter and publications like *Faith Folk and Clarity* (Smith 1967), coming from the vision of Bernard Braley at Stainer and Bell. These included some women writers, but paid no attention to inclusive language with songs like *The Family of Man* becoming popular. The performers were also men, with notable exceptions like Estelle White.

These developments followed the development of the secular protest song. This was often in the hands of singer/song writers and there was a rise of this phenomenon in religious circles. Carolyn McDade is one of those with a considerable impact in the US in particular. Much of her work is concerned with justice for women and the earth:

> A people are not hurt by strong women
> When women are strong their people are not hurt ...
>
> Dissenting towards justice.
> (McDade 1986 p. 43)

I attempt to embrace justice themes in my hymns (Boyce-Tillman 2010). One was written for my friend and worker for justice, Hugh Boulter:

> Within our hearts may justice reign
> And burn with fiery Spirit-flames,
> Creating systems that in strength
> Embody Christ's outrageous claims.
>
> And so the God of joy and hope,
> Can be revealed in humankind,
> Where politics reflect shared wealth
> And nature's growth as intertwined.
> (Boyce-Tillman 2006a p. 89)

But the one I was commissioned to write for the Jubilee was considered too radical in some circles because of its search for radical justice. The popular song writer Bernadette Farrell is involved in the justice seeking organisation London Citizens and this concern is being reflected in her current songs:

> One of Bernadette's recent songs, 'Alleluia, Raise The Gospel', epitomises the spirit of her current music and the challenges she has laid down for herself to make the world a better place:

1) engage creatively with the decision makers in one's neighbourhood, town and country;

2) embrace and promote a theology that inspires people to imagine a new future; and

3) work to create new economic institutions for our new global situation.

As Bernadette says, 'If we do nothing, we will not have a planet fit to hand on to our children.' This book collects almost all Bernadette's published songs, nearly 80 in all, dating from the 1970s to the present day. A bonus is the inclusion of seven new and previously unpublished pieces, including two sets of Eucharistic acclamations. (Farrell 2013)

From *Joy in Singing: The Hymns of Jan Parker Huber* (1983) come titles like *God, teach us peacemaking, justice, love*. Alongside these are hymns of God's nurturing; this one designed for a child's baptism:

O God Who calls, creates and leads
Whose plan provides for all our needs.
(Parker Huber 1983)

Justice is a passionate concern for the Rev Doctor Janet Wootton (2003), my co-editor of *Reflecting Praise*. She describes her hymn writing as a struggle between vision and inspiration. A number of themes run through her thinking

- The hiddenness of women hymn writers, who are often tacked on to the end of writings on hymnody:

  [But] women have played an enormous part in writing hymns, and they haven't just written ditties for children. They've written really good, radical and poetic material ...

- The life of Jesus ...

  If you look in any hymnbook, you see loads of hymns about Christmas and the birth of Jesus, and loads of hymns about Good Friday onwards, and almost nothing about the actual life and teaching of Jesus. Where is all the radical teaching and life of Jesus? The explosion of his actual life? ...

- The challenge of the Gospel:

> I don't want to write … worship hymns … I find that a lot of it is selfish – self-centred. *I want to know Jesus. This is what Jesus has done for me … Jesus has washed away my sins, and I have the victory.* [In some hymnbooks] the section beginning with the word *I* is enormous … So I've written a hymn for Homelessness Sunday, for example, which challenges the whole community to respond in a just way … I'm really looking back a long way to people like Anna Lætitia Barbauld … She wrote a lot of really good, satirical political writing, always under pseudonyms … Anna wrote prose hymns for children, and they've got some very good radical ideas. For example, she writes against the slave trade; she writes hymns about the poor Negro woman seeing her children go off into slavery, and why should she have to suffer that when other women don't. So that's quite a strong idea to put in the 18th century; … and she also talks of God as 'Mother', but, on the other hand, she was working in a school, her husband's school, and … she really – she bought into the moralising work ethic … But in the background she was writing the satirical material … against the established Church – against Britain's war effort … *We are now about – Almighty God, we are about to go out and slaughter our brothers, and we (you know) we pray for your blessing upon this effort to kill the people that you have made* … Amazing writing. I wonder if the hymn writing [reflected] a desire to be acceptable. (Wootton 2003)

She edits a publication with material for worship entitled *Worship Live*, which is published three times a year by Stainer and Bell, and critiques the material she receives as often being:

- Too challenging and not enough nurturing
- Too densely written and difficult to penetrate
- Too naively optimistic

> I do decry the 'happy ending'… the hope should be interwoven … and not tacked on at the end, as it so often is … There's a particular hymn of mine – *God is our Father, what does it mean when parents abuse and damage their children? … When Christ is the Bridegroom, what does it mean when marriages end in false – in sharp disillusion?* … the last line of each verse is *Help us make sense of the dream* … And an editor sent it back and said they couldn't use it in its present form because they wanted a happy ending. They wanted a verse … which says *Now we make sense of the dream*, and I tried ever so hard to write that verse, and in the end I couldn't do it because the reality is that parents *do* abuse and damage their children. (Wootton 2003)

Women have traditionally not had access to musical tuition and even now in an age when more women can access a musical education, women are still often unconfident in their abilities even when they have been affirmed by the examination system. There are few role models for them musically and not enough nurture to give then the necessary confidence.

Janet does not have confidence in her tune writing ability. She writes often to set tunes. Now she is moving away from established metres and even using secular tunes like *Bloody Brass Handles*.

> I wrote music at school because my music education went as far as O Level, so not enormously far but far enough to – and I can hear music and write it down, which is very helpful …

But she feels music 'is closer to my soul' and that she would find critical responses to her music very difficult. Occasionally she does create text and tune together but in collaborations is frustrated sometimes because her composers do not pick up the inflexions of her words in their tunes.

> The writers of music in history have been mostly male, and the writers of words have included a higher proportion of women than people realise … the history of art, generally, has been dominated by men, in terms of what has sold or what has been accepted, or what has been valued, and it makes me extremely angry, because it must mean that thousands of years' worth of women's creativity has been trodden under foot … In historical terms, very definitely, music writing … has been, therefore, only open to men, and … women composers have been de-valued, or women have been told that … it's not something that women can do … I'd love to be *competent* and *confident* [in music]…

Shirley Erena Murray also sees her role as challenging. In *Here to the house of God we come*, she calls for an inclusive community, including the refugee, which reminds the singers that the image of God is in everyone:

> Here to the house of God we come,
> Home of the people of the Way,
> Here to give thanks for all we have,
> Naming our needs for everyday,
> We who have roof and rent and bread,
> Sure of a place to rest our head.

> There is a knocking at the door,
> Sound of the homeless of the world ...
> (Murray in New Zealand Hymnbook Trust 1993 No 55)

She sees her role as challenging conventional wisdom:

> Church of the living Christ, people of Easter faith ...
>
> No use old wineskins now – new wine is here to stay:
> No patching up old schemes – new patches tear way.
> Old gear, old concepts have no place
> Where Christ's own presence sets the pace.
> (Murray in New Zealand Hymnbook Trust 1993 No 19)

She identifies her thinking in this hymn, identifying herself as a Wisdom theologian:

> Regarding the word concepts in that context, I was thinking of entrenched ideas, the sort that need rethinking for every generation in order to keep up with finding out 'the more'. One of the most useful clues, for me, in the Christian life, is to question conventional wisdom. So yes! To relate to the dogma which has oppressed and restricted fresh thought in the Church. And prevented the work of the Spirit! (Mann 2000 p. 12)

So women can be inspired to challenge the established order and deal with justice issues in their writing. There is also a desire to use more nurturing images for God. There is a real sense that women themselves need a great deal of nurturing particularly in the area of music to realise their potential. They fear negative criticism being given too early in their development.

4a Rational/Intuitive

The interview with Janet Wootton (2003) already cited shows the struggle to bring together the rational and the intuitive. Cultures with more trust in intuition deal in more circular rather than linear narratives. I have written hymns reflecting this. This one is based on Hildegard and Julian as well as Ecclesiastes:

> And the circle goes round,
> And we're recycled;
> And the circle goes round,
> And we are healed,
> And the circle goes round,
> And we are strengthened,
> In love encircling,
> In love enclosed.
> (Boyce-Tillman 2006a p. 99)

As we saw in Chapter 1, the intuitive is often associated with the dark and mysterious and there is need to redeem the way of unknowing in music. A more circular approach to salvation history sees darkness and light as interconnected in a cycle of de-integration and reintegration. This reduces the triumphalism of much of the traditional repertoire.[7] I have written a number of hymns connecting darkness and light, like the chorus of a new version of the triumphalist Easter hymn, *Thine be the glory*:

> Christ our companion gloriously alive,
> We can share your darkness, we can share your light.
> (Boyce-Tillman 2006a p. 16)

Written for the tune BENSON by Millicent D. Kingham (1866–1927), my hymn *Harvest of Darkness* links creativity with darkness:

> It was dark in the dawn of time ...
>
> It is dark in sheltering womb,
> Where the baby for three months lies,
> Curved like a moon near a warm woman's heart
> Till the waters roll aside

---

7   These debates have not reached many composers composing for worship like Robert Saxton (2003) who builds his whole philosophy of composition on the journey of darkness to light in his chapter entitled *Darkness to Light: Cycles and Circles: the Sacred in my music.*

> It is dark in the heart's deep cells
> Where the Spirit of Wisdom lies
> Firm are the strong rooms and bars of the mind
> Till the barriers are rolled aside ...
> (Boyce-Tillman 2006a pp. 42–3)

And each verse ends with

> As the Spirit works out her plan.

Carl Daw (2003) also attempts to address this in:

> Dark and comely, evening veils
> All the glare and blaze of day,
> Slows down frantic busyness
> Bids the faithful pause to pray:
> 'Glorious, thrilling gleam of God,
> Jesus Christ, blest holy Light,
> Brighter far than vesper lamps,
> Fill and form our hymns tonight ...'
>
> Mighty angels tend this night
> Those who work or watch or weep ...
> (Daw 1996 No 37)

Kathy Sherman moves towards instrumental music from words:

> Words seem quite incapable of expressing the depth of joy and emotion, quite inad-
> equate for describing the process of laughter, hard work and tears ... At other times
> the tunes came quite by surprise as I sat at the piano searching for a particular note
> and suddenly my fingers fell elsewhere and I knew that THIS was the right note. –
> IT FOUND ME. Sometimes I struggled for a very long time to complete a musical
> idea. The music and I had to get to know each other extremely well, intimately in
> fact ... Some days I run with unrestrained joy to greet you, and together, we catch
> ancient melodies flung by the stars. (Sherman 1998 Sleeve notes)

As with other writers, we see the delicate balance between rational and
intuitive elements in the process. For both men and women it is important
to acknowledge the way of unknowing alongside the rational processes of
shaping and crafting.

4b Embodied/Disembodied

We have seen in Chapter 1 how within feminist circles there is a perceived need to redeem the body and sexuality. Images of dancing appear and images dealing with the body (particularly women's bodies) in a way that regards it as sacred rather than evil:

> The play of the Godhead,
> The Trinity's dance
> Embraces the earth in a sacred romance ...
> (Bringle 2002 p. 128)

In a hymn about Mary Magdalene, I use the images of women's hair and clothing as icons of women's entrapment in the gaze of a male culture:

> CHORUS:
> *Mary, Mary, let down your hair,*
> *Let loose the love of God for all to share.*
>
> > Come, dancing Mary, draw near to your lover,
> > Fear has no place in the meeting of hearts;
> > Let loose your feelings and let them flow freely
> > For deep in this loving a new world could start.
>
> CHORUS
>
> See how your lover advances in springtime;
> Throw your arms widely in passion's embrace;
> Look in the eyes that are longing to meet you,
> And hold up your head; you can meet face to face.
> (Boyce-Tillman 2006b pp. 136–7)

The notion of reuniting body and spirit has resulted in the restoration of dance into liturgy. Sometimes this is liturgical dance by skilled dancers and sometimes it is involving the entire congregation. Some songs are written with the intention of being used for dance, like my text to the tune *Slane*:

> Peace flowing outward and peace flowing in,
> Draw peace from the centre in which we begin;
> Find peace in the ending, the close of the day;
> Let peace in the heart wipe the evil away.
>
> Strength flowing outward and strength flowing in ...
> (Boyce-Tillman 2006a p. 58)

Dancing is used regularly in images in hymns and songs by women. Kathy Sherman's cassette *Dance in the Dawn* concludes with the song that starts:

> Refrain: Women go forth to proclaim your stories
> Go with your visions and go with your dreams.
> Women go quickly the night is waiting
> For us to dance in the new day.
>
> We gather around Holy Wisdom
> Trusting her warmth and her flame.
> In her we are tender, fierce, loving and strong
> As one we go forth in her name.
> (Sherman 1987 sleeve notes)

The hymns and songs in the Wisdom tradition show a clear desire to redeem traditional church attitudes to the body as evil and to be subjugated. Here the body is celebrated and used for movement and dance.

Spirituality

These hymns have enabled a revival of the spiritual experience within a Christian context for many people both women and men. The widening of the view of the Divine through liberation and feminist theology has opened up a deepening and widening for many who hover on the edge of a Christian frame. It has enabled them still to find a spiritual experience within the context of Christianity – a situation that many had begun to regard as impossible.

Summary

Hymn writing has been a place where women, particularly Protestant Victorian women have found a way of getting their voices heard in worship in the past. However, their works have not always held their place in hymn collections. The work of contemporary women and those writers interested in the Wisdom tradition show the trends evident in Chapter 1 and attempt to rebalance the dominant patriarchal tradition. However, there are a number of issues that make this problematic. Those raised in this chapter are:

- Inclusive language for human beings
- Inclusive language for God
- The problems of traditional hymnody
- New subjects like ecology and the interconnectedness of creation and democratic community
- Revisiting the songs of our foremothers in the tradition
- Creating material telling women's stories
- The place of the body
- The place of diversity

CHAPTER 7

Vignette Six – Inning and Outing: Contemporary Practices

Story from Marilyn Harper

BIOLOGY

Someone has to bear and care for the next generation ...

The effect of full time caring means that any musical skills acquired may not be kept as sharp as they would be if they were being used all the time. My own keyboard skills suffered a little during my carer years but I did find later on that mentally I had matured a bit. Years of managing the lives of two dependent children and running a home sharpened my efficiency to do several things at once, including the study of something new ... All this should develop a caring and understanding managerial style. It means I can hold a demanding job down whilst maintaining home stability. Many women do exactly the same as me. Whilst more men share the caring roles the burden stills falls on the women ...

CONFIDENCE

Some girls are extremely fortunate. Those I have the privilege of teaching are especially lucky in the amount that can be spent on their education, especially on their instruments, music and lessons ... The downside of their eventually being at home can lead to a loss of confidence but the benefit of their good education means that with help and support, especially in the individual being valued, confidence can be recovered ...

OPPORTUNITY

Performance opportunities do develop girls' confidence; they learn to handle nervous feelings prior to playing or singing in public. Instrumental study needs to begin early. It is easy to see how those who miss such opportunities in their early years can feel inferior to those who do start early. Unless a late starter has a very determined approach not enough progress may be made to enable a pupil to take part in any form of music making at a time in their lives when the most fun can be had from it.

In the privileged world of the male cathedral chorister and public schoolboy a system envied the world over has been created which makes full use of a boy's musicality and intelligence. From the age of 7 he can learn to sing, follow a part, become aware of other parts. He becomes aware of them fitting together, reading the full score as well as his line. On maturity he can learn to sing another part and will have learned another instrument, including the organ. He is in a wonderful position to observe conducting, accompanying and get ahead by copying his masters. He is an apprentice at a young age when the mind is ready to absorb all these skills. Musically, it is a wonderful set up, one denied to girls until comparatively recently. Yet some old fashioned attitudes prevail and one article I read recently in a magazine devoted to cathedral music suggested that girls should never be allowed anywhere near a cathedral. The reason given was that the boys-only system perpetuates itself and provides the tenors and basses of the future.

As an organ scholar, encouraged initially in a semi-rural parish and later in an urban one, I could not understand why I felt so inadequate besides men who appeared to know the ropes. Once I began to understand something of cathedral and public school education I began to realise where I had missed out. I regret never having learned an orchestral instrument for which, if I had been a boy in a cathedral choir or pupil in a better school, the opportunity would have been there. At least I would have seen a violin before the age of 14. In my state grammar school there was no such thing as an orchestra or a string teacher at that time. Anything I have usefully learned as a potential Director of Music has been through observing others as a student, from my children and my present job.

If girls are to be denied a cathedral style musical education where are female role models? Some parishes have fabulous mixed voice choirs from which girls can be inspired. Are women directors in public schools or state schools? They are more likely in state schools as heads of music. They do marvellous work in a variety of supportive and leadership situations. Are they in our cathedrals? One or two are beginning to be appointed. Do they conduct? Many operate at a local level, some at a national level, but until a woman conducts at the Last Night of the Proms women conductors will not have arrived ... Opportunities are better now than they have ever been before, thanks to better communications, better musical activities and improving attitudes towards women already in positions of leadership. Women Directors of Music will materialise in the fullness of time when the traditions that promote musical leadership are sufficiently well developed for girls. If circumstances are favourable and a suitable opportunity to become a Director of Music appears, I will consider it. Will those who seek such a person consider me too old if by then I have attained membership of Saga?

— HARPER around 2000

Introduction

This chapter examines the controversies inherent within current liturgical practice. It is based on observation and interviews with a variety of contemporary practitioners. The information reported here was accurate at the time of the interview. The male body of God still finds its clearest expression in the songs and singers of the mainstream/public Church. As the opening email shows, in Orthodox, Anglican and Roman Catholic traditions in music, women have been systematically silenced as identified by Elisabeth Schüssler Fiorenza in *Women Invisible in Society and Church* (1985 p. 14).

The contemporary position of women's musical authority in the Church also varies considerably from tradition to tradition. The long history of Church's misogyny that we saw developing in the first 600 years of Christianity in Chapter 2 has persisted, and in many ways increased as the Church accepted the prejudices of the surrounding culture creating 'a Church and State in which women were seen as existentially evil, a fact that was enshrined in a whole web of misquoted Scripture and misappropriated neo-Platonism and Aristotelianism' (Wootton 2000 p. 24) like:

1st Epistle of St Paul to the Corinthians, xiv, 34,35 in which he writes, 'Let your women keep silence in the churches: for it is not permitted unto them to speak ... If they learn anything, let them ask their husbands at home: for it is a shame for women to speak in church.'

We have already looked at where women sit within the traditions of hymnody in the contemporary Church. The area of performing, particularly in a leadership role, has often presented another set of dilemmas for women. This account is from the Welsh Nonconformist tradition in the nineteenth century which demonstrates the problems in Wales and the relatively greater opportunities for women in the US:

CORWAS is a smallholding of about 14 acres in the parish of LLANEILIAN on Anglesey ... In the middle of the nineteenth century, Griffith and Elizabeth [Betsan] Roberts and their nine children lived there. It was quite a talented family and often entertained the neighbours with their music-making. Not only was Griffith [1822–86], a self-taught skilled engineer working in the nearby Parys Mountain copper mines, but also a gifted singer. He led the singing at Nebo chapel for some years and was accompanied by his dog on the one and a half mile walk there. The chapel had no musical accompaniment and a pitchfork, made in the local smithy, was used. It was tuned to produce the key of C and he struck it on his knee or on the wooden pew to obtain the correct volume. As Griffith led the singing, the dog's tail was constantly moving and knocked against the underside of the pew in time with the hymn tune.

Betsan [1827–1901] was always young at heart and liked to join in with the activities of her 4 sons and 5 daughters. As well as being members of a four voice family choir, they had all learnt the basics of music through the College of Tonic Sol-fa which issued certificates at the Junior and Elementary levels. They also had a flute, a violin, a piano and small organ which were played by various members of the family.

Besides being members of the family choir, the daughters were also popular as soloists. Hannah [born in 1862] had an exceptional voice and later adopted the name Llinos Eilian [Llaneilian's linnet]. In 1864 Bosra chapel was completed and is much nearer to Corwas than Nebo chapel. It is very likely that the family had been instrumental in the building of the new chapel and immediately became involved in leading the hymn singing there. Pew number 34 was allocated to them and is still used by their descendants. Two of the sons, John [born 1854] and Owen [born 1864] eventually took over the singing from Griffith their father. Hannah, however, was not happy with the situation, but because she was a woman there was little hope for her to take over. She often started singing before one of her brothers had struck the pitchfork, but was never allowed to take the lead. Eventually in 1900, she decided to emigrate to America, as she could not show her talent fully at Bosra. She settled in Chicago and became a very popular soloist and it is claimed that an evening's performance could earn her up to £100. Some years ago, there was a poster locally indicating this. It is possible that ... [her chosen repertoire was from] Welsh congregational hymn singing.[1]

This chapter will include brief overviews of where the mainstream traditions are today in terms of women's work and leadership in the areas of performing and composing but will focus on alternative liturgy groups.

The result of the influx of feminist ideas and the associated dissatisfaction with the established church, be it Orthodox, Roman Catholic or Protestant, was the burgeoning of alternative liturgy groups, many predating the ordination of women in the Anglican Church in England. Some of these meet regularly and others are just brought together or particular events and occasions (as evidenced by Ward and Wild's *Human Rites* 1995). There is a range of people who are dissatisfied by the worship diet of the mainstream churches resulting in a great variety of groups. Some of them exclude men to give women a safe space in which to share the views and opinions. These groups regard the presence of men as limiting the possibility of women's self-expression. Some include men who are sympathetic to women's position. There are a range of positions within feminism. We have already seen the more mainstream conservative position in Lisa Neufeld Thomas's project in Chapter 6. The radical position sees the need for women-only groupings, with a declared aim of completely eradicating patriarchy from society. Many of them drew their inspiration from Rosemary Radford Ruether's book; *Women-Church: Theology and Practice of Feminist Liturgical Communities* (1985) drawing on Fiorenza's theology of an *ekklesia* of women. I have chosen groups of which I have experience or whose practices I was able to access through interviews with participants.[2]

1　　The information in paragraphs 2 and 3 has been derived from a book COFIO'R BLYNYDDOEDD GYNT by the Rev G. Wynne Griffith. The book was published in 1967. The rest of it was told by various relatives to John Roberts to whom I am indebted for this account.

2　　There is a much more detailed examination of these groups in Berger (1999 and 2001).

From my observation of and participation in these groups, it would seem that music is an area where women feel disempowered. Material for the Iona Community is popular and its links with the folk tradition means that it does reflect women's traditions insofar as women have had a hand in the shaping of the tunes. The Taizé chants are also popular. It is a pity that groups do not use these as a starting point from their own creativity. And yet in other parts of the world as Janet Wootton writes:

> Very often, the very dynamism of feminist worship generates new material drawing on the talents and expertise of people who would not have thought themselves the 'type' to contribute to the development of worship. (Wootton 2000 p. 35)

The review of these practices will be explored under the value headings of Chapter 1. The stories of individual practitioners following their vocation as musicians within or outside the Church structures are also included. Here is one very good example including a number of the themes to be found in interviews:

> I wrote my first song when I was two-and-a-half years old, in my back yard, playing – we were making a tent in our back yard, my brother, my sister and I, and I'd had what was an old sheet my mother had given us. It had a big hole in it, and it fell and my eyes came out ... So I just started singing a song. *(Sings) I see the peoples and the peoples see me, I like the peoples and the peoples like me* ... Needless to say, I'm a Leo – fire ...
>
>   We grew up in a musical house ... Music was on all the time. My brother loved classical music. My father loved big band music ... My mother just liked any kind; so music was always on more than TV in our house, so we grew up with an appreciation of different kinds of music. And ever since I was a little kid, I was always attracted to the piano ... We never had a piano – we couldn't afford one – but when I was nine years old, I got rheumatic fever and I was in bed for six months, and I had to give up sports, which I loved and was very good at; I had to give up dancing lessons, I couldn't ride a bike, so my father, God rest his soul, went out and bought these little organs from Sears and Roebuck Company that had the numbers over the keys and little chords on the sides ... When I was about sixteen years old, Peter, Paul and Mary were big, and I loved them ... For my sixteenth birthday, my friends pitched in and got me my first guitar, because they were sick of seeing me play the yardstick with Peter, Paul and Mary records, and during that time, which was about 1966 ... the Church was starting to change ... I went to an all-girls Catholic High School, so we started to do Folk Masses, and that's where I really got my start and interest in liturgical music ... I played at the first Folk Mass ever at Yale University ... So I

started to play at liturgy, and ... I just started to write my own liturgical music at that point, and they were pretty male centred at that point, you know ... I wrote a song called *Come to me, Father* ... But as society started to change – you know, the feminist movement was starting – the change in the Church was giving women more voice – I, at that time, after leaving High School, went to the Sisters of Charity for seven years. From there, I did a children's TV show, so I started to write children's music, which had a spiritual bent to it. A song called *Won't you be my rainbow friend* is still very popular ... I began to realise that there was really no music that spoke of women's experience of the spiritual. It was all male-based ... I was a Campus Chaplain after I left the Community ... So, probably in the late 70s, after the first Women's Ordination Conference ... I said ... 'We need something that can be sung here.'... So from there, I really started to think about the women's experience in terms of the spiritual, and *The Blessing Song*, which is probably my most famous [was written]:

'Bless you, my Sister,
Bless you on your way ...
You have roads to roam before you're home
And winds to speak your name.' (Silvestro 1993a)

It's a very personal song. It's about woman blessing herself or us, blessing each other, and when I say the word 'bless' I always think about ... honouring the sacred in each other ... And the first time, 1983, my first album came out ... I was the National Director of the Women's Ordination Conference, and ... we were then 'being defiant' and doing liturgy all over the place ... I began to write feminist liturgical music ... [*The Blessing Song*] was sung during a healing service where Elisabeth Schüssler Fiorenza ... was going to talk to the Bishops ... and all the women automatically, tears rolling down their faces, raised their hands and blessed these women going up, and then they turned to each other – and I was very humbled by that moment, you know. 'Who am I, Lord, to be the instrument ... of this for these women?'

My music is my own spiritual journey. My first tape was called *Circling Free* ... [My students] couldn't understand why I was a single woman working on a College Campus fighting for women's ordination when basically you were already a priest ... So I wrote a song called *Spinning*:

'I'm spinning through the times of my life,
I'm not a mother, I'm not a wife,
Does that mean I cannot love you,
Does that mean I can't do what I do?'

... A lot of it came out of my own lived experience ... So [based on a friend's visit to Nicaragua] one of the verses says,

'If ever I should cry for the pain of injustice,
Let the tears I cry run down like a river and set us free,
And let the women be there.'

And that song has been used a lot, in women's communities especially ... I could
see myself getting deeper in terms of the spiritual, feminist, and sacred feminine in
myself ... My other stuff was very ... political ... It was sacred and intertwined with
more the political ... Another nun who was very famous in the Movement, Sister
Margaret Smith, died, and there was a machine message left for me, saying that –
'Our Sister, Margaret, has wrapped her arms in Mother Earth.'. And so I wrote this
song, *I am Flying*. And it says:

'I have returned to our Mother, the Earth,
And wrapped myself in the fold of her arms,
For I have seen the light of our sisters coming,
And they're all to welcome me home.'

... I have a friend who, when she 'came out' to her parents as a lesbian, was thrown out
of her house and lived in a dumpster for a year, going to college. She, presently, is on
the board of a bank in the Boston area; and she also ... had a dream of doing old-age
homes and assisted living for the gay and lesbian community, so that she said to me
that night, 'My dreams have always kept me real,' and ... it goes into a little file. So
for Christmas, I gave her the song *Myself Growing Older* ... As a matter of fact, that
song has just been used in a play about domestic violence, here in town ... There's a
song called, *Say it Sister, Don't Hold Nothing Back:*

'Say it in the morning,
Say it in the night,
Say it in the darkness,
Say it in the light.
This violence has got to stop, got to stop.'

... It really talks about domestic violence as well as:

'Tell it to the Congress, to the State House, our bodies are our own'...

So, I would say throughout all my music, I've woven the political, the spiritual and
the personal transformation [together]... We are words; we are music ... I cannot
tell you how many letters I have received from women around the world, telling
me how they've been healed by my music. Whether it actually has been physical,
mental or emotional ... [There was]... a group of psychologists who get together

weekly and pray together – women, who always used to sing *The Blessing Song*; one of them had a heart attack ... She was in a coma. So all of the women went down, and they were going to do the Last Rites for her because they didn't think she was going to make it ... So they started to anoint her and they sang *The Blessing Song*. The woman woke up out of the coma, singing *The Blessing Song*, and she's fine ... So I said, 'That's my first miracle for canonisation.' [But now] I can't go through those [Roman Catholic] doors ... I think we've gone backwards in a lot of our parishes ... We used to have people around the altar and everyone was participating, and that sort of dissipated ... The gay and lesbian issue ... forget that! I'm a hell-burner myself now ... I always think of Mary Hunt saying, 'You don't add women and stir. You don't add gayness and stir.' ... It's about changing the system ... [At the first Women's Ordination Conference] it was still male-based. Jesus Christ, and there was nothing about the Goddess; nothing about the feminine sense of Spirit ... but Ruach – the breath – is feminine, ... We did some phenomenal rituals together, and I remember the first time – one of the women ... knew all about the Goddesses ... She really got me to love the moon and the stars – the moon in the sense of feminine. So I learned a lot from her, and I remember the first time we did Eucharist together ... We were sure we were going to be struck by lightning ... For me, the whole idea of the breaking of the bread is a sense of community. That still has meaning ... – whether it be the sense of Jesus, or the sacred, or the sense of community that the Eucharist brings – I think that's important.

Some of the scriptures I still find very rich. You know, the Gospels of Justice ... I can remember preaching when I was a campus chaplain about Mary really being the first priest, because she could say, 'This *is* my body and this *is* my blood.' So the whole sense of birthing was sacred ... That's what I loved also. I loved the story of Mary and Elizabeth. You know, they welcomed the fruit of their womb ... People say, 'Oh, you're not married. You don't have children.' For me, I don't know, I've lost count – I probably have about three hundred and something songs, maybe more than that, but those are my children. I mean, they come from the deepest part of me, and that which is sacred. I know a lot of times when I'm playing my keyboard, that's not me. I know it. Singing *The Blessing Song* that first time – that wasn't me. There are many times when I know there's something beyond me that sings. I think that music is so transcendent ... I've been given a gift to musically capture the stories of women and raise them to a level that honours the sacredness of their lives.

There's a really wonderful story about when my father was dying, he was dying in a hospice in Connecticut ... I was having a very hard time in terms of he wanted – the Last Rites and here I am, his daughter, the National Director of the Women's Ordination Conference, and he wanted to bring this priest in to do the sacraments; so I really had to learn to let go, saying, 'You know, Marsie, your mother and father have been married for ... almost forty years.' I said, 'This is their faith, and this is important to them.' So I said, 'Let go, sister'... And the priest came in, and he was

wonderful ... He said. 'My name is Ed. I'm a priest,' and my father reached out and
he grabbed my hand, and it was shaking, and he said, 'This is my daughter, Mary
Ann.' He said, 'She's a priest, too.' And those were my father's last words. He sank
into a coma after that, and died the next morning. So that was my ordination ...
Here's my father – one foot in Heaven and the other on Earth. So I sang a song at
his funeral, and I usually tell that story when I'm on the road doing my conferences
... We carry a story with us ... I think women's music has helped women to have a
voice ... (Silvestro 2003)

This story from Marsie Silvestro (2003) shows how the history of women's
general authority in the Church is intimately bound up with their position
in the musical hierarchy and from it we can draw the following themes:

- The passionate connection of her creativity with her justice-seeking
- The personal as political
- The importance of powerful emotions as a source of inspiration
- Healing ways of receiving music
- The orality of her process
- The creation of a community of women through music
- The problem in finding the confidence to speak out

The rest of this chapter will concentrate on the area of Values. It will do this
primarily by means of an analysis of interviews with women ministers, priests
and song writers carried out mainly in the early part of the millennium.

1a Individual/Community

There is a strong sense of community in the alternative liturgy groups. The
wider church has a variety of attitudes to these burgeoning groups all of
which tend to favour inclusive language which receives a very varied reception in the wider church.

Some communities meet in Church halls (seldom in churches) and
others in people's homes. Some like the Brevard Episcopal Mission in

North Carolina have started in good relationships with the mainstream church but have since encountered problems with the relationship. Women Church Iceland is remarkable in that it was an initiative supported by the established Church. The Rev Audur Vilstalmsdottir (2003) at the time of the interview ran this Women's Church in Reykjavik. It grew out of a course she ran for women on feminist theology and is an independent Church inside the national Lutheran Church supported by a secretariat producing a regular Newsletter and a website. It contained 250 women members with an average congregation of 100 of all ages with preponderance of people in their 40s and 50s. They were starting a meeting for youth in the following year with candidates for confirmation and she brought a group of women in their 20s to the European Women's Synod in Barcelona in 2003. Audur provided pastoral care in the form of counselling for the members. It was a woman-only space, although there were men who would like to join. They met in various churches once a month on Sunday evenings. They also had a weekly prayer group followed by a meal and sometimes special services to support women who have been abused. The Sunday service included a sermon, and prayer. They had a professional pianist playing hymns in between them. Brought in from outside originally, the musician became a member of Womenchurch and learned the organ as well, which was used largely at the beginning and end of the service. They did not use percussion instruments but would have liked to use them to give them greater variety. Sometimes they used violins and flutes if they had people who will play them:

> [Music] has been very important for us, the music because we wanted to get to use the old hymns of Iceland – both the words and the music, and at the same time, we wanted to get new music, and we wanted to get new hymns based on feminist theology and inclusive language ... So we got the women in the Women's Church, and all the women outside, to make new hymns for us, either to translate them or just to make them using traditional tunes and material from other collections like the Canadian Hymn Book.

They used hymns, songs and Taizé chants with English, Nordic and Latin texts. Traditional hymns were left with their non-inclusive language. Otherwise the majority of members always referred to God as 'She'. There

was a stress on people being free to do what is right for them. In relation
to the regular services of the Lutheran Church in Iceland the services were
freer making use of the congregation's gifts which worked out the priesthood of all believers in a new way. They did have a choir, open to everyone, which once sang in two parts but now sings in unison, its role being
to support the congregation. Sometimes a woman soloist came in to sing
a black spiritual or an Icelandic song which was much appreciated. They
did it for love. The design of the churches was not conducive to dancing
although they had included it; sometimes they used drama.

    We see here a church, officially sanctioned, committed to feminist
ideals and principles, serving a large congregation that includes young
women. It embraces diversity, has primarily a piano accompaniment and has
a real pastoral concern and concern with a democratic structure. The choir
is seen as intimately related to the congregation. Not only is this an example
of a functioning community in good relations with the Lutheran Church
but also we see within it a real attempt to involve everyone particularly
in the singing; the choir's function is seen only in this light. There is also

- A limited amount of available musical expertise – a recurring theme in this chapter
- An embracing of a variety of styles
- An embracing of inclusive language and feminine images of God, particularly
  in contemporary material
- A desire to teach women about the Wisdom tradition

    The church community can often be very critical of people who break
away from the established norms of a tradition. Joy Webb is a Salvationist,
who set about using idioms accessible to the wider public. Her desire for
inclusivity did not get acceptance for her work in some Christian circles. Her group – called *The Joystrings* – played in the Playboy Club; she
described this as a nightmare that she only went through because she felt
God's call to this particular ministry;[3] she had not then considered the

3   'We were all used to going into pubs and clubs with The War Cry, and so we were
     not afraid from that sense. We were just scared because, you know, everything was
     new, and we were frightened. It's no good saying we weren't. And we used to get

sexual overtones of the uniform. It brought her a great deal of protest from Salvationists in the UK and even more from the US. But people who remembered the beginning of the movement, applauded their opening up of the message to a whole new group of people:

> The old people saw William Booth, doing his thing, you know, reaching to the masses. They would pray for us and support us – 'Oh, it's like the old times!' ... and the kids loved us ... and in the Church, I've been spat on ... Lovely, isn't it? The thought of it now is comical. Oh, yes. Twice I was spat on ... by my fellow Brothers and Sisters in the Lord! (Webb 2003)

Joy became very well known in the 1960s through her establishment of the band that featured well in the pop charts of the day entitled *The Joy Strings*. She described how right from the beginning women had equality of status within the community of the Salvation Army, but after the equal opportunity of the first generation of Salvationists the band quickly became an all-male preserve; in some areas particularly in the area of the marriage of officers this did not apply. A woman officer could not hold a rank above her husband, nor could she marry a layperson. At the time of the interview these rules were slowly changing.

I have been exploring in my own composing new ways of creating community. In the area of ecology I created a work designed to encourage our community with the earth entitled *The Healing of the Earth* (Boyce-Tillman 2001a) which has been performed in several situations including with 500 children aged 6–16 for the Queen's Jubilee in Battersea Technology College, London, UK.

The starting point of the piece was in the areas of Value and Spirituality. It is a piece with an intentionally ethical system based on the valuing of diversity and connecting with the environment. This drew on feminist theoreticians of music discussed in Chapter 1 (especially Subotnik 1996). It is based on a notion of community musically within a single musical

---

Army cadets – all two hundred of them – together, and say, "Promise us, you'll be praying for us at *that time*," you know, and they'd set their alarm clocks, bless their hearts, to get up and pray while we were playing in The Playboy Club and The Blue Angel. Terrific support from the young people.'

event in which through participatory performance professional musicians and children work together with integrity (Sharp 2000). There are few examples in the music making traditions of the West where adults can behave as adults and children as children and they can both be included in a musical event. There are situations, like the cathedral choir, where children have to behave like adults to be accepted. Other situations, like nursery classes, ask adults to behave like children to facilitate group music making. In this work, I tried to develop an inclusive structure, in which experienced musicians played quite complex textures, while children had sections which they themselves devised.

The Valuing of the environment is reflected in the titles of the nine movements: Wisdom, Water, Knowledge, Fire, Technology, Earth, Compassion, Air, and Communication. Many of the pieces include theological and musical ideas taken from Hildegard of Bingen (see Chapter 3). The themes of the songs are ecological but this ecology includes the recycling of ourselves and our experiences alongside the care for the environment. It is extended to include personal and community transformation.

This pluralistic Value system is reflected in the range of cultures from which the songs are drawn. These include Native American, Urdu, Israeli, Yoruba, Muslim, and Christian sources. These fit alongside newly composed material in a more Western classical style. Diversity is put together with respect for both the differences and common elements. Music now provides an example of how Values might work in the wider society.

The Value systems of the Western classical concert with its separation between the composer, performer and audience are, in this work, balanced by a more democratic approach to creation and performance. There are the devised sections – so the performers have a hand in the compositional process. The players and singers are placed around the audience, who also have to sing. The notion of a musical performance as something packaged by a conductor at one end of a space and then propelled to the other where it is received by an audience, is now replaced by one in which each member of the audience has to construct their own listening experience; this will depend on which group of musicians are near them. So we all collaborate together – performers, composers and audience – to make things happen musically and also ecologically.

In the area of Construction I chose a modular format. Construction in the dominant Western Classical tradition had often been managed by notation, tonality and harmony. I had to find a structure that could contain material from a variety of sources – both instrumental and sung material as well as pieces devised by the children. I, therefore, developed a structure that retains as far as possible the character of the original pieces. So there are a variety of accompaniment textures, such as ostinati, drones, and chords. There are 'holes/windows' in the piece for the devised episodes, a technique developed in an earlier piece (Boyce-Tillman 1998) The structure is intended to reflect the multi-cultural nature of our society, including notated and non-notated – literate/orate – elements. The modular structure enables the piece to be rehearsed in sections and then put together in a final rehearsal. It is the task of the composer/conductor to make the connections work effectively; so the role of director/composer becomes more that of a weaver than a benevolent dictator.

The Materials used are deliberately simple. It is accompanied by a flexible ensemble consisting of a high, low and two middle instruments using whatever players are available. A great deal of the musical Material involves the human voice and the other Materials are left to the choice of the participating schools. In this performance we had a devised piece using steel pans.

The valuing of the area of Expression is apparent in the inclusion of sections devised by the children themselves. These improvised sections included movement, dance and drama. The performance included artwork in the form of mobiles and banners on ecological themes created in association with a local art gallery. This reflects an interdisciplinary view of the arts, balancing the discrete approach to them espoused by the dominant value system.

I followed up this performance by semi-structured interviews with children, teachers and parents to see how far my ecological intentions particularly those in the areas of Values and Spirituality had been realised. Various themes emerged from these.

The valuing of diversity was clearly reflected. In a school in which the head teacher had said that the citizenship agenda could only be delivered through discussion and debate, a 10-year-old boy started his reflections with: 'It was like peace on earth. Everyone did their own thing but it all fitted together'.

The piece clearly valued the notion of community above the individualism of the National Curriculum in the UK. This was why a number of the head teachers agreed to participate in the project. They commented on the effect the piece had had on children's community building skills. A head teacher in a zone designated as one needing special educational resources, commented:

> It improved the children's co-operative skills. I saw them supporting one another and encouraging other schools in their work. This is unusual for our children whose poverty often makes them quite self-centred.

In the domain of Expression and emotional literacy, there was the development of empathy through music. A 10-year-old girl said that she sings the setting of an African prayer every night. I had told them about the community in Gugulethu where I had found the prayer. She said: 'I felt close to the people in Africa whose prayer we sang. Now I continue to sing it and think of them.'

Teachers often commented on the improvement in their pupils' ability to use music for personal expression. One statement ran: 'It encouraged me to encourage children to make their own music and value their pieces.'

The importance of the Spiritual domain appeared regularly. A ten-year-old girl commented: 'There was this power there. I don't know what it was. It was simply a power.'[4]

This has been followed by a number of works based on this model and attempting to express a truly inclusive music-making tradition (Boyce-Tillman 2007b). Some of these have excited hostility among the traditionalists in the musical community.

So we can see that the notion of building a more inclusive community can sometimes find a ready acceptance by mainstream churches and at other times provokes hostility and results in the forming groups separate from the mainstream churches.

---

4   These findings formed the basis of the *Space for Peace* project which includes people from a great variety of faiths in a large scale event described in Boyce-Tillman (2013a).

1b Unity/Diversity

Inclusive community often involves the embracing of diversity. Flois Knoll Hicks (2003) is an African American who has devoted a great deal of her professional life to forwarding the cause of Christian unity by embracing a diversity of singing traditions. She acknowledged her love of diversity as originating from an early music teacher. When she went to Germany in 1973, she worshipped in a church with very diverse congregations – Korean Presbyterians, an African congregation and a Serbian Orthodox congregation as well as a German congregation of varied ethnic extraction. Here they celebrated ecumenical services using German, even though many of them could not speak it. In 1981, she established a choir, of about sixty people, mostly students. They called themselves *The Ecumenical Choir*, believing that the earth is made for everyone to live decently, with peace and justice, and that the earth belonged to everyone to take care of. The title was taken from the motto from the World Council of Churches – Peace, Justice and the Integrity of the Creation – which links human beings and the natural world in a community of justice. They often sat mingled with the congregation rather than separated out as a separate group. She saw music as a way of affirming identity:

> I realised that, by singing a particular Korean song, people opened up, and you could see that their spirit opened up, and they were very appreciative that we tried to do something in their language. ... And I started ... finding little liturgical pieces from the world over, and we did this and celebrated services in different congregations; we found ourselves often being invited to different congregations – sort of like to spread the news that it could be done. (Knoll Hicks 2003)

For her the characteristic of good liturgical music is to embrace variety. She enjoys including improvisation in her practice which she draws from the black spiritual or jazz tradition, working orally most of the time:

> I do just improvising warm-up exercises so that they can just use their voices in a different way than we are used to ... listening to each other. (Knoll Hicks 2003)

For Flois, music is an important way of creating inclusive community by embracing people who have little vocal skill:

> In the black traditions, the melody is the basis for the embellishments ... The harmony is made up and some people who are singing might even sing ... [what we might call a] monotone ... They don't have a good ear but because everybody else is improvising, then this one, who may not have a good ear, is integrated. (Knoll Hicks 2003)

Her own composing is through these improvisatory practices which she describes as:

> When we are improvising liturgy ... that's a spiritual relating which is uplifting ... We're experiencing God. (Knoll Hicks 1999)

She sees her work in women's groups as part of a concern from *justice* rather than simply for feminism. In Flois's work we can see

- The deliberate embracing of diversity through her passion for justice
- The breaking down of the division between choir and congregation
- The embracing of inclusive language
- The use of music for nurturing
- The embracing of process-based ideas like improvisation rather than product based approaches

Many Christian denominations protect their identity by maintaining a unity of style. Just as there is a great variety of practice between Christian traditions on the subject of women's authority and consequently in ordaining women; there is a similar diversity musically. What is interesting, however, is that groups of women who gather for worship from different Christian denominations often share a considerable unity of purpose. The first woman minister was ordained in England in the Unitarian Church (the minister Gertrud van Petzold) and then the Congregational Church; the Salvation Army had women in positions of authority from the outset.

In the Orthodox traditions the situation is very different and reflects the Platonic principles of the silencing of women:[5]

> In many churches, men and women sit separately. Often the women are upstairs away from the men. The cantors are men. Except on high days when women may sing in the choir, some are the readers, chant the psalms and prayers and read the epistle, those who process the icons and carry the candles. Their sons are altar boys ... Women are passive in the pews, for the responses to the prayers are left to the chanters, but their voices can also be heard whispering the liturgy,[6] which they know so well from decades of faithful attendance. (Liveris 1995 pp. 160–1)

This is not a tradition with which I am familiar and, in my more recent experience, these traditions are starting to wane. I have heard women chanting in some churches but have also experienced all-male groups.

In the Nonconformist traditions, however, the sacred song did allow the mature woman's voice to be heard in worship from the very beginning and linked with a large raft of music making including festivals and singing competitions associated with Sunday school activity. The soloist was billed just below the name of the preacher on the church noticeboard and the repertoire was often the religious version of the Victorian bourgeois ballad with its pattern of three verses – one introductory, one more sad and then one more joyful. The piano accompaniments were quite demanding and reflected a time when playing the piano was a necessary domestic accomplishment for women. It is suggested that the decline in the tradition is due to the decline in the number of people with the piano technique necessary for the accompaniments of the songs of the bourgeois ballad type which made up this repertoire (Methodist Women 2004). Here the older women's voice can still be heard and celebrated in worship, although it is a tradition not as vibrant as it once was.

The Christian traditions that have their roots in the African-American traditions still retain within them the concept of the strong women singer or group of singers, linking them with the pre-Christian traditions of the

---

5   But also see the work of Susan Ashcroft Harvey in Chapter 3.
6   When Hildegard (1098–1179) was excommunicated near the end of her life she would have had to whisper the liturgy.

spirit possession traditions of the African continent. There is here, however, among some singers a sense that the accommodation to European culture has meant the loss of some of the inspirational elements of the original traditions (Catlin Reid 1997). Here the sound produced by the women is a full-bodied sound often associated with movement and using a wide compass, including a powerful lower register.

However, the sound cultivated by the convent traditions of Anglicanism is often that of the pre-pubescent girl in the same way as their vow of celibacy might be seen as a way of trapping women into this condition even though the average age of many of these communities is now well over fifty. The singing style within the convents also reflected this. A woman experienced in singing German Lieder entered an enclosed woman's religious community. She thought that her voice was what she really had to offer God. She was soon told that that style of singing was unacceptable in the 'pure' sound of their liturgical singing.

The Unitarian tradition has always been a singing tradition and has encouraged women's ministry. Not surprisingly it has produced hymn writers like Love Maria Willis, most famous for *Father, hear the Prayer we offer* which despite its first line is a break from the tradition of peaceful quiet devotion that characterises many women hymn writers of the period. The current Unitarian/Universalist tradition has produced a fine collection in *Singing the Living Tradition*, drawing on:

> humanism, feminism, mysticism, natural theism, the Jewish tradition, many other world faith traditions, and the skepticism generated by this century's disillusioning woes and wars (Unitarian/Universalist Hymnbook Resources Commission 1993 p. vii)

It includes such titles as *Mother Spirit, Father Spirit, where are you?*, *Lady of the Seasons' laughter* and *Faith of the larger liberty*. I was privileged to play in a drumming circle of women and men for the ordination of a Unitarian minister in a US service that included traditional hymns alongside our drummed interludes.

In the Roman Catholic Church after Vatican II the move towards a more folk style in worship drew more women into contributing to worship situations both as cantors or composers. Leading the tradition in the

UK was Estelle White with songs like *Trust is in the Eyes* (Boyce-Tillman and Wootton 1993 pp. 38–9) and Bernadette Farrell (2009) with very popular songs like *Christ be our Light*. It opened up the way for the less literate singer/songwriter – a genre always favoured by women. One of the leading women in this area is Carolyn McDade who was attached to the Dominican sisters in Plainville US for some ten years. She started an imaginative women's ecological project with women in two centres in the US and one in Canada. This self-funded project was an elaborate one involving a large group of women mostly in their 50s and 60s.

The more folk-like styles and the worship-song tradition developed by the more charismatic churches are often despised by the Anglican upholders of the cathedral tradition under the heading of 'happy clappy.' As Judith Blezzard writes at the opening of her book *Borrowings in English Church Music 1550–1950*, there are 'two extreme and opposing views to church music':

- Any music, irrespective of its origin, can be used as a vehicle for worship.
- Church music ought to be separate and distinct from music of any other kind, particularly secular. (Blezzard 1990 p. 1)

Women have tended to find a greater place in traditions that embrace a variety of styles rather than those who support the position of the 'separateness' of the liturgical traditions.[7]

The Episcopal Divinity School in Cambridge, Massachusetts is a theological College training ministers from many church denominations. When I was a Visiting Fellow there, the chapel included a great diversity of traditions in its worship. The tone of the College was set by the Principal, Bishop Stephen Charleston (2003). From a Native American background he saw

---

7   An American Episcopalian Patricia Woods (2003) from Albuquerque said that she had initiated what she called a 'blended service', which involved two traditional hymns and some Taizé chants and then other songs for which she had an assortment of instruments. She let the children come and play with her whatever they wanted. She also said The Episcopal Church has some beautiful music, a lot of it unsingable. She asked when we would learn simplicity, as children know it as in *Jesus loves me this I know*. She represents a position that many women worship leaders can identify with.

the drum as 'a profoundly powerful liturgical instrument' which the West is rediscovering. His own belief system is eclectic, to which the statues of Crow woman and the Virgin Mary on his desk testified. He encouraged the diversity found in the Chapel:

> You may find Taizé chant one week and very traditional Anglican hymns the next week, and Africa drumming the third week, and I think that eclecticism is important, particularly in a seminary setting – a theological education setting – because it gives students a chance to really learn about the varieties that they may bring to bear in a worship setting. It builds a deeper respect and knowledge of other cultural forms and expands their theological varieties, and it allows them to make mistakes and to learn from their mistakes within the Chapel setting ...

He raised the issue of whether diversity needs to be in separate services or whether it can be contained within a single service. He saw the separate services as ghettoising people – Spanish-speaking at one time, English-speaking at another, and sees the integration of difference within a single service as part of the formation of an ecclesia. He examined the area of naming God as well:

> There's a pastoral dimension here, not only theological. *Shouldn't we all be one community* is the theology. The pastoral side is *But – Well, how do you do that?* ... And for me, the mission is to try and find ways to let that happen ... I personally feel that, when people step out of their boxes for a while, they learn about one another ... I want them to realise that, *Yes, you can call God, 'Father', and that's fine, but you can also call God, 'Mother', and that's just as fine* ...
>
> Personally ... because I come from a very matriarchal, matrilineal culture, and grew up understanding the feminine divine and respecting it from childhood, I think the day needs to come when that is as common in Western culture, ... where our children grow up feeling, from the very beginning, that that's quite acceptable and understandable, that the whole imagery of God as feminine – as female ... We need to redress the balance because we've been weighted to one side.

Jane Ring Frank (2003) at the time of the interview had been the musical director there for five years. Although not an Episcopalian, she had worked in a variety of traditions from Unitarian to Presbyterian. She saw the chapel as the meeting point for the problems of the College, a place where they could both be expressed and also worked through in a safe place, where mistakes can be permitted. She was pleased at having created a singing community. She embraced a diversity of styles rather than the more authoritarian style of previous leadership regimes:

> Diversity in music is a double-edged sword because – in liturgical music, people's hearts are with what they know from their childhood … Their memories and hearts and good feelings about being in the Chapel are so rooted to actually a very few pieces … so it was very important to bring joy to diverse music …

She opened up the styles used in chapel, including drumming. It showed the richness that can be created in a climate where:

- Diversity is embraced as a positive feature
- Participation is encouraged
- The principles of the Wisdom tradition are joyfully embraced

Some women have operated a syncretic approach to the development of their faith drawing on a variety of traditions. Laime Kiskun (2003) is a visual anthropologist and works with women's ritual groups in Vilnius, Lithuania, which she describes as having only sixteen hundred years of Christianity and as being the land of 'the last remaining European pagans'. She challenges the Christian traditions of her country, regarding the Catholic priests as narrow-minded and hierarchical. The Lithuanians, in her opinion, are naturally pagans, still celebrating festivals, like the Summer Solstice. In the past she had run a music theatre group with a spiritual dimension. She had also been part of an Ashram which was closed down. This informs her practice with creating rituals, often for women's events like puberty and childbirth. They use lullabies and ancient Lithuanian songs called Sutartines – songs that were special to women for such tasks as cutting corn and domestic tasks. They have a particular structure involving four women's voices entering one by one and forming a distinctive harmony. The words she says are still appropriate for contemporary rituals and designed to create community with the natural world. They use elements like the sun, moon, morning star, trees and the serpent which is a symbol of femininity, wisdom. She stands outside the confines of the Church and wishes to use ancient women's music to nurture Lithuanian women.

Other Christian women have been active in the area of interfaith dialogue musically. Ana Hernandez, who specialises in chanting, delights in musical diversity:

> Music is just music ... I'm happy in all styles, just because they're all good for something. They all move different parts of you, I think. (Hernandez 1999)

She works in interfaith settings and at the time of the interview, was working towards *The Interfaith Sound Initiative*, a bi-weekly chant session in a cathedral in special formations drawn from Sanskrit traditions:

> like [one in which you] form a cross with a garnet at the centre, and you sing in that formation, and what you do is you pick one person, usually like the person most in need of [help] at that time. And you sit him in the middle, and he's the garnet, and then you all just line up, facing the centre ... with the guy facing east and you do that mantra four hundred and eight times. To be able to do that – those kinds of things in a space like a Cathedral would be beautiful and I think will move the people ... That's really powerful ... (Hernandez 2003)

Others have been concerned about the oppressive unity of colonial Christian traditions like Sister Robyn Reynolds in Nugalinya College in Darwin, Australia. She was concerned in embracing and studying diversity and wrote her thesis on *Catholic Sacrament Engaging with Wadeye Ritual*. It looked at a Christian initiation ceremony incorporating a Wadeye ritual. She was very much in favour of indigenising the Mass and disliked the aping of Western practices in aboriginal Christian worship. She acknowledged the variety of practices that the missionary activity has created:

> I would have loved that Mass down at the camp on the ground, in the – not the dirt – the earth – on the earth, sitting round, having the basic – the beautiful symbols of our Catholic liturgy, but having just them in their purity and not cluttered up with, you know, chasubles and bells ... We've just got to respect where ... those wise elders are ... There are many different answers to it because [there are] so many different cultures in the Australian Aboriginal and Torres Strait Island communities, ... (Reynolds 2003)

In the piece called *The Call of the Ancestors* (Boyce-Tillman 1998) I started to explore the notion of structures with 'windows' in them to contain a diversity of musical styles which I developed in *The Healing of the Earth* described above. It included improvising groups of various kinds (non-notated orate traditions), which in this performance were Kenyan drums, a rock group, a Thai piphat, a Western brass quintet, a moot horn (an Anglo-Saxon instrument), and a large four-part choir (in this case the combined choirs of the participating colleges). The orate traditions had spaces in the piece for improvised episodes. The groups were placed around the Cathedral with the choir and brass group at the East End, the rock group at the west end and the drums and piphat in the North and South aisles. The audience was thus enclosed by the music which appeared to 'move.'

To summarise, there is a variety of musical traditions associated with the various Christian denominations and the place and the sound (tone quality) of women's singing that is acceptable varies from one to another. Individual services tend to be more uniform musically. The challenge is to contain diversity within a single service. This is a theological as well as a musical challenge.

2a Public/Private

The general invisibility of women in positions of authority in the various denominations is reflected in the roles played in musical performance leadership and composition. Some of the arguments used against women's priests in the debate in the Anglican Church in England have greater power when applied to a group of women singing in a choir. One of these is the so-called 'problem of the male gaze'. Graham Leonard, Bishop of London, identified the problem of a woman preaching being that male members of the congregation would only be able to think of hugging her (Harris 2002 p. 4). How much more true would this be of a group of girls in a choir who would also serve as a distraction to the male choristers?

English church music inherited Luther's misogyny which found its expression in boys' choir schools that were established during the reformation to serve the main churches and the cathedrals. Many voices in the world of the cathedral choir are still unhappy about the presence of girls. This choral tradition was a self-perpetuating tradition in which the boys who came through it, continued in charge of it as organists. There is a belief that women will destroy the church music tradition just as there was about the priesthood. At Oxford University I read music in the 1960s. There were 6 women and 36 men in my year. At the time I saw it as a great privilege to be accepted into this world of men. Most of the men whom I sat beside had experienced the wealth of church music (in the style of which we had to write) day in day out as cathedral choristers. They had proceeded to Oxford as choral scholars where they were able to continue in this wonderful form of music education. As a member of that previous all-male preserve I came to the conclusion that one of the reasons that choirs have stayed male is social. The social structure cannot accommodate women. It is built on male ideas and the mores are male; it is like a men's club with its songs, pubs and cricket. This produces two dilemmas for women:

- The absence of role models
- The inability to find a place in a community consisting largely of men

Diana Harris's article in this area starts with economic issues:

> Economics are coming to the aid of women. Historically, cathedral schools were set up to educate the choristers. In time they took in other boys to supplement their income and now many also take girls. Westminster Abbey is now the sole school to teach just choristers. Salisbury and Wells now also have girls in the choir, as has St Mary's in Edinburgh. Some churches however are taking backward steps. In Bury St Edmunds, Harrison Oxley ran boys and girls successfully for several years before a new dean ordered its cessation. Oxley thereupon resigned in protest. The fear at the back of this reluctance to accept women and girls is seen by many women as an acknowledgement that they could do the job just as well. There are, however, problems to look at in respect of girls in choirs. In some churches where this has been tried the boys have left. The main reason for this is that boys feel uncomfortable with girls. Girls develop earlier and are more proficient at language skills than boys at a similar age. There is also the question of the natural cut-off age. When boys' voices break they leave the choir but often return as men when their voices mature. Girls do not have this problem and there would be no need to leave the choir. They would remain as sopranos or altos allowing no new spaces for either boys or girls. If the boys left because they did not feel comfortable with the girls there would be no tradition to come back as men. Although men and boys together can fulfil all the parts in the choir, women and girls could not and the music would suffer ...

> As in many walks of life, the question of what is in the public or the private domain is often of the essence. At the top of the Church of England the important salaried positions are all male. Beneath this, in the less prestigious unpaid jobs, and in many non-conformist churches, it is the women who are keeping the church music going both as organists and in the choir. (Harris 2002 pp. 6–7)

There are still not women's voice choirs serving the cathedrals of the Anglican tradition in the UK; and whereas men can sing in the main churches from the age of seven well into their middle if not their old age, women must still leave around the age of puberty. As I write this, headlines proclaim that a 'Choir of female voices performs at Canterbury for first time.'[8] It was with some excitement that I read this and then I found that the women/girls are aged twelve to sixteen. I can only hope that it is the beginning of a journey that in the end will include mature women's voices. This phenomenon of exclusion results in such curious anomalies as the song of a pregnant woman, the *Magnificat*, sung regularly to settings by male composers by an all-male choir (see below).

In the view of the wider society, the result of this has been that choirs including men have been regarded as more worthy of attention than the women's voice choir. This has more often been the subject of ridicule where they exist in such organisations as the Mother's Union and the Townswomen's Guild. Only in women's barbershop traditions and in black women's choral groups has this tradition been developed, using women on the lower parts, in a compass usually associated with the male tenor. Contemporary women like Adey Grummet and the Curate's Egg and Barbara Thornton and Sequentia are working hard to right this balance but there is scope for much more work here.

Because of the power of the value systems prevailing in this tradition, the average English parish church choir, short as it usually is of men, does not solve this by developing a women's voice tradition, but carries on with

---

8   Mail Online Feb 1st 2014 <http://www.dailymail.co.uk/news/article-2546452/
     Hallelujah-Its-girls-allowed-Choir-female-voices-performs-Canterbury-time.html>
     Accessed Feb 1st 2014.

the struggle to continue the mixed-voice choir tradition. But the tradition has a stranglehold:

> The Kings College Cambridge choral tradition has done for church music what Barbie has done for women.[9]

The results of this are that local choirs consisting primarily of women still aspire to use the same repertoire as an ancient university choir backed by huge financial resources. Why are there not diverse repertoires that suit different constituencies and levels of experience? Why do we have a single standard that all aspire to? How much dissatisfaction and how many hierarchies have been generated by having a single style that governs the notion of what is good? The advent of the worship song has, to some extent, broken this mould by using a totally different style; but there is potential for a greater variety rather than simply the two styles.

Only in some female religious communities has the development of a women's voice tradition occurred. Ironically still, as we saw in renaissance Italy in Chapter 4, the process of enclosing women both put them in the control of the prevailing patriarchy, and also gave women within them a freedom not possible anywhere else in a patriarchal culture. One enclosed woman's community in the UK had as its Mother Superior a gold medal pianist from the Royal Academy of Music. She established there a fine distinctive chanting tradition. Nowhere else in the musical world of the 1920s would she have had sufficient standing to have such musical authority. The Community of the Sisters of the Church produced a beautiful collection based on the considerable amount of material that they produce for such events as the Advent meditation (Sisters of the Church 1996). It is, indeed, arguable that women-only areas have been demolished too quickly in English culture; such institutions as single-sex schools or women-only religious communities gave real opportunities for female musicians.

9   This quotation comes from a monk from S.S.J.E. speaking in the US. It has caused a great deal of mixed responses – discussion, anger and rejoicing. It is interesting that it does not originate from feminist circles but from a male religious.

Composing for mainstream churches is even less open to women than performing. This reflects the wider world of music making as seen in Chapter 2. Diana Harris's survey in this area revealed: 'of the women composing music, few seem to be writing religious music' (Harris 2002 p. 1).

This is partly because music in the Protestant traditions has to be accessible to amateur choirs and even the cathedral choirs contain young children. There is therefore a necessity for a simplicity of approach that does not come easily to contemporary composers. Therefore many women choose to write pieces for the concert hall based on religious and spiritual themes, like Louise Talma, born a Protestant converted to Catholicism. She has written much liturgical music but chooses texts from the bible and religious poems. Here women run into the same problems as their sisters who choose secular themes:

> Some of the reasons for the lack of performance of church music written by women are secular. Kendal Kirkland has written a Requiem for soloists, choir, organ and rock band, with libretto by Ian Florance and arranged by Rod Iliffe. She does not come from a musical background although she has always sung in choirs and written songs for her rock group. Her Requiem, written as a memorial to her father, is a mixture of different styles ranging from Gregorian chant to heavy rock. One of her problems in getting performances, publication or recording, is that it does not fit into a category. (Harris 2002 p. 15)

This was a problem we saw in Chapter 1. When women do write pieces for liturgy it is difficult to get them used. The book *Composing Music for Worship* (Darlington and Kreider 2003) contains 9 chapters by men and only 2 by women writers – Janet Wootton on the hymn and Roxanna Panufnik on writing a Mass for Westminster Cathedral. Seeing the number of women writing today for a variety of occasions, it is lamentable that the balance is so poor, and weighted so much towards classical composers and university professors. The patriarchal control of the public face through the old boy network shows no sign of relaxing its control.

It was for this reason that I set up the Magnificat project, as a millennium project to encourage some settings by women of the canticles for Evening Prayer. My original application ran:

> The Magnificat, which was originally sung by a woman delighting in her pregnancy, has been regularly sung in churches throughout the millennium. It is allied with the Nunc Dimittis – the song of an old man. This demonstrates a beautiful balance of experience within the service. Sadly this balance is not reflected in the music used for these two canticles. (Publicity sheet for the Magnificat Project Boyce-Tillman 2002b)

Startup funding was provided by Women in Theology and the commissioning money was provided by Women in Music supported by an Arts Council of England National Lottery award. Initially I approached a range of women from various styles and traditions. A screening committee included a principal and assistant cathedral organist (a woman), a woman cathedral canon, a representative of the Royal School of Church Music and a woman composer with experience of church music. One problem was that some of the leading women composers, although they may once have been interested in writing liturgical music, they no longer feel comfortable doing so. Many had given up on the perceived misogyny of the Church and saw more possibilities in the secular world.

Other aspects of the project were not as straightforward as I had expected. Women's exclusion from the world of church music has led, as described above, to them not having the long firsthand experience of the tradition. Indeed, many of the women I asked were so angry about the Church's general treatment of women that they were not interested in the project. Because of the link with Women in Theology which was committed to inclusive language I wanted to use versions of the canticles which were inclusive. But it soon became clear that cathedral Evensong is locked into the 1662 text from the Book of Common Prayer and that settings using other texts would not be used. Somewhat regretfully, I had to accept this decision.

The committee often showed a variety of views on the issues. The central argument was that the important thing was not who it was by, but whether it was good. There was no room for discussion about who set the standards by which 'good' was defined. The men had the positions of power and they set the standards. This was considered by some of the committee to be unproblematic. There was a dispute about the necessity for role models for women; for some of the Committee this was no problem; all women needed to do was to learn to write in the appropriate style.

It became clear that feminist debates had either not reached or had been resisted by some of the Committee, in a way that is familiar to women composers in many situations.

In the end we had six settings (some for SATB and some for SSA). The pieces were from women from a variety of traditions – some well-established classical composers, some from more popular traditions, and some with more experience in the area of liturgical music. Few of them still had a relationship with the Church. All of them found it difficult to write simply enough for a situation that includes children as young as seven with limited rehearsal time. In general, the pieces are quite complex for this context but some have been sung in liturgical settings. It has been quite difficult to get the settings around the cathedrals. As I tried to get the compositions better known I moved rapidly between from being hopeful to being discouraged, as I felt by the weight of the male-dominated tradition closing around me.

Martha Ann Kirk's doctorate, carried out 1980–86, was one of the first in the area of women in liturgy. She is a Roman Catholic Sister of the Order of the Sisters of Charity of the Incarnate Word of San Antonio, Texas, which she entered in 1962. Her thesis drew attention to the absence of women's work from the standard hymnals in the public domain:

> Oregon Catholic Press, for instance, had about one or two percent. They had some Bernadette Farrell songs, some had Susan Toolan's[10] *and I will raise you up ...* I ever did things like call the General Editor of GIA, the major liturgical publisher in th United States ... I can remember him on the telephone, saying 'But people don't wai or need women's music,' and ... so many things would make me so angry, and I wou say, 'Now try to transform the anger into creativity. Don't get stuck in the anger. I this feeling that you have, give you the strength for doing creative things.' (Kirk 20

Like Marsie Silvestro, she was empowered by the movement for wom ordination in the Roman Catholic Church in 1975:

> 'What is women's place in liturgy? Are the words of women used in official lit of the Church?' and so ... I was searching official liturgical books – some Comn services that mediaeval nuns led or Offices that women led; I kept saying, '

---

10   These women wrote both text and tune together.

words of women in official prayers of the Church?' and then another aspect of
this would be, 'Are women's words in hymns – have women been the composers of
hymns?' So, again I was so delighted when I found Hildegard. And ... I've started a
book on liturgical dramas; I was trying to find out if women were authors of miracle
or mystery plays, or other liturgical dramas ... I was excited about Hildegard doing
musical dramas, and things like that. (Silvestro 2003)

She sees the problem in the public domain as lying in its patriarchal nature
which excludes women from positions of authority:

[The situation in the hymnals] has improved ... but not enough. It – and the whole
Catholic music world – is so political ... It really doesn't have to do with talent. It has
to do with connections, and then when they have big conventions, it's the companies
trying to make money that sponsor the persons who are doing workshops and doing
major presentations at conventions – so it's sort of a self-perpetuating world of the 'old
boys' club'. But there are, you know, some women getting in; I think my point is it's
not that women are not talented and women are not creative, but it's that they don't
have the networks to get into the major hymnals; the major liturgical conferences ...

I was asking these questions. 'Have women ever done official liturgical books in
the history of the Church?' I would go to the male professors, and they would start
laughing, like they thought it was some sort of absurd question. And I was, like
'Well, it's an important question.' I mean, we're half the people in Christianity, and
our voices and our thoughts and our emotions, and our expressions are important
... I was looked upon as a troublemaker. (Silvestro 2003)

However, alternative worship groups can be a place for women to find a
more public voice. Mary Ermey (2003), musical director of the Hildegard
Community in Austin, Texas, was working on a music drama based on
Mary Magdalene, drawing on Gnostic sources when I interviewed her. She
outlined how the community had helped her find her voice:

It's a story of a woman who found her voice and I think I feel like St Hildegard's has
been a place for me to find my voice and – through music, and in other ways as well ...

This was the finding of a voice that she thought she had lost through child
bearing. She described how bearing her child had affected the public expression of her musical creativity, causing her to abandon her doctorate in
Composition. (Ermey 2003)

At the Society of St Margaret in Boston, Massachusetts, I met the Mother Superior, Carolyn Darr, and Sister Christina Frances (2003). Sister Christina is setting about making public the compositions of the nun composers we have already met in Chapter 4. She was very excited about finding these pieces in the Harvard library and found it amazing that music of this quality had not survived the processes of music history.

Carolyn Darr (2003) had been a choral conductor and organist before she joined the order. She described an encounter with a visiting conductor from the Royal School of Church Music in England who was surprised to find a woman conductor of her standing conducting a choir of boys and men. Trained in the US, her experience of England was that it was a far more difficult place for women than the US. She had tried to open up the roles available to the sisters in the Order and had seven cantorixes. She allows sisters like Sister Christina Francis to go out to sing in the wider community when appropriate. All the nuns are encouraged to sing in order to establish the community, and this is considered more important than a 'perfect' sound. They sing a great deal, sometimes importing two men to make a four-part choir, otherwise singing in two or three parts. Sometimes there is a space in the service for people to initiate music spontaneously. There is some attempt at inclusive language, although male words for God are acceptable. Here we see a deliberate attempt to rebalance the dominant culture by:

- increasing the amount of freedom
- encouraging an inclusive community and allowing people to realise their potential
- rediscovering women's music from the past

So the more public spaces in Christianity (as in the wider society) are often difficult for women to enter. However, smaller alternative worshipping spaces may have an important part to play as a route to more public expression and a reclaiming of musical creativity after times of domestic engagement like child-rearing.

2b Product/Process

Many of the alternative liturgy groups are working in an orate way musically as they lack anyone with a grasp of musical notation. There is a desire in such a situation where people lack confidence to 'play-safe'. This often leads to music being tailor-made for particular situations and reworked by various leaders of the group. The publication *Women Included* grew out of the St Hilda Community in London. They use traditional hymns and carols, Taizé chants, and sometimes other chants (e.g. Peruvian) taught by members of the group. They sometimes make up dances to music but 'have not got very far in writing our own hymns' (St Hilda Community 1991).

For the Britain and Ireland School of Feminist Theology in Liverpool Hope University entitled *Dreams for a Dazzling Millennium* I put together a liturgy throughout the week from offerings that women chose to give to me. These included songs, ideas, names of people, and issues of justice. I was putting it together as the conference progressed and it included improvised musical episodes such as a group hum holding the energy of the group while people sang or spoke their prayers over it. It included the use of improvised sounds as we crossed over the River Jordan to the land flowing with milk and honey. Although for me too there is a security in knowing where you are, many participants enjoyed this method of group creation which led to a great variety of material being used for various liturgical acts.

Carl Daw (2003) of the American Hymn Society saw a technique of holding a chord and improvising a petition over the top, a possibility I had explored with children in *New Orbit* (Smith and Boyce 1972 pp. 154–7). He saw it as easier with children and those brought up in the call and response traditions of Africa. It was hard to get started with adults without this experience.

Diann Neu (2003) in her women's group called WATER[11] in Washington DC uses more chants than actual hymns. It is mostly professional and white in its makeup which is a sadness for Diann Neu with the

11   WATER acronym = Women's Alliance for Theology, Ethics and Ritual.

amount of racism in Washington DC. Her liturgies are for smaller groups where she considers them more appropriate than hymns. Sometimes she uses a soloist for chorus songs. She identifies the lack of musical expertise in the group, but sees the situation as improving as more women get to know the repertoire. She claimed not to be a composer herself although she had composed as a child. However, at the time of the interview she had a child of her own and talked about making up lullabies and other songs to amuse and nurture her baby.

Caroline Wilkins (2003) is an African American who at the time of the interview was musical director of the Jazz Service at First Church in Cambridge, Massachusetts. From her experience of the jazz tradition she was able to use the process of improvisation effectively in worship. The Service which took place at 5.30pm on Sunday in the Church Hall had been running for about four years. Each week she had a budget to hire two people to form a jazz trio with her as pianist, usually a saxophonist/bass and a drummer. She saw music as vital in worship because it allows us to get in touch with emotions and energies that are not easily expressed. Her background was in religious music as the granddaughter of a minister:

> One of the exciting things about this [the Jazz] Service was that I was given the freedom to be able to choose the kind of music that I wanted, as long as I felt that it would fit, without having to be sort of in a straitjacket ... A lot of Churches that have gospel, for example, do not have jazz because they feel that jazz is a secular music, whereas Gospel is a sacred music. So this Church, since it was a new service and a new thing, I think they were a little more open to just allowing all different kinds of things to come in as long as the intent was worshipful and respectful of this place ...

She saw that in this service process and product were balanced with set pieces and improvisatory at different points in the service:

> When I was in the Baptist Church – [they prized] 'get the Spirit'! No, no, no, no, no. Forget about that. I think the fact that they clap [in this service] is a big accomplishment! ... You can't allow yourself to be overcome too much because then you lose control ... This kind of service is not like a Pentecostal Service or something where you could get excited and shout ... You can't do that. This is a Congregational Church. Our Service starts at 5.30 and goes to a quarter of seven. So, you know, there's a certain element of control, and I think that there's a certain level of emotion – over-emotion

– that people are not necessarily comfortable with. So my job is to be able to feel the energy, feel the connection with Spirit and bring that through and translate it into something that people do feel comfortable with and that works for them.

In Caroline's work, we see a number of themes:

- A discovery of a more process based musical experience through jazz
- The sense of an inflowing Spirit informing her creativity
- The desire to have more structure than the freer practice of more free charismatic traditions
- An embracing of variety

So women's groups use and have developed an orate tradition, arising often from their sense of inadequacy musically. This has not led to an improvisatory tradition, but has resulted in people willing to try out new material within them. So the women become an important part of the process of musical creation.

3a Excitement/Relaxation

We have already seen how as an antidote to the triumphalism of much music in the mainstream churches, expressed in loud organs and on ceremonial occasions by brass instruments, has been that softer sounds have been validated and some instruments have acquired gendered characteristics. This is sometimes associated with the notion of acknowledging women's suffering and vulnerability and also pacifistic belief systems. So at the Women's Synod in Harare in 2001 there was a real reluctance to include a trumpet in the liturgy, and at large gatherings in venues with an organ and someone to play it, a debate often ensues about how patriarchal an instrument it is.

The London group of the Catholic Women's Network (now Women Word Spirit) has been meeting regularly for many years. It is all women, many of them Roman Catholic, but including several Anglicans. Its meetings start with a liturgy and end with a shared meal. The music used varies from singing to or listening to tapes. The singing is often unaccompanied although there is sometimes a guitar. Sources are Iona songs, my songs, *Reflecting Praise*, Miriam Therese Winter, the Taizé tradition, Carolyn McDade and specially written songs. Circle dances are regularly used. There is an established character of softness and gentleness associated in the minds of the planners with nurturing. Occasionally I bring the drum which changes the energy but there is an awareness that this is a radical change from the norm.

Since I have taken to playing the drum it has been interesting to see how some communities accept and embrace it while others do not. The long tradition of women not playing the drum seems to still be present in the psyche of western women who would feel themselves emancipated in many ways. It is, in my opinion, an indication of where Christian women stand in relation to their suffering, particularly that inflicted by the Church. There sometimes seems to be a desire to stay in that suffering tradition rather than claiming the power through the use of the drum. Gradually I am hoping that this might change. I find it exciting to enter the male tradition. A London taxi driver lifting my drum bag remarked on its weight; I told him it contained a drum. 'You are the last sort of person I thought would be carrying something like that' he commented. 'Well, you learn a new thing every day' I replied. I felt proud of challenging the tradition, and saw myself returning to the time when the women of Europe might have played the drums.

I spoke to Elisa Lucozzi (2003), who was brought up in the Roman Catholic Church; she sang in the church and school choirs which she enjoyed as an intergenerational activity. She learned the drum at Emerson College, US. She called it 'Recovering our Spirit'.

I decided I was going to go play the drum on my own. It's a little bit of a rebellion from the way I grew up – 'You must be pious; you must be quiet; you must be silent, to praise God.' ... I'm an extrovert ... The drum somehow connects with my Lesbianism ... It's about bucking stereotypes ... The drum is always considered more of a masculine instrument, and when you play correctly you can't sit ladylike

You feel that, once you get into Church, you've got to move to a product model, but there's nowhere for process ... I think eventually you come to the place where, 'O.K. Let's just move to the music, and whatever comes out, comes out.' (Lucozzi 2003)

There is a freedom to experiment in her philosophy and to take risks. She questions her inspiration, valuing her intuition:

You know, a piece of music was poured into me from above, but I definitely feel like it churns inside of me and ... it comes together with my own experience, and, 'What is the message? What is God trying to teach me? What's God trying to show me?'

I have in my life, through my kind of journey of recovering from sexual abuse, had times where all groups of us have gotten together and created rituals around whoever we were now healing. (Lucozzi 2003)

Elisa's story shows her finding her own power through the drum (which is connected with her sexuality), and using it for healing rituals. It shows her love of the process-based liturgy. Ana Hernandez trusts the power of the drum as the conduit of the Spirit:

Drums are the external manifestation of your heartbeat ... I'm not really sure whether there's a theology of the drum, but rhythm in general is very important for people's health. (Hernandez 2003)

Diann Neu in WATER in Washington DC uses music with a variety of expressive characters:

In the Peace Liturgy book ... I really went back to chant there, the chants of the sixties, interfacing with the Gregorian Chant, into some of the peace songs that the Women's Movement had created ... I put spirituals in frequently, and you get ... the laments through the spirituals, and ... *We shall overcome* ... When that song was written, the way that it was sung was to cross your wrists in front of you with the right over the left, and to hold onto people – hold hands, to keep the circle tight, so, in fact ... the police couldn't break into that circle. So, when I teach that song, I always teach the history of it. (Neu 203 interview)

She uses drums sometimes for themes associated with violence but warned about the problem of appropriation of Native American traditions. So the use of more energising instruments can produce a sense of empowerment but some groups are not entirely comfortable with their character.

3b Challenge/Nurture

Many of these alternative groups see the nurturing of their members as paramount. The Chapel of Holy Rood House,[12] Yorkshire is committed to health and healing based on the Wisdom tradition. It uses *Reflecting Praise* (Boyce-Tillman and Wootton 1993) and *A Rainbow to heaven* (Boyce-Tillman 2006a) regularly and is a mixed community. Because the Rev Elizabeth Baxter who leads the community has a confident singing voice, the songs are often unaccompanied. New material is embraced and written by members of the community and guests. If there are suitable members of the house team a singing group is formed. Music is regularly played on tape when the healing ministry of the laying-on of hands is administered; the community uses circle dances regularly. Music is used therapeutically with the guests, which sometimes means that there are instrumental improvisations in Chapel. There is a real sense here that music is there to nurture guests and make them feel accepted so that crying is accepted as a regular part of liturgies.

The work of contemporary modernist composers with its challenging dissonances finds no place in these groups although contemporary composers like John Tavener do find a place.[13] There is some use of pieces from classical and romantic periods and Hildegard of Bingen recordings are popular for listening and as a background for meditation. I find it sad that

---

12   <http://www.holyroodhouse.org.uk/>.
13   John Tavener would not regard himself as a modernist composer (Interview 2004 *A Portrait of John Tavener*).

some of these groups are unaware of the rediscovery of women composers of these periods – like Clara Schumann and Fanny Mendelssohn – which are now recorded and available. Although they would try to use prayers and poetry by women,[14] they are happy to use music by men. Again, their lack of confidence often results in a clinging to the familiar.

There has been a problem with modernism in more public worship, although modernist composers – both men and women – have written for worship. There is a sense in which in a challenging world, worship needs to be nurturing and the dissonances of avant garde composers are not that in the minds of many congregations. So the more dissonant sounds of both male and female contemporary composers have not been readily accepted. This is problematic for a generation of women composers who were brought up in modernism. So when they write for the Church (as in the Magnificat project) the music is regarded as too difficult. As there is no music from women of the past for liturgy, it is difficult to see where settings of liturgical texts by women are going to come from.

Ana Hernandez (2003) specialises in the use of chant in liturgy. She has a strong sense of the healing, nurturing power of music:

> Those things [chants], they really work on you. They change you.

She has a strong sense of the spiritual origins of her creativity and of approaching community and holiness through encouraging congregational singing to lead to:

> that magic place – that ineffable 'Godness' – that mysterious place that we try to get to all the time. I try to get everybody to go there ... and not just have the congregation listen to the choir going there ... I want the people to feel the vibrations in their bodies because I think that, only when you feel your own vibrations, do you have a sense of how much of God there is in you. (Hernandez 2003)

Her God is undoubtedly feminine but Ana is critical of feminism:

---

14   There are exceptions. Dianne Neu in WATER in Washington DC (see Embodiment/ Disembodied below) has a strong policy only to use women's music in the liturgies as a way of educating people in what women have created.

[God] is only feminine for me because of that whole thing of being made in God's image; when I look in the damn mirror, I see a girl ... My family is fairly matriarchal ... And I think I've just always loved that phrase of '... being made in God's image.' ... I just know we are, and I have no doubt about that ... I also trust that when Johnny looks in the mirror, that he's made in God's image too ...

I find that feminists are still fighting to get out of the box ... I just play in it sometimes, but I don't have to live in it ... And sometimes I feel, when I'm in Church, I'm playing in the box. But God is what's outside of the box as well; and so I spend most of my time outside of the box ... I tend to find people who are wonderful everywhere ... I've been told on numerous occasions that I'm not a Christian by lots of people who call themselves Christian, but you know that's that Church thing. There's a joke ... saying 'You're a Christian because you go to Church is like saying that because you're standing in a garage, that you're a car'... I have been a part of a number of worshipping, separate groups, both women's and mixed and ... they tend to have their life and then lose steam, and then people go their separate ways. (Hernandez 2003)

She sees God as inclusive:

You know how the Church can be ... God's big – inclusive – quirky as hell, but being inclusive ... I am a priest, but not in the normal kind of a collar. A number of priests call me a priest, but you know, I laugh at them and I say, 'No, you are a Priest. I am a musician.'
   ... I really don't like the hierarchy. I really don't like to be under anybody's authority except God. God and I get along just fine. I don't want to put anybody else in the way. (Hernandez 2003)

Ana has a profound sense of God through an intuitive creativity. Various themes emerge from her story:

- The relationship of music with nurture and healing
- The need to democratise worship
- A dissatisfaction with the hierarchies and formal structures of the Church
- A natural embracing of a feminine dimension of the Divine
- The use of a variety of instruments and expressive character in worship

In terms of inclusive language, women practitioners are divided about it – often because this makes an added difficulty in getting their material accepted by the wider church community. The jazz composer Carolyn Wilkins does use both male and female images for God in her own writing:

'Mother, give me strength to make it through this day. Give me the power to overcome my weaknesses. Mother, guide my feet along the upward way. Spirit, fill me
with your love.' ... That's mine, and that reflects, you know, my own kind of personal
feelings about spirituality, and a nice thing about this church is that they've been
open to doing that; some of the more traditional churches ... it wouldn't work. It's
welcomed here. (Wilkins 2003)

Martha Ann Kirk, a liturgical dancer, described a number of projects like her
dance to the song *Bakerwoman God*, which was followed by *Washerwoman
God*. Here she explored more nurturing feminine images for God

We call you 'mighty God, leader of armies, King of Kings',
But you are Washerwoman God,
We know you when the water is splashing, laughing free.
If you didn't clean the mess, where would we be?
Splashing, laughing, dancing God,
Freeing you and me,
Make our hearts as white as snow,
Wash us through and through,
Washerwoman God, Let us be like You ...

Think about the sacramental system – men washing away our sins, and tears, and
God washing the earth with rain, ... If it's all right to have metaphors of God as war-
rior and God as a bulwark, and, you know – God as king, why can't we celebrate the
metaphors of God who is cleaning and purifying us? One verse is ... 'You wash the
dirty diapers', and I like to think a lot that Grace is like our mothers who washed
us and our dirty diapers. While we were still in our sin, God loved us and came to
us, and while we were in our dirty diapers, someone loved us first, and it is that first
love – it is that first Grace that gives us a chance to grow and draws forth love and
draws forth goodness in us.
    I think one of the most important uses of that song *Washerwoman God* has been
at the Nevada nuclear test site ... I was invited as the main liturgical dancer to be a
part of things there. So, on the edge of the test site, he and one of the Franciscan
leaders were presiding at Eucharist; I was invited to read the liturgy of the word, and
do a ritual with a very large globe where there's sort of a poetic reading about how
we have been polluting the air and polluting the water and polluting the top soil,
and I'm sort of miming the putting of this gook – this mud – all over this globe as
this poetic reading is going on, and then ... I talked about at the Last Supper, Jesus
started to wash the feet of His Disciples, and Peter got angry, and we know that
servants washed feet, but also wives washed feet. So Jesus was acting like a woman;

he was acting like a slave, and that made Peter angry because he was upsetting the power system. And this continues through the ages, that people get upset when we flip over the power system, and so we need to remember Christ who washed feet. We need to clean up the nuclear messes in the world; we need to clean up other messes, and perhaps the God that we need is 'Washer Woman, God', and I go into dancing that. (Kirk 2003)

She exhorts women hymn writers to celebrate the nurturing God – who washes feet, cleanses us, teaches us to wash dirty diapers, the cleaning God. This is also a God who cares for our bodies:

> We are the body of Christ, birthing, feeding, touching, weeping,
> We are the body of Christ, mending, healing, dancing.
> Glorify God in your bodies.
> Glorify God in your loves. (Kirk 2003)

She delights in the woman's body using images like the Renaissance nuns in Chapter 4:

> We are the body of Christ, birthing ... and all the imagery of Baptism is new birth and life. The mediaeval mystics so often look on the wound in Christ's side and the Eucharist as nurturing from the breast as a mother nurtures from the breast; so I was working with that image. (Kirk 2003)

She loves the image of the darkness of the womb:

> The Hebrew word ... – compassion ... [comes] from the root word for womb, and ... we're saying that God is like someone who has a womb; and I can remember praying in the dark Chapel at night, and having this sense of being in God's womb of mercy where I am re-created and renewed, so that next morning I would be fresh and new and vibrant and exuberant, and not loaded down with incoming doubts and burdens ... So then I was doing visual art, then I was doing sort of a dance, drama, ritual of being born from God's womb, and then Colleen was seeing this dance/drama ritual, and she wrote a song *(sings)*
>
> 'Rahamin, Compassion. Rahamin, Rahamin.
> Womb of God, Compassion. Rahamin, Rahamin.
> Even if a mother forgets her own child,
> I will never forget you.' (Kirk 2003)

Sister Robyn Reynolds (2003) saw the problems of introducing inclusive language into Nugalinya Chapel in Darwin, Australia. She tried to change existing songs like making the Spirit 'she', which did not always find acceptance with the aboriginal women's position. They are concerned about the men in their communities and wish to retain the masculinist words to support and encourage them.

4a Rational/Intuitive

The alternative worshipping groups often encourage discussion and it is a place where people can explore and discuss experiences which they might find difficult to share in the wider society. They are places where the more intuitive is valued and the more circular forms of music – repetitive and meditative – can find a place.

This is also happening in liturgical music in more public spaces. Here the more rational crafter tradition of the hymn is being challenged by the rise of repetitive, meditative chanting traditions. This has made more repetitive forms of construction more acceptable in church music of many denominations.

This is partly due to the influence of events outside of Christianity. Chanting is an important part of New Age culture (and has influenced Christian groups of one kind or another). The chants are drawn from a variety of traditions. Hindu mantras are popular alongside a revival of Gregorian traditions and the Native American traditions provide a very popular source. The practice of overtone chanting has been adapted from traditions found among Tibetan monks and Siberian shamans. Jill Purce has produced her own particular synthesis of singing techniques from many traditions, specialising in overtone chanting in order to 're-enchant' Western culture (Purce 1998).

The Hildegard Community, Austin, Texas, US, at the time of my visit, used a variety of material reflecting a balance between the rational and more intuitive approaches to liturgical music. The musical director was Mary Ermey who was originally Organist and Choir Director at an Episcopal Church (Members of the Hildegard Community 2003). The main differences she saw between the Hildegard Community's music and that of a traditional Episcopalian Church were:

- The focus on congregational singing. Almost entirely everything is sung by the whole congregation and there is no choir. There are sometimes solos, including the Exultet at the Easter Vigil. In the traditional Church she saw people as just following the organ. In the Community she uses the guitar which puts a greater responsibility on the singers. She sees singing as 'a genuine sacrament of community'. (Ermey 2003)
- The notion of diversity of languages had been an issue because of the Episcopal Church's commitment to worship in the language of the people. They use other material from Africa, Mexico, Cuba, South America which sees Christianity as a global family.
- The openness of the Hildegard Community to new material.
- The feeling of being part of a team 'and not just have to do what I'm told.'
- An ecology of the feminine in God who she thinks of 'less as a single individual person as this concept of spirit and kind of this all-encompassing metaphor for goodness that I can relate to in a personal way ... There's kind of no limits for me as to what God is.'
- The spiritual discipline with regular meetings with her accountability partner and commitment to physical health, psychological health. (Members of the Hildegard community 2003)

She had a real sense of her music coming from a God within.

So these alternative spaces can favour more circular forms of construction and more intuitive ways of working. People can still talk about being inspired by the Spirit without fear of the ridicule that they would meet in wider musical circles including those associated with liturgy. More repetitive, meditative music is finding a place in more public worship largely through the popularity of Taizé traditions and composers like Margaret Rizza (2004).

Practitioners' accounts of their own processes do include the intuitive. Joy Webb (2003), the Salvationist, values the intuitive, seeing her work as driven by the Spirit and describes how she receives the songs in the silence.

But that does not preclude hard work which she does at the piano; so she values the crafting process alongside the initial inspiration. She always writes things down, sometimes writing on buses with the pencil and the paper that she always carries. She criticised the younger generation for not being prepared to work hard enough at the songs they write.

Ana Hernandez has a highly intuitive approach running through all her practice. She trusts intuition in her creativity:

> I'm just banging around on these … drums with two … mallets and playing a pattern, and all of a sudden a tune will show up and then I'll realise – 'Hey, this really works.' And then, I would sit for hours on the door jamb to the back yard, trying to be able to sing them and play them at the same time. (Hernandez 2003)

Noirin ni Riain now lives and works at Glenstal Abbey:

> Glenstal is a wonderful place to live out that expression of the divine. I'd been coming here way before I met any of the monks. (Ni Riain 2013)

She describes how she found her confidence to sing through finding a power beyond herself:

> Then I found the answer – it's not you. It's not my will be done, it's thy will. There is a force – call it whatever you will – much bigger than us … You just go into a space, beyond yourself. I find that's the same for singing. I just go into a different space, so I don't worry about any of the things I used to worry about – 'will I break down? Will I forget the words? Will anyone like me?' That all goes. I am just the outlet for that sound to communicate. (Ni Riain 2013)

This has led her to a project leading chant workshops around the world:

> Clearly, despite being now 62, Noirin has no plans for a quieter life. Quite the opposite. 'I've never been as busy in my whole life as I am now, but it's a lovely busy-ness,' she says. As well as teaching two days a week in Limerick, she runs regular chant workshops in Glenstal, and most recently has begun leading groups to sacred sites around the world.
>
> 'We're starting in Ireland, then going to Iona, then Jerusalem,' she said …
>
> What does she think is the secret to her extraordinary vitality, a kind of self-contained dynamism that hums within? 'I do think about my age all right,' she says, 'but I think meditation, alone-ness which is different to loneliness, it enhances your being …' (Ni Riain 2013)

Noirin's work includes both Christian and pre-Christian Celtic material alongside material like *Abide With Me*, *Regina Caeli* and Kyries. She laments women's position in the Church:

> 'God herself', she sometimes says – so how does she reconcile that with a Church where women are not fully welcome? 'It is weird', she says. 'By its silence, the Church is perpetuating the idea that women are inferior. And I don't think that is going to change. Certainly not in my lifetime. That's what draws me to Glenstal – you don't have that misogyny.' Does she really not feel that here? There is a long pause. Then, 'No ...', another hesitation, 'There is something here that has great respect for women. Of course it's very clear that I can't be a member of a community, because of my earthly genitalia. And that's the only reason. But here, in Glenstal Abbey, it's about a new time, new beginnings.' (Ni Riain 2013)

So in Noirin's work we see themes we met in other singers – a lamenting of the Church's misogyny and a strong intuitive sense of the presence of the Divine.

4b Embodied/Disembodied

Dance and dramatic elements using the bodies of participants has found a ready acceptance in these alternative groups. Circle dancing is very popular; simple dramatic gestures, such as putting flowers in a pot for intercessions or bringing sacred objects to create a sacred place, are common aspects of the liturgies. Many groups are concerned with embodying feminist principles.

Diann Neu (2003 interview) was concerned with embodying a passion for justice making when she started WATER in 1983 with Mary Hunt. They were forward-thinking enough to know that it needed to be ecumenical and interfaith in its make-up, and so they gathered a group of thirteen women together to create the Women's Alliance for Theology, Ethics and Ritual, so producing the acronym WATER, a powerful feminist symbol.

They consistently had a Women's Ritual Group that met once a month. At the time of the visit, they were meeting on Sunday evenings every couple of weeks and are the oldest women-based community group in the United

States. It first started as Catholic women and from it has come many publications. *Women's Rights, Feminist Liturgies for Life's Journey* (2003) looks
at a woman's life's journey and starts from the birthing all the way through
to the crone, which has not been covered in traditional liturgies of the
Church. Its liturgies include – *A prayer for conception, Choosing an abortion* and *A blessing for a mother-to-be.* A whole section honours *Women's
Blood Mysteries*, moving from celebrating the beginning of menstruation,
through celebrating women's monthly cycle to the honouring of a crone
(Neu 2003). They often use movement in the liturgies at WATER which
Diann sees as the movement of the Spirit. She often uses circle dances and
also uses more dramatic ways of using readings and prayers.

Margarita Medina (2003), a Lutheran Pastor and art therapist, at
the time of the interview was organising liturgies for women's healing in
northern Germany:

> I am using music ... in my therapy [and liturgy] groups ... using the voice. I've dis-
> covered a very beautiful new CD, and it's called Ninna Nanna ... CD with lullabies
> from the 12th until the 20th Century. I had a group ... to help [participants] to grow
> better ... a mixture of liturgy group ... and therapy group ... I try a very special mix-
> ture ... It's not only therapy, and [its intention is] to develop the root forces every
> woman has, even if she had had a very bad trauma. So, for example, I choose only
> certain pieces of music to help them to get in contact with some hidden resources
> [like the lullaby]... I led a project ... called *The Voyage on the Rainbow* and we had
> twenty-five women for one year in a fixed group ... Women came directly from their
> work, and they got a glass of water to enter, and they had to pass through a golden
> cloth, to leave behind their daily life, and then the room was very specially arranged.
> We were sitting on the floor. This was a hall ... in a Church house ... In the middle
> there was like a big bowl with water and flowers and candles, and then they had to
> choose one cloth which might fit their mood ... unroll it, and knot it into a golden ...
> weave ... together ... This was a symbol for the group ... There was [recorded] music
> when they enter the room – maybe something African, Indian, Armenia. We tried
> to choose something ... not too strong, but unknown to them [to go into] a different
> space. We have some silence ... and some singing ... We always used to finish this first
> sharing [with a song]. It's a single line melody – a repetitive thing ... No percussion;
> no piano? Just voices ... We stood ... embracing – altogether, and ... (Medina 2003)

This description shows the desire to embody worship with a number of
sensual images. She was at pains to point out the democratic nature of the
group community. The power was coming from the song which had a line

that there should be a time for miracles. They had one drum. They started with grounding exercises and afterwards, after the music, they wrote poems in defined structures. To deepen the experience, they used an ocean drum – a drum with seeds inside that flow over the skin of the drum. In the main group they had a finger piano associated with a relaxation exercise. They used improvisation. All texts used inclusive language for human beings and God, including Shekinah, Sophia, or Holy Ruach.

Sister Robyn Reynolds (2003) of the Order of Our Lady of the Sacred Heart has worked within Central Australia with the aboriginal Arrernte people of the desert country there 'all of her living life'. She was a dancer before she entered the community. In 2003 she worked at Nungalinga College which is for the training of aboriginal leaders, including theology, textile studies and management. It is a mixed, ecumenical College. All the clients are adult aboriginal people. The relationship of music and dance to her life is important and coloured by her own experience of life with aboriginal people:

> Ballet gave me my first love of music, because I'm a dancer first of all ... Now the Aboriginal music and the dance ... taught me about life, because when you watch those Wadeye dancers – you see people together in a good, beautiful way, how life could be, because there's the uniqueness of each dancer ... There's a unity and an awareness of one another and a coming together at times ... [and] music is all part of this – not distinct from it, enhancing it, just carrying it along ... It's just when I look at those dancers; it's just how life should be ...
>
> I can ... hardly hear music without wanting to dance. I have to hold myself – no matter whether I'm on a tram or driving a car. Often I'm driving a car – I'll dance as I'm driving the Lincoln. You know, tap my feet ... I move the car with the dance. (Reynolds 2003)

She explains the universality of the dance creating community from different traditions:

> I remember my younger sister came once. She used to dance. She came to have a holiday and she danced to Stravinsky and Chopin. She did two different ones – up in the Hall one night and, oh! You could have heard a pin drop. People still talk about that – the old people. They would not have seen ballet before ... But my sister danced for them ... The next morning, up to the Convent the old men came to invite us down to the Creek camp that night, and they gave her a beautiful dance back in return. (Reynolds 2003)

Martha Ann Kirk is an embodied liturgist; she teamed up with Colleen Fulmer to use song and dance together. She is a woman who is able to use her body effectively as a tool:

> [I am] comfortable in my body. I started taking dance lessons when I was five years old, and so I did tap a little, but then I did more ballet and modern, and some jazz and acrobat ... It seemed perfectly natural ... Other children might play Monopoly or something like that ... when I went to that first Women's Ordination Conference ... she [Carla de Sola] danced in a Vespers Service ... I am fifty-seven, and it gets better all the time ... I am aware that I can't run as fast and jump as high as I could before; but I think I am also aware that my spirituality has deepened, and the most important thing is not running as fast and jumping as high. (Kirk 2003)

Martha has been concerned to embody the Gospel in a number of art forms. She has been concerned with a number of the themes we have seen in the work of others:

- The inclusion of feminine images of God
- The notion of creativity as a gift to be shared
- The idea of widening access to the Gospel
- The association of the arts with a passion for issues of justice

As a performer and composer, I have experimented with using feminist principles as the basis of performances. They include story, song, movement and instrumental improvisation in forms characterised by circular structures and explorations of themes like the medieval women mystics. Much more movement was introduced in the form of dances that were sung as I grew more confident in the use of my rotund and aging body. I had always wanted to be a dancer but was never the shape that is deemed necessary for progressing in Western traditions. I had admired more 'earthed' traditions like the dances of African women. I was also being increasingly aware that by performing as a middle-aged woman, I was challenging the perception that women of my age and shape do not perform in public. After performances, middle-aged women would come to me and say that I had transformed their world. I was initially perplexed but then realised that I challenged all the preconceptions about the female performing body that Western society has laid down. *Lunacy or The Pursuit of the Goddess* (Boyce-Tillman 2002b) became a clear way of presenting the subjugated ways of knowing outlined in the first chapter as a performance piece especially the goddesses of the underworld. After the performances, people are often not sure what they have just experienced: Was it a performance, or a meditation or storytelling? I am glad that I have developed a form that is different from those developed by patriarchy, based on the following principles:

- Circularity. Storytelling rather than the lecture is their basis.
- Interdisciplinarity. They all use as many different art forms as possible integrated one with the other.
- The role of the audience. The audience becomes more like a congregation, involved in singing, making sounds and moving. Most of them include a circle dance including the audience
- Empowerment. I do not use the trappings of the conventional theatre like lights and makeup. I wish to be as part of the audience as possible so that the audience feels 'I could do that'.
- Women and the body. It uses what my distinctive body can do.[15]
- Images of older women. It challenges contemporary images of women who have to appear young in order to appear in public.
- The context. I do not perform it in theatres but religious spaces (or out of doors). Here I use the surrounding iconography rather than carrying scenery and amplification with me. The concept is of a contextualised performance – using what is there rather than starting with an empty stage and filling it with props.

So women's liturgies and liturgical performances are attempting to use dance to bring together the body and soul again. This is less apparent in the more public spaces in the Church. After the popularity of liturgical dance in the 70s and 80s in the UK, it is now less in evidence. Some churches do attempt circle dances in worship and cathedrals will host days of circle dancing, seeing it as a form of prayer. Nevertheless, the layout of the average church is not conducive to it, especially if pews and steps are involved. The smaller groups with their flexible seating and often circular layout are more conducive to exploring embodied ways of worshipping.

---

15 I extended this idea by recording my own songs unaccompanied entitled *The Voice of Experience*. It was based on the idea that my body contains all my experience which is expressed through my voice without extending it by instruments.

Spirituality

The empowering of women in the more private musical sphere of alternative worshipping groups away from mainstream contexts has opened up all areas of musicking – composing, performing and listening – to a wider group of people. It is interesting to reflect that much of the work in this area has been done by women who were once or still are religious women in the Roman Catholic tradition, thus linking with Chapter 4 and the place that a life choice of celibacy plays in freeing women up for creative work. This widening of the pool of writers has opened access to the Spiritual/liminal experience to a wider group of people. It has removed some of the barriers set up but a patriarchal misogyny to women's access to this domain. So we find some women worshipping only in alternative groups where they see themselves having greater power of the ritual which includes the music. Most of the differences between these alternative groups and more public rituals have been in the area of Values as discussed in this chapter; but there are changes also in the instruments used and the greater use of unaccompanied singing. There are simpler forms in use – Construction uses more repetition. These changes have widened access to the Spiritual domain.

Summary

The examples that this chapter has drawn on show very different situations, all of them embracing feminist principles in one way or another in the context of communities. The themes that we see are:

- The sense of an alternative supportive community run on democratic lines with women claiming their authority
- A firm connection with the natural world
- The use of material from a variety of sources including interfaith ones often reworked from a feminist perspective like *Miriam's sisters rejoice* (Neu, Shapiro,

Cullom and Hoffman 1988), which reworks Passover from a feminist perspective. The embracing of inclusive language and feminine images of God
- The desire to make the work of women better known and sometimes the exclusive use of material by women
- The production of material for events in women lives like the menopause
- Varying degrees of privacy (Some groups are deliberately private and others deliberately more public to make women's work better known; some are officially sanctioned while others are opposed.)
- The problem of a lack of musical expertise and the use of oral ways of working (but little confidence in improvisation)
- The use of a variety of portable accompanying instruments including the drum[16] and a predominance of softer pieces
- A stress on justice-making alongside a desire to nurture its members
- An embracing of both rational and intuitive ways of knowing
- The use of the body in dramatic and dance elements in the rituals given appropriate expertise

This chapter has seen the development of an, at least partly, underground movement rebalancing the patriarchal structures of the institutional church. They often deliberately embrace Wisdom theology and certainly use it to underpin their liturgies. They challenge the musical structures of patriarchal religion and give women a chance to do it 'their way' and have some musical authority.

---

16 The use of the drum by women is fairly recent, from the late twentieth century. It was used to wonderful effect in Durham cathedral in the liturgy celebrating the decade of women in the church in 1998. There is fine book entitled *When the drummers were women* (Redmond 1997), documenting how women were systematically deprived of musical power in sacred situations. Drums were central to some of the pre-Christian traditions but Christianity has always feared the power of the drum. Even today many churches welcome a church band consisting of flutes and acoustic guitars but are unhappy when a drum kit is introduced. This was at its clearest when the black slaves taken straight from Africa were not allowed to use their drums. The drum represents power and those who control the drums often have control of the power. In workshops many women tell the story of always having wanted to play the drums but never getting them because the boys shouted louder and the teachers wanted a quiet life.

CHAPTER 8

Conclusion: Musicking Wisdom's Ways

Story

> 'Dancing in the hours of Wisdom' or 'Waltzing in Wisdom Ways' [means] step-
> ping and twirling – creating an interpretive, communal dance and breaking out
> of the rhythm of culturally ascribed steps. I visualize a diverse group of women
> dancing in a circular formation inside the pillars of an open-air house – their
> dance circle open, ready to accept the reader inside. The dance could be edifying
> to the mind, body and spirit of the reader.
>
> — ELLISON quoted in Fiorenza 2000 p. 18

Introduction

This book has been about making women more visible in the history of
Christian liturgical music. I searched Michael Wilson Dickson's *A History
of Christian Music* (1992) – a popular text with those who wish to examine this area – to see how women are represented. In the pictures women
feature as:

- Angelic figures
- Children
- Nurturers of children
- Spouses of central figures

In none of these positions do they have any real authority or have control of either the theological or musical traditions. As angels they mediate Divine patriarchy, on the one hand serving a male God and on the other acting as Muses to male composers. As children they are indoctrinated into the conventions they have little control over. As nurturers and teachers of children they are required to teach the conventions they have little control over. As spouses they are required to live out the conventions they have little control over. The only significant pictures including them are a Salvation Army women's orchestra (a tradition that was very early obliterated and only revived in times of war) and Ann Lee's Shaker women dancing in a group opposite the men. Jeremy Begbie in his book *Resounding Truths* (2007) – described on its jacket as a definitive history of Christian music – includes not even Hildegard of Bingen in the theologians of music. His later book with Steven Guthrie (2011) entitled *Resonant Witness: Conversations between Music and Theology*, includes more chapters by women; but it does not address the challenge of feminist theology to a theology of music. Much more inclusive is *Christian Congregational Music* (2013) from Monique Ingalls, Carolyn Landau and Tom Wagner. In the introduction its intention is declared as:

> a polyphonic collection – with moments of consonance and dissonance – Christian Congregational Music seeks to model what we believe to be a crucial aspect missing from much scholarship on Christian congregational music: a multi-voiced dialogue between methodological approaches, disciplinary perspectives and the positioning of scholars in relationship to the communities they represent. The volume's focus on fluid, dynamic aspects of music in and as performance calls for scholars and practitioners to use a range of analytical methods that extend beyond textual analysis of music and lyrics. (Ingalls, Landau and Wagner 2013 p. 10)

Congregational Music (2013) has a greater variety of perspectives than other literature in this area and includes more women in its views of congregational music. However, this book has attempted to concentrate on women's experience and to tell the stories of women (often deliberately in their own words) and of those who share their love of Wisdom theology. It has outlined the controversies that bedevil the history of women in liturgical music. From examining the work of feminist musicologists in Chapter 1 and allying this with a model of conceptualising society as a centralised core of accepted conventions with a number of marginalised ways of knowing, it has moved to show how these ideas are reflected in various vignettes in the history of women in various church traditions. Here we have found how difficult it has been for these ideas to penetrate to the main (or male-) stream thinking which has been shaped by a patriarchal society.[1]

The early history of Christianity charts the processes of this marginalisation, while the next three chapters have shown three communities inspired by the visions of Wisdom and how they related to the surrounding culture. Hildegard, for example, was alternately praised and excluded. The nun composers of Renaissance Italy found a place as the spiritual holders of their culture but have been ignored by the history of liturgical music. Mother Ann is respected by her community but persecuted by the wider society. The women hymn writers of Europe have been systematically ignored by historians of church music but lately made more visible by publications like Wootton (2010). In Chapter 7 we have found women and also some men, often at the margins of the mainstream churches, attempting to be true to the musical vision as they see it. They receive a mixed message of acceptance and rejection. They have re-acted with a variety of responses ranging from delight and freedom to anger and resignation.

This is perhaps inevitable as liturgical music-making sits within the highly gendered sphere of liturgy:

> Christian worship has historically been deeply gendered, but … liturgical historiography has all but ignored this fundamental gender differentiation … Gender analysis in liturgical historiography is a multifaceted enterprise, encompassing not only human beings who worshiped but liturgical time and space, texts and structures of rites, as well as constant reflection on the conceptualization of its subject matter. (Berger 1999 pp. 5–26)

This chapter will draw on the value systems outlined in Chapter 1 to suggest ways forward that will enrich the musical life of the whole Church, acknowledging the gendered character of its history. To aid this process, discussion questions are provided at the end of each section.

---

1   Rachel Bennett (2001) in her article on *The English Choral Tradition: Lawful discrimination* shows how these inequalities are supported by the law.

1a Individual/Community

We saw in Chapter 1 how contemporary society favours individualism and the importance of rebalancing this with a rediscovery of a wider community including the natural world.[2] The growth of individualism has been expressed in some parts of the Church by a separation of musicians from the other members of congregations. Throughout this book the theme of the valuing of community has been prominent in the work of female liturgical musicians.[3] Contemporary developments in musicology have seen the rise in the significance of the area of Values and with this the appreciation of the significance of context in all music making.

The first six hundred years of Christianity saw the narrowing of the musical community with congregational singing being devalued in favour of choirs and musical hierarchies. In the Middle Ages there was a profound spiritual sense of music being part of the stuff of the cosmos. This was clearly reflected in Hildegard's theology of music. The development of counterpoint in European music meant the loss of the visionary woman singer tradition because it required access to education. This was available to aristocratic women, who were able to use it in conventual situations where they were freed of familial responsibilities. Congregational singing formed a central plank of the Protestant reformers' belief in the priesthood of all believers, but this did not allow women to rise through the hierarchical musical structures of choir schools which launched their participants into leadership roles in liturgical music. Indeed legal systems often defined and still do define this exclusion (Bennett 2001). In the Victorian period in the UK, women found a way getting their voices heard in the Church through writing hymn texts in Protestant traditions including translations from Latin and other vernaculars. The Second Vatican Council asked Roman Catholic

---

2   These ideas are still not widely accepted in Christian circles and people are reluctant to express them.

3   To a certain extent it would be possible to say that the Christian Church as a whole presents a challenge to the dominant culture by its notion of creating community (koinonia and ecclesia) and the prominent place that sound has played in this process.

congregations to sing and women came through the system as cantors and musical encouragers. Contemporary writers have regained the sense of both a natural world and a human community held together by music.

The Salvation Army started with a strong vision of an all-inclusive musical community but the band room soon became male. However, it has shown itself willing to embrace more popular idioms in the interests of evangelism through the work of figures like Joy Webb. Their acceptance in the more evangelical traditions has meant that the combination of a very 'male' theology and the deeply gendered world of popular musics have not offered much scope for challenging gender representations in the tradition.

Worship songs in a more popular style have had a mixed reception in Christian traditions which have embraced the so-called 'standards' (more accurately conventions) of the world of classical musicians. However, the rock world, in general, has been no more open to women than the classical world. Women are likely to be found singing in music groups but less often playing instruments or managing the group. However, we still often have a unison line that is high and not easy for a congregation.[4] The classical hierarchy is also often reflected in a struggle between organist and priest/minister (often still both male), both claiming the moral high ground for controlling the total liturgical experience.

The contemporary alternative worshipping scene where women are in control has established more democratic ways of liturgy construction and in the absence of women with confidence in their musical ability; the resulting liturgies have been closer to the experience of the participants and closer to their musical abilities. There has been an overt desire to include people, the natural world and experiences that the church has excluded. Simple repetitive music has played an important part in this in the use of chants from the Taizé community and the work of composers like Margaret Rizza (2004).

Elizabeth Theobald (1997) sees that the necessary skill of the liturgical composer is to integrate the community effectively:

---

4   The loss of the gallery choir traditions where all could sing a line of appropriate pitch or the notion of free harmonisation by congregations (still alive in some branches of Methodism) was serious in this respect.

- To successfully and musically integrate untrained singers and trained musicians
- To appreciate the strengths and weakness of such a combination
- To write music that engages all those assembled with scope for the assembly to make the music their own (for example, by adding harmonies)

There needs to be a continual flow between the two polarities of individualism and community if we are to create an ecclesiology based on more circular 'democratic 'ideas of the Divine rather than systems based on hierarchies with power concentrated at the top. Then both individuals and communities will acquire an identity. Individuals need empowerment in the area of music which can be done by a mixture of education but, more importantly, confidence building – as the developing community choir tradition clearly shows (Morgan 2013). This is best done by means of musical engagement with a community and the smaller alternative groups are a good stepping stone to wider public worship. There needs in these to be a space for both solo and small group work and congregational singing. Women in leadership positions can see their leadership as empowering an inclusive community – inclusive and celebrating of experienced musicians and also of people who have self-identified as non-musicians. As a woman gains confidence by creating material and leading music in that context she will be able to claim her identity as a musician. There needs to be a place for individual women to take their place as leaders and soloists, not only in women-only groups but also in the 'grand' worshipping situations of the Churches; but there is also a case for the development of alternative situations in which musical democracy can be encouraged and in which all people can gain confidence in the musical God Within – Sophia Wisdom.

Questions for discussion

- How far does your worshipping congregation embrace diversity?
- How far is the musical community inclusive or exclusive? Who feels excluded?
- Does everyone engage with congregational singing?
- Is there scope for women to take positions of musical leadership?

1b Unity/Diversity

A truly creative tradition is able to keep a flow going between diversity and unity. There needs to be greater acceptance of diversity in various areas – whether it is a variety of genders, sexualities, disabilities and so on, or the chaos of change and transformation. The concentration on unity in every area of the Church's life whether it be in the nature of the Godhead, the worshipping community or between different denominations has not served the Wisdom cause well. It has supported exclusivity in the interest of unity, not only in the area of priesthood but also in other areas like music. We have seen how the 'standards' movement of church music reflects a fracturing of humanity and divinity, placing most human beings in a state of continual failure that resembles musically 'original sin' at a cosmic level. It has often meant the imposition of the conventions of the world of Western Classical music-making on situations which are profoundly different and often closer to orate community music-making. It has also meant the imposition of Western values in terms of construction on traditions where these are inappropriate and limiting. Those sections and denominations of the church that have sought out a different style have often been despised by the upholders of traditional values who have set themselves up in some exclusive but united hierarchy.

The early Church clearly had a variety of traditions and the narrowing of the vision was a narrowing of acceptable musical styles. The missionary movement was often as responsible for the imposition of Western musical values and styles on colonised groups, reflected in the establishment of Western curricula in the musical academies of these cultures.

The establishment of alternative communities like The Shakers has usually meant the establishment of a new musical tradition. Christian denominations have often been defined by their musical style. The distinctive sound of the Salvation Army band, the clapping and swaying of the gospel choir, the full choral sound of Parry's *I was glad* – all of these musical idioms have served to define particular traditions, often embodying its underlying theology. Diversity has often been located between traditions rather than within them.

But there are signs of change. The installation of Rowan Williams as Archbishop of Canterbury in the Anglican Communion with its dance, Welsh harp music, traditional hymns and modern anthem showed what diversity within a single service in a liturgical context might look like – one reflective of a world in which people of differing backgrounds often live side by side or even collide and John Sentamu's installation as Archbishop of York was similarly various. Alternative worshipping communities usually reject the dominant notion of musical control and of necessity draw on the diverse experiences of their members. As denominational boundaries and even faith boundaries mean little in these groups, there is a greater variety to draw on. The challenge is to keep a sense of coherence that is not based on uniformity within the music of a tradition. This can be expressed in services at different times and different denominations and also through the containing of diversity within a single service. This may mean the development of new musical structures and ensembles to enable this. We saw in the life of the Episcopal Divinity School in Cambridge Massachusetts how such developments can enrich the worshipping community and lead to new spiritual insights.

In the life of an individual musician, it may mean a rhythm of times of uncertainty and times of security as part of the development of the inner musician. These times can be reflected in terms of hymn texts that include notions of vulnerability.[5] This is a regular part of the composing process, but both performers and listeners need to take on board the challenge of different styles and traditions; they also need to be helped through that process. It can be a creative process bringing growth and fruitfulness. It challenges a position of extreme musical conservatism and allows for the possibility of change.

---

5   At the end of my hymn to Wisdom I attempted to express this:

Tremendous and fascinating is the mystery
Dancing in truth before creation's start;
A strong vuln'rability is Wisdom's paradox:
Power and weakness entwined in God's heart. (Boyce-Tillman 2006a p. 60)

There is an issue around the acceptability of feminine images for God and whether these can be accepted alongside the male ones established over 2000 years. There is a call from feminist theologians and hymn writers to expand the range of metaphors for God, bearing in mind that it is idolatrous to think that God can be contained in any single image. (This raises huge questions around the preponderance of the word Father as a descriptor of God.) There now exists a body of hymns calling God 'mother', 'sister', 'midwife' and so on, but it is debatable whether they will find a ready acceptance in the mainstream churches, although references to Mary, the Mother God, can be acceptable in some traditions.

There is a case now for an acceptance of variety both within (which is the more difficult) and across liturgical situations as a true reflection of a God who embraces the chaos of human existence as much as the order, renaming it variety and creativity, deintegration and reintegration – a spiritual value system that embraces and values chaos as well as order.

Questions for discussion

- How much diversity can you tolerate?
- Do you have favourite pieces of music in the classical canon? Are they to some extent 'holy' to you?
- Do you have pieces of music that have a special personal significance for you? What style are they in?
- How comfortable do you feel with the challenges of this book?
- What is your reaction to inclusive language? For human beings? For God?
- Where would you place yourself in the value systems outlined in Chapter 1?
- Which musical tradition do you prefer (Look at your own collection of recorded music)? Do these tastes carry over into religious music?
- Reflect on your own experience of religious music. Can you see feminine religious elements in it, like devotion to Mary, female saints, or to Christ's suffering or the Eucharist (see Chapter 4)?

2a Public/Private

There needs to be a connection in our lives between the public and private with a flow between them. The history of the musical liturgy of the Church has seen women in more public positions alongside men in the early years; that authority was steadily eroded as women were pushed into semi-public spaces such as graveyards and finally into their homes. It has been in the private spaces afforded by the convents that women's musical creativity has flourished in Europe and because of varied attitudes towards the clausura, these were sometimes quite accessible to the surrounding community. Ann Lee again achieved authority within the space of her community but was subject to ridicule in the wider society. In terms of the publicity of the history books these women's traditions have often been hidden in the private, secret domain, even when in their own times women liturgical musicians achieved a measure of public acclaim.

The contemporary Church in western culture today still often reflects this polarisation: most public spaces = white men in control, the more private spaces = women in control. The UK here lags behind other cultures. There are some women organists in British cathedrals and there are some US cathedrals including choirs of women as well as girls. There are plenty of women in smaller churches in unpaid less high profile positions and the average church choir has more women than men. The Church, in general, will support isolated women like Hildegard or women clearly separated from the surrounding society like the renaissance nuns. The conventual tradition made that a valid and freeing choice for women; it is arguable that the loss of that tradition, first of all in Protestantism and then its decline within Roman Catholicism has deprived women of valuable creative semi-public spaces; marriage has offered them a much more limited private space for their creativity, now associated largely with children. Current large gatherings of women in public spaces, like women's voice choirs or large liturgical gatherings like synods have been seen as more threatening by church authorities. However, many women are happier in the private sphere, hidden and free to do their own thing with impunity, with only occasional longing glances at more public roles. It is a place where emotion and trauma can be more readily integrated into liturgy than in the larger public arenas. Indeed, many radical Roman Catholic women have seen their exclusion from public authoritative roles as the work of the Spirit and a chance for real reform.

The result of the alternative liturgy movement has been to make women's contribution to the musical traditions of the church better known and to give them a platform for their creativity. It is nonetheless a sadness that women have been denied access to such resources as the well trained choirs and large acoustic spaces, where notions of canonical musical texts have played as disempowering a role for women musically as the Bible has theologically. While access to large public spaces is seen as part of the process of valuing by the wider culture, women will be seen as devalued in their inability to access them.

In the lives of human communities there needs to be private and public spaces – spaces for experiment and spaces for bringing those experiments into a more public domain. This is particularly true of musical activity and it is necessary for women to have the opportunity for a bridge between private experimentation and public exposure of their work. A mature community has such channels open and a flow between them, so that change for individuals and communities can be negotiated safely and in a way that enables people to mature.

There is a role for the private and the public. The private space is often a place of experiment and risk-taking but the location of all the Wisdom exploration in the private sphere and all the more patriarchal traditions in the public sphere has deprived many of positions of authority and access to the range of experiences that constitute the total sphere of action for the Christian gospel.

Questions for discussion

- Do any of the themes in this section resonate with your contemporary experience?
- Do you sing regularly in your home?
- Do you wish you could lead music in church?

- Can you relate to an experience of being silenced in your own life in public worship?
- Have you had an idea for a song that you have been afraid to share?
- Where do you think you might have more freedom to control a spiritual musical tradition?
- Have you ever wanted to be a musical leader but lacked the confidence?
- Do you use music privately – in your home for example?

2b Product/process

The concentration on product is well established in Western society and is often identified with literacy and a literate culture that gives value to product, ignoring and devaluing process. Its value systems are concentrated in the perceived perfection of the product. Yet the process is embodied in the product and many contemporary products reflect the shallowness of the process.

The establishment of the canonical texts of Christianity identified Christianity with literacy, leaving behind and subjugating the orate traditions of its founders. The first six hundred years saw the establishment of this canon theologically, although the musical traditions were oral. It was the work of Gregory the Great to standardise the musical traditions in a notational form. But from this moment on, the mainstream musical tradition has been as identified with notated scores as the theological tradition has been with the written text of the Bible; the oral has been despised and subjugated. This has progressively located power musically in the hands of those who had access to musical education. In Hildegard's day, this was a very limited number of people but ecstatic visionary, improvisatory song was still a possibility in a monophonic tradition. Because of the limited availability of the skills of musical literacy, this could, at a later date, be written down if someone was prepared to pay for the services of a musical scribe. With the establishment of counterpoint and harmony as the dominant musical styles of Europe, the situation limited Christian liturgical music to the aristocracy.

But the loss here is of a genuinely contextualised tradition where material is continually reworked to be appropriate for particular situations. The result has often been bizarre, such as the location of J.C. Crum's hymn *In meadow and field the cattle are good* with its references to rabbits and primroses in an African context where little would be known of the English landscape that generated it.[6] An orate tradition would have thrown up material appropriate in that context, encouraging the people within the tradition to be creative rather than importing products from other cultures. Less experienced musicians have felt unconfident about leading or initiating music activities; as the liturgy came to need books for the congregation, there were requests for written music to be available for congregations as well. And yet these very texts may actually serve to destroy confidence further, as pitches are now fixed and cannot be moved in relation to the mood or general disposition of a congregation and texts may be outdated or inappropriate.

Successful liturgical music has always to be appropriate for context. Elizabeth Theobald (1997) drawing on her review of music in the Roman Catholic Church post Vatican II suggests:

- The music is appropriate for the function within the liturgy being served
- The music is appropriate for the abilities of the assembly and music ministers[7]
- The music is flexible for differing resources and times

6   In meadow and field the cattle are good
     And the rabbits are thinking no evil.
     The anemones white are refined and polite
     And all the primroses are civil.

     Oh, once in a while we obey with a smile
     And are ever so modest and prudent,
     But it's not very long before something is wrong
     And somebody's done what he shouldn't.
     (J.G. Crum original edition of Hymns Ancient and Modern)

7   This was a real problem in the Magnificat Project discussed in Chapter 7 where the women composers had had insufficient experience in the cathedral choir tradition to write music that could be learned within the allocated time slot by children singing

- The music fully engages the assembly and each individual
- The assembly is able to relate to the type and style of music being used
- [Attention needs to be paid] to the type of music used within the liturgy and that used elsewhere – the corporate taste of the assembly
- [The music needs to represent] the society and culture of the members of the assembly

A number of these challenge the Church in relation to how women represented in the musical traditions of the Church. In this area the music has lost its relation to its context – it has lost a Wisdom dimension.

The subjugation of musical orality has led to the loss of improvisation in many traditions. However, improvisation is often used as a metaphor for the way life is lived:

> Living in love is always a risk, and in its tradition of improvisation, jazz music expresses this well. The chord structure underneath the melody remains the same, but improvising takes a risk in creating something in the moment that is new and that may not work. There are decisive moments in our lives: when we move into a new situation that can't be reversed; when we have children; when we make vows or when we fall in love for the first time; when we lose someone we love – something changes in us for ever. But we still live day to day – improvising life – making it up as we go along. The familiar chords – the building blocks of our lives – underpin us, but we find our own tune and sing with our own voice.[8]

Richard Holloway (1999) also uses improvisation as a metaphor for the way in which we operate morally in a 'godless morality':

> Is morality a science or an art, a technique we can learn my mastering rules and applications, or is it more like mapping a strange country by a process of exploration, trial and error? To change the analogy, is the moral life like playing from a fixed text or is it closer to the improvisations of jazz? (Holloway 1999 pp. 22–3)

---

alongside adults. Their lack of experience in the tradition made this imaginative leap very difficult.

8   The sound of Freedom <https://vulpeslibris.wordpress.com/2010/02/17/our-sound-is-our-wound-by-lucy-winkett-a-prophetic-voice-in-a-world-of-noise/> accessed Dec 30th 2013.

If it is such a good preparation for life there is an argument for its inclusion liturgically. It was clearly there in the early Church and included the possibility of communally 'singing in tongues.' There are indications that this more ecstatic improvisatory tradition was part of women's traditions in biblical times. It has been retained in the black congregations drawing on their largely orate culture; here we see women soloists and choral directors more in evidence and a notion of 'singing in the spirit'. The notated songs of the Shakers appear to have been skeletal melodies that were ornamented freely by singers.

The advent of the women singer/songwriters with limited notational expertise, led to

- songs being transmitted orally by groups like *Sweet Honey on the Rock*
- more repetitive structures like Taizé chants that function as ostinati for improvisation

These are signs that the tradition is beginning to rebalance itself including process as well as product and so more accurately representing the assembly of God. The advent of composing/improvising in the school curriculum in the UK means that children can now contribute musically in terms of composing to worship, while in alternative groups lacking musical expertise material learned from literate sources is freely reworked for a variety of purposes. The rediscovery of such techniques as the power of the group humming can provide a powerful basis for extemporary prayer. This freedom also opens up the way for experimentation with new forms and ensembles rather than those established by convention and practice, exploding the canonical structures and delighting in playing with the tradition. It means revisiting the linear views of construction that have characterised the classical canon in favour of more circular cyclic forms.

The discovery of spontaneity balances the order of the notated traditions with the freedom of the Spirit; it can make worship a playing space freed from the constraints of a product-based surrounding culture, where people can freely offer a representation of themselves musically.

Questions for discussion

- How far are there improvisatory elements in your own worshipping tradition?
- Can you see the progress towards a loss of spontaneity in any other religious traditions?
- Do you enjoy exploring religious ideas by singing them?
- Are there ways of helping people in the congregation refine their ideas musically and turn them into polished products?
- Are there communal ways of creating music that you could explore?
- Is there a balance in your liturgies between sections that are carried out orally as well as parts which are presented in literary form? Are there times for people to share their own spiritual experiences orally – e.g. small discussions?

3a Excitement/Relaxation

Different denominations within Christianity have created their own rhythms for worship. At the extreme ends, there is the excited vibrancy of the Pentecostal traditions and the silence of the Quaker traditions. Each of these traditions within an individual service would also have an emotional curve of some kind. This can be managed by means of the music. Lucy Winkett (2010) calls for greater silence in worship to balance the noisiness of the contemporary world:

> The Christian Church has an historic role expressed in this story – to call people into silence in the presence of God. It is a role that has particular meaning at a time of tragedy, but, given society's increasing noise, has more contemporary urgency and focus in today's world. To fulfil this role, the churches must practise silence in order to create something for others to join ...
>
> A silence that is underpinned by love, by a willingness to wait, by a level of attentiveness that accepts where we are and who we are now before God, is a gift that the churches can give to such a distracted world.

The Expressive character of a piece of music is often dictated by its speed, volume and the materials used to make it, like instrumental accompaniment. Early worshipping groups appear to have used unaccompanied voice and whatever instruments were available. Drumming and percussion instruments seem quite early to have been identified with the greater excesses of paganism and this has been true wherever Christianity has established itself over and above the indigenous pagan traditions. In these traditions, women seldom had access to anything but the smaller softer instruments; the drumming traditions, in particular, are, or have been until recently, often tightly controlled by men.

But having abandoned or criminalised/outlawed the drum (Eluyefa 2010), Christianity was responsible for the development in its public spaces of an instrument capable of a huge range of emotions with which it could influence its audience in the shape of the organ. But this has been alternately embraced and smashed by mainstream traditions as it vies for a place alongside more unaccompanied traditions; these, certainly in the eyes of the more radical Protestant reformers, were closer to biblical precept. Before an age of amplification, the organ was probably the loudest single instrument in the Western collection of musical instruments and associated with the triumphalism of mainstream theology; at worst it bludgeoned congregations into a musical order resembling the emotional battering of the perceived ethics of Biblical texts; at best, it offered a huge range of levels of support, judged according to the needs of a particular context.

Rock has found an outlet in the more evangelical Christians, often allied with the triumphalism of their more apocalyptic elements. The charismatic evangelicals in the UK flock to Spring Harvest where the excitement of the tradition is now allied with Christian fervour. But triumphalism is also dominant theologically in these louder sounds, although more gentle sounds are added in devotional songs. Some local churches have embraced these, replacing pipe organs with electronic keyboards and guitars, and choirs with rock groups. Elsewhere, the drum is still suspect and anything involving a drum kit can be difficult.

Many local churches have resorted to a middle way in terms of Expressive content – not too loud and not too soft, not too slow and not too fast (often dependent on the musical expertise of the organist or musical leader of some kind). For many congregations where the average age of worshippers is going up, it proves a welcome reassurance that something in society has stayed the same.[9]

Many women's traditions have been unaccompanied because of their limited access both to instruments and technical training. Only the aristocratic women of the Renaissance had sufficient access to wealth to enable them to gain instrumental expertise, but the fact that the teachers were male posed problems for their encloistered status. Alternative groups often use unaccompanied singing for the same reasons. The guitar has proved an easily accessible and (very importantly) portable instrument, but there is still a strong feeling that women's music should be soft and gentle as we saw in Chapter 2 in the critiques of composers like Ethel Smyth.

I was asked to write a hymn to celebrate 100 years of women's ordination in the UK – starting with Gertrude van Petzold in the Unitarian Church. I found that she had been a suffragette and wanted to capture some of that spirit, choosing the tune associated with Fanny Crosby's hymn, *To God be the glory*:

CHORUS
We rejoice, we rejoice in our foremother's faith;
We rejoice, we rejoice in an inclusive Grace;
We'll keep pressing onwards in courage and love
And soar on the wings of God's free flowing dove

God groans as she watches us struggle and fight;
Her belly is stretching and aching for right;
Tears flow in her travail; her pain is revealed;
She waits and she hopes that her wounds may be healed.

CHORUS

9   The issue here is a theological one – the balancing of the stability of a God who stays the same with the ever-changing contextualising Wisdom traditions, remade anew in each situation and responding to individual and communal needs. It may be argued in a culture where change is so rapid that people attend Church for this sense of stability. Here to debate these issues may enable there to be a greater balance within liturgy of stability and change, both musically and theologically. I have attempted to do this in *Space for Peace* (Boyce-Tillman 2013a).

God's wings are enfolding and circling the earth;
She dreams of the time when she brought it to birth,
Laments how the systems of patriarchs' pow'r
Have stopped her from bringing her world into flow'r.

CHORUS

God bristles with anger and rage in her bones;
Her body is raped and emitting deep moans;
Her energy rises; she raises her arm
To regain the power for all who are harmed.

CHORUS

God joys in our leaping our dances of faith;
She laughs as she opens her arms in embrace;
We gather within her as sisters in grace;
Our strength is increasing as we find our place.

CHORUS

(Boyce-Tillman 2006a p. 77)

When I first sang it to a close friend she commented that that it was not the sort of hymn that the women in the women's groups liked because it sounded too triumphalistic and militaristic. However, when we sang it to this powerful tune at a conference on feminist theology, someone asked me if it was a suffragette song. I was glad that I had captured the spirit of struggle that characterised those early women who were prepared to give such commitment to a cause in which they passionately believed. Singing it in that mixed congregation were also our Roman Catholic sisters still struggling for ordination and Anglican woman priests who might one day follow in the footsteps of the inspiring Bishop Baerbel from the German Lutheran Church who had us standing to applaud her own courageous story. She warned us in her address that it would be at least two generations before radical women had positions of authority (and that would include musical authority) in the Church.; so the controversies identified in this book will remain.

It is a pity if women, in the interests of regaining the gentler softer sounds, then fail to regain the stronger ones; through these they can regain some of their power. The use of drums has gone some way towards this but the stereotypes die hard. The Wisdom tradition has both gentler but also more powerful aspects. If we, as women, fail to lay claim to the louder instruments, as well as embracing unaccompanied singing and more gentle instruments, we fail to tap into a deeper source of power with the universe.

The history of power in the Church is that it has after the earliest years been male; associated with this has been a certain triumphalism expressed in musical terms by stronger louder sounds. Women have not had access to the powerful instruments and have therefore associated themselves with either gentler instruments or no instruments. Now women do have access to musical education, it is possible to see that the power of instruments like the drum and the organ do not necessarily have to be associated with 'power over' but can be used for empowerment – to support struggles for justice and the telling of subjugated truths.

Questions for discussion

- How far do the traditions of Church music that you are familiar with give you a sense of security?
- How happy are you with changes in the music in regular worship?
- How does your tradition use and value the more powerful instruments in worship? The gentler instruments?
- Is there an emotional curve in your liturgies reflected in the music?

3b Challenge/Nurture

There is a direct link between these issues and the previous section. In this section there is both the question of the texts and the music. On both fronts, liturgical music has been remarkably resistant to challenge its own thinking, for the Church plays its part in supporting people in a dominant culture that is already perceived as too challenging. Indeed, some would link the Church with the escapist tendencies of the entertainment industry. As congregations in the UK become older, this tendency is reinforced and there is real resistance to new hymnody or music of whatever kind. This has been a particular problem for the inclusion of women's work into the established repertoire (as indeed it has music of classical women composers into the classical canon). If the museum of liturgical music is already filled with works that offer some escape from the struggles of the market place, there is no space even for other master or mistress-pieces of the past and certainly little for the present.

The inclusion of elements of social justice has always been part of some hymnody. There are certainly elements of challenge within Hildegard's gender characterisation of the Virtues as female in her opera *Ordo Virtutum*.[10] Women hymn writers, like Anna Laetitia Barbauld, were also social activists (although there was a great outpouring of hymns of private devotion by Victorian women). In the 1960s the protest movement was reflected in the Church with such male Wisdom writers as Sydney Carter[11] and Fred Kaan, alongside Estelle White. Some women came through in this but still hymns in this area are considered problematic. Preferred hymns for the millennium, for example, emphasised God's supporting hand throughout the past years, rather than addressing contemporary social issues.

There was much challenge to the sexual mores of the surrounding culture in those songs of Mother Ann extolling the virtues of celibacy, which freed women from the continual round of child bearing. Hildegard and the nuns of Renaissance Italy also present a challenge in this area. The issue of celibacy for women is indeed a vexed one; but there is no doubt that it enabled women's musical creativity to flourish in a way not open to married women in Europe until the advent of reliable methods of contraception in the twentieth century.

10　A friend of mine attending an opera of mine with sections of *Ordo Virtutum* in it, remarked that to see the young women's bodies as virtuous and not seductive went against a great deal of his training at theological college.

11　It is a strange irony that *Standing in the rain* which accuses Christians of being 'always willing, never able' is now sung happily by the very Christian congregations that Sydney sought to satirise.

The worship song has proved an innovative phenomenon that has found ready acceptance in some circles and an equally powerful rejection in others. Started in the 1960s with writers like Geoffrey Beaumont and Patrick Appleford at the Twentieth Century Church Light Music group, it brought the popular (rather than pop) idioms of the secular world into the Church. The traditional metre of the hymn and the compressed theological statement that comprised the text of much traditional hymnody was replaced by free flowing texts (often with non-metred Biblical texts used as they stood) associated with tunes that were not interchangeable with other texts in the way the hymn tune traditions had traditionally been. Some resisted the bringing of the world of entertainment into the church and saw the pieces as facile – more nurturing perhaps – and commended the challenging nature of the theological treatise that was often compressed into a hymn like *Hark the herald Angels sing*. But as we saw in Chapters 4 to 9, the worship song is often beloved of women singer/song writers because it frees them from the constraints of patriarchal metric forms.

The challenging discords of the avant garde classical composers have also not been readily accepted in church circles and hymnbooks like the *Cambridge Hymnal* have not found a ready acceptance. However, composers like John Tavener (Holbrook and Poston 1967), having left their more discordant earlier idioms, have found a place with a return to older traditions that they have been able to synthesise with their own personal style. There is, however, very little chance that new religious music for choirs will get published, as the market for it in the UK is regarded as too small. The museum of the past is overflowing, and the simpler less discordant sounds have often been dismissed as of lesser value than the complex musical construction devices of the Classical canon.

In terms of nurturing the musical skills of the Church, periodically the various denominations move to improve congregational singing (and indeed choral singing in churches). This was particularly true in the Roman Catholic Church post Vatican II, when groups of people who had never sung before were suddenly expected to sing. The Royal School of Church Music in the UK has attempted a similar task mostly with Protestant choirs and instituted a series of tests that child choristers can go through to educate them musically. In my experience, this was quite empowering, although I personally shall never be comfortable with a testing environment.[12] In the US, there are many more courses in Liturgical Music in universities around the country, which does enable at least potential musicians to examine the musical and theological issues involved in music for worship.

Alternative liturgy groups have brought about their own balance of challenge and nurture. The feel of them is often nurturing but within the songs themselves (both text and tune) there is often a real sense that the issues that have produced the vulnerability of certain groups in society, including women, need to be challenged. This balance offers some guidance to the mainstream churches on how to both nurture people in the arms of a life-giving Wisdom but also shout the challenges of Jesus' life to contemporary society. Only when the liturgy of the Church can find some way of both nurturing and challenging people – both musically and in terms of subject material – will the church be able to grow both musically and theologically.

Questions for discussion

- What do you think is the value of the vow of celibacy – in the past and in the contemporary world? Do you know anyone who has taken such a vow?
- Are there social justice issues you would like to see present in hymnody?
- What do you feel about experimental liturgy?
- Are there events either professional or global that you would want to have liturgies for?
- Do you feel the Church should provide liturgies for occasions where people need nurturing in difficult times in their life or when they are facing difficult issues like divorce and abortion? Would you feel comfortable with creating them?
- Do you long for music that is more representative of the issues of contemporary society?

---

12 My experience is that it produces more failures than successes.

4a Rational/Intuitive

The history of Western culture during the last two thousand sees a move from a trust in intuition towards the primacy of rationality and a consequent ridiculing of intuition. The outpouring of the Spirit that characterised the birth of the early Church resulted in an early trust in intuition. But very quickly the very rational Graeco-Roman tradition became dominant within the Church. Even so, women visionaries (and to a lesser extent men) had an accepted place, and music was sometimes given as part of that experience. Their music (like that of indigenous shamans) was construed as coming directly from a spiritual source. All creative acts of expression were God-given.

The Enlightenment saw the final establishment of the primacy of reason over intuition in Western culture. Mother Ann mounted a final challenge to this with her community of Shakers. Current practitioners often have a very intuitive approach to composition, although see the role of rational crafting in the process and talk about a tension between the two that has to be worked out in the creative process.

The music of Christian traditions has often been in the hands of classically trained musicians who have been educated in a tradition that has valued the more rational Construction elements over the more intuitive spiritual and expressive ones. Elements of Construction have been very much a part of evaluative processes. 'It matters not who writes it but whether it is good' said the cathedral organist of the panel deciding on settings of the evening canticles by women composers; and 'good' is usually conceived of in structural terms. Denominations like Black Pentecostalists have used the more free-flowing structure of improvisation and have been able to exercise their right to subjugated ways of knowing more easily than the white-led churches of all denominations. The encouragement of improvisation from the congregation and choir members has created a different approach to constructional issues in the music.

Similarly, in the Construction of hymn texts, great stress has been laid on metre, rhyme and theological logic. We have seen how women writers have moved away from hymns encapsulating abstract theological statements to hymns based on experience and action, sometimes in freer forms. Pastoral theology found its expression in the hymns by women writers (and some men). The one musical tradition where the woman's voice was regularly heard in worship was the soloist in the Free Church traditions in UK when the soloist (usually an older woman) was billed on the noticeboard next to the preacher. The songs were often of the Victorian bourgeois ballad school, with a strong emotional charge. These were often degraded by the dominant culture as sentimental and emotional (Methodist women 2004). Unfortunately those practising it did not often have the confidence to level the charge of cold impersonality at the dominant hymn traditions. Women liturgical music theorists see it differently. 'The emotional associations which the music has for members of the assembly adds to the liturgy' (Theobald 1997 p. 39).

Many of the more popular traditions on hymn singing have been characterised by more emotional approaches to the gospel and the most rational member of a congregation is often secretly glad to have a chance to sing such pieces as *What a friend we have in Jesus* or *The Old Rugged Cross*. The evangelical traditions have always been more comfortable with emotional hymns and songs and have used them for evangelistic purposes (which has not helped their status in more academic circles). The crusades of Billy Graham are filled with such numbers as Fanny Crosby's *Blessed Assurance*, in which the simple rhythmic repetition and the Romantic, simple harmonies bring tears to many eyes. The Salvation Army too has cultivated a more emotional approach to their singing and songs.

Alternative liturgy groups have seen a greater inclusion of emotional elements within liturgy and offer ways on how this can be done with integrity and dignity. The valuing of elements of Construction and Expressive character equally may offer models for examining and structuring more public liturgy to include the more difficult lived experiences of its members within public worship. It may pave the way for an examination of experiences received more intuitively and enable them to be examined using more rational processes; so they can be rooted in everyday life. When the rational and intuitive are separated there is a risk of visions of a fundamentalist nature being followed unquestioningly, as a counterbalance to a cold reasoning power divorced from lived experience. When the wit and the will can work together in harmony to discern right action, whether it is musically or theologically or both, then there is a real understanding of the nature of Sophia Wisdom.

Questions for discussion

- Have you had a visionary experience? Did it involve music?
- What are your favourite hymns? Are they related to your childhood memories?
- Do you have hymns that make you cry and is that acceptable in your worshipping tradition?

4b Embodied/Disembodied

The history of Western culture has been one of a split between mind, body and soul, drawing on ancient Greek notions of the soul. The roots of this can be laid, at least partly, at the door of Christianity. Traditions privileging mind and soul over a licentious body are scattered through the history, and the woman's body has come in for particular censure, because of its apparently seductive nature for men, drawing on the myth of Genesis One.

For music making, the body is the basic raw material of sound resonating with parts of the natural world, although Western musicology has not always seen it like this. Although dance appears to have been present in early Christian traditions, it soon seems to have been associated with more pagan traditions. As rational elements started to dominate theology, the soul became associated with mind and the tradition became more intellectual. The body and its activities became viewed as evil – to be persecuted and controlled by the perfection of the soul.

Music and, in particular, singing did keep an important bodily activity as part of worship. This was central to Hildegard's theology and to the Benedictine way that she followed. Mother Ann Lee saw the importance of embodied work in her community – the labour that led to the Shaker tradition of furniture – and this was intimately bound up with her worship, where songs reflected this holistic approach to belief and action.

The place of celibacy was critical to Hildegard, the Renaissance nuns and Mother Ann. Far from it being a denial of the body, it can be seen as a freeing of the body for social and creative action. Many of the singer/songwriters of the contemporary world explored in Chapter 7 are Roman Catholic religious who are also directly involved in social activism. The devaluing of the tradition of celibacy can be seen as putting women more tightly in the hands of a male culture whether as wives, mothers, partners or 'one-night stands'.

The Cartesian split is deep in western musicology and theology rooted as it is in the Enlightenment Project. For many Classical trained professional Anglican Church musicians the splits are perfectly intact and unchallenged, despite the publications of feminist theologians and musicologists. Protestantism was an Enlightenment project and has the splitting deep in its heart. The Oxford Movement with its rediscovery of ritual, did something to restore sensuous gestures to Anglican worship, but the gestures are always tightly controlled and ritualised. Interestingly, so are the gestures associated with white charismatic worship where the freeing Spirit seems to move people to remarkably similar gestures.

The Roman Catholic tradition was always a more embodied tradition with its retention of sensuous elements such as incense, visual images, gestures and instrumental and vocal music interwoven. But what could be done and by whose body it could be done by was tightly controlled. In a recent visit to the Vatican, I attended High Mass celebrated by a cardinal one afternoon. There were also a large number of bishops and archbishops concelebrating. They were all men except for the religious sisters who did the intercessions. The men used their bodies to raise and lower their hands. After supper, in the same space, there was a concert by a choir of young girls. They had planned the concert for a secular space and were concerned about the dancing included in their programme. In front of the same altar, I saw young girls' bodies moving freely in dance and movement from their folk tradition, and using actions they had generated themselves. It seemed extremely interesting that one set of gestures and bodies had been validated by the church authorities – men in flowing robes raising and lowering hands – and the other had not; it was interesting to reflect on the forces that made this so; it was, in my opinion, a pure cultural construct.

The Pentecostal traditions have a greater sense of approaching the spiritual experience through embodied sensuous movement, drawing on rituals indigenous to African culture and adapted for Christian use. Embodied possession by the spirit is a part of these traditions and associated with ecstatic singing traditions.

Liturgical dance has had a chequered history within the mainstream churches. Professional companies have developed certain fairly stylised ways of performing it, with the intention that it be watched as part of worship, in much the same way as the choir is to be listened to. Involving a congregation in dance is an interesting experience. In my one woman performances, I often include a circle dance at the end and it is interesting to see who will actually get involved and who will not – for a variety of reasons. Some people are still very uncomfortable with any form of dance in worship, seeing it as mere entertainment or too sensuous.[13] St Paul's somewhat equivocal attitude to his body dies hard in Christianity! Contemporary discussions about dance have shades hanging over them from the earliest debates in Christianity and its relation to the surrounding pagan traditions.

Alternative liturgy groups try to include dance if at all possible. They are also often tightly linked with social action of some kind, bringing the theology of the mind and heart together with embodied action. They give some pointers to the way in which Christianity might address the very real problems of embodying Wisdom. Our society is desperately in need of a Christianity that can help with the Cartesian split that permeates almost every aspect of our culture. The rediscovery of the embodiment of the voice, where mind and soul infuse the body and work in harmony with it, and a moving body, where mind and soul inform the gestures and from deep natural springs.

13   Recently (2013) in a Baptist context I was told that to dance in their chapel would defile it.

Questions for discussion

- What gestural components are there in your tradition? Are they associated with music?
- What is your attitude to liturgical dance, done by a limited number of skilled dancers? How does this compare with the inclusive circle dance traditions?
- Are you aware of the breath and the resonance of your own body while singing?
- Are you involved in social activism, embodying the Gospel and does that flow into songs and hymns?

Spirituality

This book has set out the limitations imposed by the Values of the dominant culture both in the secular world but also within Christian contexts. It has set out a model of the musical experience that requires participants to be able to relate to the totality of the musical experience. It has drawn on the literature and interviews with a diverse range of musicians to illustrate how many women (and men) feel excluded by the dominant Value systems and are therefore unable to access the realm of the spiritual/liminal; there is regularly a mismatch between their chosen value systems and those offered to them by the tradition. It has set out ways in which these dichotomies can be overcome, drawing on the Wisdom traditions of theology. It has importantly made available voices representing women's spiritual experience. As these have so often be hidden in and excluded from established histories, this is an important contribution that this book makes to the narratives of Christian liturgical traditions.

Summary

The subjugated value systems examined in Chapter 1 need to be associated with those of the dominant culture in a creative synthesis. This book has suggested some ways in which this might happen in the context of liturgical music:

- An acknowledgement of circular cyclic forms of music in the formation of inclusive communities involving human beings with one another, the natural world and the spiritual (however this is conceived), reflecting the immanence of Wisdom in her creation alongside the more separated linear transcendental view of patriarchal traditions
- An embracing of diversity and novelty as positive and creative, alongside the stress on unity and conservation as a marker of excellence, reflecting the diverse forms that Wisdom can take as well as the single source from which s/he/it emanates
- An acknowledgment of the interface between public and private and the need for opening of both spaces for all, exploding canonical systems that limit freedom of access so that the hiddenness and the revealed nature of Wisdom is clear
- A delighting in the making of ephemeral oral music for their own sake alongside the valuing of the beautiful product carefully rehearsed from notated sources and effectively performed reflecting Wisdom's playfulness – contextuality as well as order and permanence
- A validating of the strong and powerful sounds of triumphalism with their sense of optimism alongside the gentler sounds of vulnerability with their emotional charge, reflecting the power and weakness of the Wisdom of emotion
- A sense of music as a justice-making activity as well as a peace-making one, reflecting the prophetic as well as the nurturing roles of Wisdom
- A valuing of the intuitive visionary experience of musicking alongside the processes of reasoned crafting as a source of authority, reflecting the immediacy and the restraint of Wisdom
- The mutual agreement of mind, body and spirit in musicking, reflected in an alliance with movement and gesture, to complement the great works where dance and music are separated, reflecting the mystery of humanity and divinity entwined at the heart of Wisdom

Hildegard's antiphon to Wisdom (see Figure Four) contains a fine vision of a three-winged figure that may lead us a new Trinitarian theology based on the resolution of these polarities. Two wings in it appear to express the polarities of heaven and earth but the third is flying everywhere. This third wing is what is needed in theology and musicology to reconcile the polarities and keep the flow between them that is needed for a society that is to be truly balanced – one that will keep the marginalised in some relation to those in positions of power:

> O the power of Wisdom,
> You, in circling, encircle all.
> You are embracing everything in such a way that is life-giving;
> For you have three wings.
> One of them reaches highest heaven and another is sweating in earth and the third is flying everywhere.
> Therefore it is right to give you praise, O Sophia wisdom.
> (Hildegard of Bingen translated by Boyce-Tillman 2000b)

I hope that this book has enabled us to see how this figure is worked out musically and where we can locate that 'missing third wing' in our polarised society by bringing the polarities into flow with one another. Then we shall have a theology in which God the Creator and Wisdom are continually dancing together as they have from the beginning of time and our music will reflect this theology. This will not, however, be achieved without addressing controversies identified here. But in the struggle lies the creativity.

Bibliography

Amar, Joseph P. (ed. and trans) (1995), 'Jacob of Serug, "Homily of Ephrem"' (5th or 6th century) *Patrologia Orientalis 47*, pp. 5–76.

Andrews, Edward D. ([1940] 1962), *The Gift to be simple: Songs, Dances and Rituals of the American Shakers*, New York: Dover Publications.

Archbishops' Commission on Church Music (1992), *In Tune With Heaven: Report of the Archbishops' Commission on Church Music*, London: Church House Publications.

Assagioli, Robert ([1974] 1994), *The Act of Will*, London: Aquarian/Thorsons.

Aston, Margaret (1990), 'Segregation in Church'. Chapter in Sheils, W.J. and Wood, Diana (eds) (1990), *Women in the Church, Studies in Church History* 27, Oxford: Basil Blackwell pp. 237–94.

Aubert, Jean-Jacques (1989), 'Threatened Wombs: Aspects of Ancient Uterine Magic', *Greek, Roman and Byzantine studies* 30, pp. 421–49.

Aune, Kristin (2005), 'Being a "real" heterosexual man: British evangelicals and hegemonic masculinity'. Paper presented to the *British Sociological Association Study of Religion Group*, 11–13th April, University of Lancaster.

Baird, Joseph and Ehrman, Radd (translators) (1994), *Letters of Hildegard of Bingen, Vol. I* Oxford: Oxford University Press.

Barkin, Elaine (ed.) (1981–2), 'In response', *Perspectives of New Music 20–21* pp. 288–329.

Barthes, Roland (1972), trans by Annette Lavers, *Mythologies*, London: Jonathan Cape.

Barthes, Roland (1985), *The Fashion System*, London: Jonathan Cape.

Bauer, Walter (trans Achtemeier, Paul et al.) ([1934] 1971), *Orthodoxy and Heresy in Earliest Christianity*, Philadelphia: Fortress Press.

Beecham, Sir Thomas (1943), *A Mingled chime: An autobiography*, New York: G.P. Putnam's Sons.

Begbie, Jeremy (2007), *Resounding Truth: Christian Wisdom in the World of Music* Ada, Michigan: Baker Academy.

Begbie, Jeremy S. and Guthrie, Steven R. (2011), *Resonant Witness: Conversations between Music and Theology*, Grand Rapids, MI: William B. Eerdmans Publishing Company.

Bennett, Rachel A.J. (2001), *The English Choral Tradition: Lawful Discrimination?* Paper submitted as part of BA (Hons) Law Part II, Trinity College, Cambridge.

Berger, Teresa (1999), *Women's Ways of Worship: Gender analysis and liturgical history*, Collegeville, MN: The Liturgical Press.

Blezzard, Judith (1990), *Borrowings in English Church Music 1550–1950*. London: Stainer and Bell.

Bowers, Jane (2000), 'Writing the Biography of a Back Woman Blues Singer'. Chapter in Moisala, Pirkko and Diamond, Beverley (2000), *Music and Gender*, Urbana and Chicago: University of Illinois Press pp. 140–65.

Bowers, Jane and Tick, Judith (eds) (1986), *Women making Music: The Western Art Tradition 1150–1950*, Urbana: University of Illinois Press.

Bowie, Fiona (1998), 'Trespassing Sacred Domains: A Feminist Anthropological Approach to Theology and Religious Studies', *Journal of Feminist Studies in Religion*, 14, 1 pp. 40–62.

Bowie, Fiona and Davies, Oliver (1990), *Hildegard of Bingen: An Anthology*, London: SPCK.

Boyce-Tillman, June (1993), 'Women's Ways of Knowing', *British Journal of Music Education* 10, 3, November, pp. 153–61.

Boyce-Tillman, June (1994), *In Praise of All-encircling Love*, London: Hildegard Press and The Association for Inclusive Language.

Boyce-Tillman, June (1995), 'The Role of Women in the Passing on of Tradition and its implications for the School Curriculum' in *Musical Connections – Tradition and Change, Proceedings of the 21st World Conference of the International Society for Education, Tampa, Florida*, pp. 282–91.

Boyce-Tillman, June (1996a), *In Praise of all-encircling Love II*, London: Hildegard Press and The Association for Inclusive Language.

Boyce-Tillman, June (1996b), 'A Framework for Intercultural Dialogue in Music'. Chapter in Floyd, Malcolm (ed.) (1996), *World Musics in Education*, Farnborough: Scolar.

Boyce-Tillman, June (1998), *The Call of the Ancestors*, London: Hildegard Press.

Boyce-Tillman, June (2000a), *Constructing Musical Healing: The Wounds that sing* London: Jessica Kingsley.

Boyce-Tillman, June (2000b), *The Creative Spirit – Harmonious Living with Hildegard of Bingen*, Norwich: Canterbury Press.

Boyce-Tillman, June (2001a), *The Healing of the Earth*, London: Hildegard Press.

Boyce-Tillman, June (2001b), 'Sounding the Sacred: Music as Sacred Site'. Chapter in Ralls-MacLeod, Karen and Harvey, Graham. (ed.) *Indigenous Religious Musics*, Farnborough: Scolar pp. 136–66.

Boyce-Tillman, June (2002), *Lunacy or the Pursuit of the Goddess* Unpublished performance.

Boyce-Tillman, June (2004), 'Towards an ecology of Music Education', *Philosophy of Music Education Review*, 12, 2 Fall pp. 102–25.

Boyce-Tillman, June (2006a), *A Rainbow to Heaven*, London: Stainer and Bell.

Boyce-Tillman, June (2006b), 'Music as Spiritual Experience', *Modern Believing: Church and Society*, 47, 3, July 2006, pp. 20–31.

Boyce-Tillman, June (2007a), *Unconventional Wisdom*, London: Equinox.

Boyce-Tillman, June (2007b), 'Peace Making in Educational contexts'. Chapter in Urbain, Olivier (2007), *Music and Conflict transformation: Harmonies and Dissonances in Geopolitics*, London: I.B. Tauris pp. 212–28.

Boyce-Tillman, June (2010), *Revealing Hidden Wisdom – Women Finding a Voice in Hymnody*, Occasional Paper Third Series No 3 the Hymn Society of Great Britain and Ireland.

Boyce-Tillman, June (2013a), 'The Dignity of Difference', Chapter in Reason, Peter and Newman, Melanie (eds), *Stories of the Great Turning*, Bristol: Vala Publishing pp. 169–77.

Boyce-Tillman, June (2013b), 'Tune Your Music to Your Heart: Reflections for Church Music leaders'. Chapter in Ingalls, Monique, Landau, Carolyn and Wagner, Tom, eds (2013), *Christian Congregational Music, Performance, Identity and Experience*, Farnborough: Ashgate pp. 49–66.

Boyce-Tillman, June and Wootton, Janet (eds) (1993), *Reflecting Praise*, London: Stainer and Bell and Women in Theology.

Braidotti, Rosi (1994), *Nomadic Subjects*, New York: Columbia University Press.

Braidotti, Rosi (1995), *The Body as Metaphor: Seduced and Abandoned: The Body in the virtual world*, Videotape quoted in Mantin 2002.

Branham, Joan R. (2003), 'Bloody women and bloody spaces', *Harvard Divinity Bulletin* <http://.hds.harvard.edu/dpa/news/bulletin/articles/branham.html> accessed 14 February 2013.

Bright, W. (1903), *Age of the Fathers*, London: Longmans, Green and Co.

Bringle, Mary Louise (2002), *Joy and Wonder, Love and Longing: 75 hymn texts*, Chicago: GIA Publications.

Brock, Sebastian P. (1994), *Bride of Light: Hymns on Mary from the Syriac tradition* Kerala: St Ephrem Ecumenical Research Institute.

Brown, Peter (1981), *The Cult of the Saints: Its rise and function in Latin Christianity*, Chicago: University of Chicago Press.

Bruit Zaidman, Louise (1992), 'Pandora's daughters and rituals in Grecian Cities'. Chapter in Pantel, Schmitt ed. (1992), *A History of Women in the West Vol 1: From Ancient Goddesses to Christian Saints*. Cambridge, MA: the Belknap Press of Harvard University Press pp. 338–76.

Buber, Martin, trans Walter Kaufmann (1970), *I and Thou*, New York: Charles Scribner's Sons.

Bynum, Caroline Walker (1987), *Holy Feast and Holy Fast: The Meaning of Food in Medieval Religious Women* Berkeley: University of California Press.

Campion, Nardi Reeder ([1976] 1990), *Mother Ann Lee, Morning Star of the Shakers*, Hanover and London: University Press of New England.

Carr, E. Hallett (1963), *What is history?* New York: Knopf.

Carr, Sister Frances A. (1995), *Growing up Shaker*, US: United Society of Shakers.

Carrette, Jeremy (2000), *Foucault and Religion: Spiritual Corporality and Political Spirituality* London: Routledge.

Citron, Marcia, J. (1993), *Gender and the Musical Canon*, Cambridge: Cambridge University Press.

Clarke, Chris (2002), *Living in Connection: Theory and Practice of the new world-view*, Warminster: Creation Spirituality Books.

Clement, Catherine (Trans by Betsy Wing) (1989), *Opera or the undoing of Women*, London: Virago.

Collin, Matthew (1997), *Altered State: The Story of Ecstasy Culture and Acid House*, London: Serpent's Tail.

Cook, Nicholas (1990), *Music, Imagination and Culture*, Oxford: Clarendon Press.

Cook, Susan C. and Tsou, Judy S. (1994), *Cecilia reclaimed: Feminist Perspectives on gender and music*, Illinois: University of Illinois Press.

Csikszentmihalyi and Csikszentmihalyi (1988) as summarized in Haworth, John T. (1997), *Work, Leisure and Well-being*, London: Routledge pp. 84–5.

Darlington, Stephen and Kreider, Alan (2003), *Composing Music for Worship*, Norwich: Canterbury Press.

Daw, Carl P. Jnr (1996), *New Psalms and Hymns and Spiritual Songs*, Carol Stream: Hope Publishing.

Dijk, Denise J.J. (1997), *Praying with our eyes open: Women. Language and Liturgy*, unpublished paper.

Downing, Edith Sinclair (1998), *A Season of Clear Shining: Hymns by Edith Sinclair Downing*, Kingston, NY: Selah Publishing.

Drinker, Sophie (1948) (reissued 1995), *Music and Women: The Story of Women in their relation to Music*, City University of New York: The Feminist Press.

Duchesne, L.M.O. (1909), *Early History, of the Christian Church: From its Foundation to the end of the Third Century*, New York: Longmans.

Duck, Ruth (1993), 'Sin, Grace, and Gender in Free-Church Protestant Worship'. Chapter in Procter-Smith, Marjory and Walton, Janet R., eds, (1993), *Women in Worship. Interpretations of North American Diversity*, Louisville KY: Westminster/John Knox, pp. 55–71.

Dunmore, Ian (1983), 'Sitar Magic', *Nadaposana One*, London: Editions Poetry.

Ellingson, L. (2009), *Engaging Crystallization in Qualitative Research: An Introduction.* London: Sage.

Eluyefa, Dennis (2010), *The recontextualisation of the dundun tradition*, Unpublished PhD thesis, University of Winchester.

Episcopal Standing Committee on Church Music (1997), *Wonder, Love and Praise: A Supplement to the Hymnal 1982*, New York: Church Publishing Inc.

Escot, Pozzi (1990), 'Hildegard of Bingen: Universal Proportion' in *Sonus* 11, 1 Fall pp. 33–40.

Farrell, Bernadette (2009) (ed. Stephen Dean), *A Bernadette Farrell Song Book*, Brandon: Decani Books.

Farrell, Bernadette (2013), *A Bernadette Farrell Songbook*, Brandon: Decani. Available at <http://www.musiccorner.co.uk/Choral-Music/p. 112687/A-Bernadette-Farrell-Songbook/product.html> accessed February 1st 2013.

Fassler, Margot (1998), 'Composer and Dramatist.' Chapter in Newman (ed.) (1998), *Voice of the Living Light*, Berkeley, University of California Press pp. 149–75.

Fiorenza, Elisabeth Schüssler (1985), *Women Invisible in Society and Church*, Edinburgh: T & T Clark.

Fiorenza, Elisabeth Schüssler (1990), *In memory of Her: A Feminist Theological Reconstruction of Christian Origins*, New York: Crossroads .

Fiorenza, Elisabeth Schüssler (2000), *Jesus and the Politics of Interpretation*, New York and London: Continuum.

Foucault, Michel/Gordon, Colin (ed.) (1980), *Power Knowledge: Selected Interviews and Other writings 1972–77*, Hemel Hempstead: Harvester Wheatsheaf.

Foucault, Michel (trans Blasius, Mark) (1980), 'Subjectivity and truth' and 'Christianity and Confession', Dartmouth lectures, 17/24 Nov. 1980 (including Howison lectures, Berkeley, 20–21 Oct.). Originally published as 'About the Beginning of the hermeneutics of Self: Two Lectures at Dartmouth' in *Political theory*, vol.21, no.2, May 1993, pp. 198–227.

Fox, Matthew (ed.) (1987), *Hildegard of Bingen's Book of Divine Works, with Letters and Songs*, Santa Fe: Bear and Co.

Frend, W.H.C. (2002), *Orthodoxy, Paganism and Dissent in the Early Christian centuries*, Farnborough: Ashgate Variorum.

Frith, Simon (1987), 'The industrialization of popular Music'. Chapter in Lull, James (ed.) (1987), *Popular Music and Communication*, California: Newbury Park, pp. 50–64.

Gage, Matilda Joslyn (1893/1998), *Woman, Church and State: A Historical Account of the Status of woman through the Christian ages with reminiscences of the matriarchate* ed by Sally Roesch Wagner. Aberdeen, SD: Sky Carrier Press.

Galloway, Kathy (1993), *Love Burning Deep*, London: SPCK.

Godwin, Joscelyn (1987), *Music, Magic and Mysticism: A Sourcebook*, London: Arkana.

Goehr, Lydia (1992), *The Imaginary Museum of Musical Works: An Essay in the Philosophy of Music*, Oxford: Clarendon Press.

Gooch, Stan (1972), *Total man: Towards an Evolutionary Theory of Personality*, London: Allen Lane, Penguin Press.

Greeley, Horace (1838), 'A Sabbath with the Shakers'. In *The Knickerbocker, or New York Monthly Magazine* Vol. XI p. 537.

Green, Lucy (1988), *Music on Deaf Ears: Musical Meaning, Ideology and Education*, Manchester and New York: Manchester University Press.

Green, Lucy (1997), *Music, Gender, Education*, Cambridge: Cambridge University Press.

Grey, Mary (1989), *Redeeming the Dream, London: Feminism, Redemption and the Christian Tradition*, London: SPCK.

Grey, Mary (1993), *The Wisdom of fools: Seeking Revelation for Today*, London: SPCK.

Grindal, Gracia (1996), *We are one in Christ: Hymns, Paraphrases, and Translations by Gracia Grindal*, Kingston, NY: Selah Publishing.

Hardy, Alister (1966), *The Divine Flame: An Essay Towards a Natural History of Religion*, London: Collins.

Harper, Marilyn (around 2000), 'Story' Written on the web when she was Co-ordinator of Academic Music, James Allen's Girls' School and Organist, Christ's Chapel, Dulwich, London.

Harris, Diana (2002), *When will hymns be hers*, Unpublished article.

Harvey, Jonathan (1999), *Music and Inspiration*, London: Faber and Faber.

Harvey, Susan Ashbrook (2000), 'Women's service in ancient Syriac Christianity'. Chapter in *Mother, Nun, Deaconess: Images of Women according to Eastern canon Law, Kanon XVI, Yearbook of the Society for the Law of the Eastern Churches*, Egling: Edition Roman Kovar pp. 226–41.

Harvey, Susan Ashbrook (2001), 'Spoken words, voiced silence: Biblical Women in Syriac tradition', *Journal of Early Christian Studies 9:1*, pp. 105–31.

Haworth, John T. (1997), *Work, Leisure and Well-being*, London: Routledge.

Hay, David (1982), *Exploring Inner Space*, Harmondsworth: Penguin.

Hay, David and Nye, Rebecca (1998), *Spirit of the Child*, London: HarperCollins.

Herndon, Marcia (2000), 'Epilogue' to Moisala, Pirkko and Diamond, Beverley (2000), *Music and Gender*, Urbana and Chicago: University of Illinois Press pp. 347–60.

Heyward, Carter (2003), Unpublished Diagram from a Christology seminar at the Episcopal Divinity School, Cambridge, Massachusetts.

Hill Collins, Patricia (1998), *Fighting Words: Black women and the Search for Justice*, Minneapolis: University of Minnesota Press.

Hills, Peter and Argyle, Michael (1998), 'Musical and religious experiences and their relationships to happiness', *Personality and Individual Differences*, 25, pp. 91–102.

Holbrook, David and Poston, Elizabeth (eds) (1967), *The Cambridge Hymnal*, Cambridge: Cambridge University Press.

Holzman, Lois (2002), '*Practising a psychology that builds community*, East Side Institute for Short Term Psychotherapy, New York, NY' Delivered as the Keynote Address, APA Division 27/ Society for Community Research and Action (SCRA) Conference, Boston, March 2002 <http://www.eastsideinstitute.org> accessed January 2003.

Homans, M. (1986), *Bearing the Word, Language and Female Experience in Nineteenth-Century Women's Writing*, Chicago: University of Chicago Press.

hooks, bell (1994), 'What's passion got to do with it?' Chapter in *Outlaw culture: Resisting representations*, New York: Routledge. pp. 30–42.

Hunt, Stephen (2005), 'Basic Christianity: Gender Issues' in the *Alpha* Initiative, Paper presented to the *British Sociological Association Study of Religion Group*, 11th–13th April, 2005, University of Lancaster.

Ingalls, Monique, Landau, Carolyn and Wagner, Tom (eds) (2013b), *Christian Congregational Music, Performance, Identity and Experience*, Farnborough: Ashgate.

Isherwood, Lisa and Stuart, Elizabeth (1998), *Introducing Body Theology*, Sheffield: Sheffield Academic Press.

James, Jamie (1993), *The Music of the Spheres Music, Science and the Natural Order of the Universe*, London: Abacus.

Jarrett, Keith (1997), 'The Creative Power of the Moment'. Chapter in Toms, Michael (ed.), *The Well of Creativity*, Carlsbad, CA: Hay House.

Johnson Reagon, Bernice (1986), *Compositions: One*, Washington DC: Songtalk Publishing Company.

Julian (1925), *Dictionary of hymnology*, London, John Murray.

Kendrick, Graham (2003), 'Worship in Spirit and Truth'. Chapter in Darlington, Stephen and Kreider, Alan (2003), *Composing Music for Worship*, Norwich: Canterbury Press pp. 86–103.

Kendrick, Robert L. (1996), *Celestial Sirens: Nuns and their music in early modern Milan*, Oxford: Clarendon Press.

Kerman, Joseph (1985), *Contemplating Music: Challenges to musicology*, Cambridge, MA.

Kim, Grace Ji-sun (2002), *The Grace of Sophia*, Cleveland: The Pilgrim Press.

King, James (1885), *Anglican Hymnody, being an account of the 325 standard hymns of the highest merit according to the verdict of the whole Anglican Church*, London: Hatchards.

Kirwan, Michael (2004), *Discovering Girard*, London: Darton, Longman & Todd.

Kisliuk, Michelle (2000), 'Performance and Modernity among the BaAka Pygmies' Chapter in Moisala, Pirkko and Diamond, Beverley (2000), *Music and Gender*, Urbana and Chicago: University of Illinois Press pp. 25–50.

Koskoff, Ellen (1993), 'Miriam sings her song: the Self and the other in anthropological discourse'. Chapter in Solie, Ruth A. (1993), *Musicology and Difference*, Berkeley and Los Angeles: University of California Press pp. 149–63.

Kraemer, Ross S. (1988), *Maenads, Martyrs, Matrons, Monastics: A Sourcebook of Women's religions in the Graeco-Roman World*, New York: Oxford University Press.

Kung, Chung Hyun (1990), *Struggle to be the Sun again*, Maryknoll, NY: Probis Books.

Kwok, Pui Lan (1995), *Discovering the Bible in the Non-biblical world*, Maryknoll, New York: Orbis Books.

Lacan, Jacques (Mitchell, Juliet and Rose, Jacqueline, eds) (1982), *Feminine Sexuality: Jacques Lacan and the Ecole Freudienne* Basingstoke: Macmillan; New York: Pantheon Press.

Laeuchli, Samuel (1972), *Power and Sexuality: The Emergence of Canon Law at the Synod of Elvira*, Philadelphia: Temple University Press.

Lamb, Roberta (2000), Adapted from an essay originally published in *Orbit* music education theme issue, vol. 31, no. 1 (Spring 2000) (38–9). Roberta Lamb in the Gender and Music Education listserv, website <http://post.queensu.ca/~lambr/>

Langer, Suzanne (1953), *Feeling and Form: A Theory of Art*, London: Routledge and Kegan Paul.

Lapsley, Jacqueline E. (2001), 'Pouring Her Soul before the Lord: Women and Worship in the Old Testament'. Chapter in Blount, Brian K. and Tubbs Tinsdale, Leonora (eds) (2001), *Making Room at the Table*, Louisville, KY: Westminster John Knox Press pp. 3–12.

Le Fanu, Nicola (1987), 'Master Musician: an Impregnable Taboo?' *Contact 31 Autumn 1987*, pp. 4–8.

Leppert, Richard (1993), *The Sight of Sound: Music, Representation and the History of the Body*, Berkeley: University of California Press.

Leppert, R. and McClary, S. (eds) (1987), *Music and Society*, Cambridge: Cambridge University Press.

Lerner, Gerda (1986), *The Creation of Patriarchy*, New York: Oxford University Press.

Lindley, Margaret (1995), 'Competing Trinities: The Great Mother and the Formation of the Christian Trinity'. Chapter in Barton, Julie S. and Mews, Constant (1995), *Hildegard of Bingen and Gendered Theology in Judaeo-Christian Tradition*, Monash University: Centre for Studies in Religion and Theology, pp. 29–40.

Liveris, L.B. (1995), 'Feminist Ecclesiology: An Orthodox Perspective from Australia', *Ortega* pp. 152–63.

Lorde, Audre (1984), *SisterOutsider: Essays and Speeches*, New York: Crossing Press.

Lovelock, William (1952), *The Examination Fugue*, London: A. Hammond and Co.

Lykke, Nina and Braidotti, Rosi (1996), *Between Monsters, Goddesses and Cyborgs*, London: Zed Books.

McClary, Susan (1991), *Feminine Endings*, Minnesota: University of Minnesota Press.

McClary, Susan (2001), *Conventional Wisdom*, Berkeley: University of California Press.

McClary, Susan (2003), Lecture in Leeds University, UK, March.

McDade, Carolyn (1986), *This tough spun web: songs of global struggle and solidarity*, Plainville, MA: Womancenter.

McDade, Carolyn (1990), *This Ancient Love*, Plainville, MA: Surtsey Publishing.

Macdonald, Margaret Y. (1996), *Early Christian Women and Pagan Opinion: The Power of Hysterical Women*, Cambridge: Cambridge University Press.

Mace, John H. (2007), *Involuntary Memory*, Oxford: Wiley-Blackwell.

McEwan, Dorothea, Pinsent, Pat, Pratt, Ianthe, Seddon, Veronica (2001), *Making Liturgy: Creating Rituals for Life*, Norwich: Canterbury Press.

Mann, Helene (2000), 'The Hymns and Carols of Shirley Erena Murray', *Music in the Air: Song and Spirituality*, Summer 2000 pp. 6–13.

Mantin, Ruth (2002), *Thealogies in Process: the role of Goddess-talk in feminist spirituality*, Unpublished PhD Thesis, May 2002, Southampton University.

Marshall, Kimberley (1993), *Rediscovering the Muses: Women's Musical traditions*, Boston: Northeastern University Press.

Martin, Madeline Sue (1998), *Bring the Feast*, Cleveland, OH: Pilgrim Press.

Maslow, Abraham. H. (1967), 'The Creative Attitude'. In Mooney and Razik (eds) *Explorations in Creativity* New York: Harper and Row pp. 40 –55.

Meyer, K. (1917), *Der Chorische Gesang der Frauen*, Leipzig: Breitkopf and Haertel.

Midgley, Mary (2003), *Myths We Live By*, London: Routledge.

Moisala, Pirkko (2000), 'Gender Negotiations of the Composer Kaija Saariaho in Finland: the Woman composer as Nomadic subject'. Chapter in Moisala, Pirkko and Diamond, Beverley (2000), *Music and Gender*, Urbana and Chicago: University of Illinois Press pp. 166–88.

Moisala, Pirkko and Diamond, Beverley (2000), *Music and Gender*, Urbana and Chicago: University of Illinois Press.

Morgan, Sarah (2013), *Community Choirs – A Musical Transformation*, Unpublished DProf thesis, University of Winchester.

Mossi, John P. and Toolan, Suzanne (1996), *Canticles and Gathering Prayers*, Winona, MN: St Mary's Press, Christian Brothers Publications.

Murray, Shirley Erena (1992), *In every corner Sing*, Hope Publishing. Accessed by CD rom *Hymnquest*, Stainer and Bell in September 2003.

Murray, Shirley Erena (1996), *Every Day in your spirit*, US: Hope Publications.

Murray, Shirley Erena (2003), *Every Day in your spirit*, Hope Publishing. Accessed by CD rom *Hymnquest*, Stainer and Bell in September 2003.

Myers, I.B. (1993), *Gifts differing: understanding personality type*. Palo Alto, CA: Consulting Psychologists Press.

Myers, I.B. and McCaulley, M.H. (1985), *Manual: a guide to the development and use of the Myers-Briggs Type Indicator* (2nd edition) Palo Alto, CA: Consulting Psychologists Press.

Myers, Margaret (2000), 'Searching for data about Ladies Orchestras'. Chapter in Moisala, Pirkko and Diamond, Beverley (2000), *Music and Gender*, Urbana and Chicago: University of Illinois Press pp. 189–218.

Nash, Wanda (1997), *Gifts from Hildegard*, London: Darton, Longman and Todd.

Neu, Diann L. (2003), *Women's rites: Feminist liturgies for life's journey*, Cleveland: Pilgrim Press.

Neu, Diann, Shapiro, Mindy, Cullom, Barbara A. and Hoffman, Tobie (1988), *Miriam's Sisters rejoice: A Holy Thursday and Passover Feminist Seder*, Washington DC: WATER.

Neuls-Bates, Carol (ed.) ([1982] 1996), *Women in Music: An Anthology of Source Readings from the Middle Ages to the Present*, Boston: Northeastern University Press.

New Zealand Hymnbook Trust (1993), *Alleluia Aotearoa*, Raumati Beach: New Zealand Hymnbook Trust.

Ni Riain, Noirin (2011), *Theosony: Towards a Theology of listening*, Dublin: The Columba Press.

Ni Riain, Noirin (2013) interview: 'Noirin Ni Riain – a serene path in valley of tears' by Emily Hourican, *Independent.ie*. Available at <http://www.independent.ie/entertainment/music/interview-noirin-ni-riain-a-serene-path-in-valley-of-tears-29777432.html> accessed December 28th 2013.

O'Grady, Helen (2005), *Woman's Relationship with herself: Gender, Foucault and Therapy*, London and New York: Routledge.

O'Malley, J. (1991), 'Was Ignatius Loyola a Church Reformer? How to look at early modern Catholicism', *The Catholic Historical Review*, 77, pp. 177–93.

Ong, Walter (1982), *Orality and Literacy: The Technologizing of the Word*, London and New York: Methuen.

Panufnik, Roxanna (2003), *Beyond a Mass for Westminster*. Chapter in Darlington, Stephen and Kreider, Alan (2003), *Composing Music for Worship*, Norwich: Canterbury Press pp. 76–85.

Parker Huber, Jane (1983), *Joy in Singing*, Atlanta and Louisville, KY: The Office of Women and The Joint Office of Worship of The Presbyterian Church, USA.

Pollock, John L. (1984), *The Foundations of Philosophical Semantics*, Princeton: Princeton University Press.

Procter-Smith, Marjorie (1995), *Praying with our eyes open: Engendering Feminist Liturgical Prayer*, Nashville: Abingdon Press.

Proust, Marcel ([1871–1922] 2002), trans by Lydia Davis, Mark Treharne, James Grieve, John Sturrock, Carol Clark, Peter Collier, & Ian Patterson *In Search of Lost Time (À la recherche du temps perdu)* London: Allen Lane.

Purce, Jill (1998), Publicity leaflet for *The Healing Voice*.

Quasten, Johannes (trans by Ramsey, Boniface O.P.) ([1973] 1983), *Music and Worship in Pagan and Christian Antiquity*, Washington, DC: Guild of Pastoral Musicians.

Rahn, John (1994), 'What is valuable in art, and can music still achieve it?' Chapter in Rahn, John (ed.) (1994), *Perspectives in Musical Aesthetics*, New York: Norton.

Reardon, Colleen (2002), *Holy Concord within Sacred Walls: Nuns and Music in Siena 1575–1700*, Oxford: Oxford University Press.

Redmond, Layne (1997), *When the drummers were women – A Spiritual history of Rhythm*, New York, Three Rivers Press.

Reich, Nancy (1986), 'Clara Schumann'. Chapter in Bowers, Jane and Tick, Judith (eds) (1986), *Women making Music: The Western Art Tradition 1150–1950*, Urbana: University of Illinois Press pp. 249–81.

Rizza, Margaret (2004), *Awakening in Love*, Stowmarket: Kevin Mayhew. <http://www.kevinmayhew.com/Product_16985> accessed Feb 12th 2005.

Robertson, Carol E. (1993), 'The ethnomusicologist as midwife'. Chapter in Solie, Ruth A. (1993), *Musicology and Difference*, Berkeley and Los Angeles: University of California Press pp. 107–24.

Rouget, Gilbert (trans. Biebuyck, Brunhilde) (1987), *Music and Trance: A Theory of the relations between Music and Possession*, Chicago and London; University of Chicago Press.

Ruether, Rosemary R. (1985), *Women-Church: Theology and Practice of Feminist Liturgical Communities*, London: Harper and Row.

Rye, Gill (2003), 'Motherhood without sacrifice The sacred without sacrifice: Julia Kristeva's new model of mothering – an exploration'. Paper presented at AHRB seminar, *Gender, Myth and Spirituality*, April 6th.

St Hilda Community (1991), *Women Included*, London: SPCK.

Sawyer, Deborah F. (1996), *Women and religion in the first Christian Centuries*, New York: Routledge.

Saxton, Robert (2003), *Darkness to Light: Cycles and Circles: the Sacred in my music.* Chapter in Darlington, Stephen and Kreider, Alan (2003), *Composing Music for Worship*, Norwich: Canterbury Press pp. 51–65.

Scheid, John (1992), 'Religious Roles of Roman women'. Chapter in Pantel, Schmitt (ed.) (1992), *A History of Women in the West Vol 1: From Ancient Goddesses to*

Christian Saints, Cambridge, MA: The Belknap Press of Harvard University Press pp. 377–408.

Schüssler Fiorenza, Elisabeth (1990), *In memory of Her: A Feminist Theological Reconstruction of Christian Origins*, New York: Crossroads.

Schüssler Fiorenza, Elisabeth (2000), *Jesus and the Politics of Interpretation*, New York and London: Continuum.

Sharp, Ian (2000), *Classical Music's Evocation of Childhood: Studies in the History and Interpretation of Music Vol. 78*, New York: The Edwin Mellen Press.

Shepherd, John (1993), 'Difference and Power in Music'. Chapter in Solie, Ruth A. (1993), *Musicology and Difference*, Berkeley and Los Angeles: University of California Press pp. 46–65.

Shillor, Irit (1993), *Jewish Women's Music*, Seminar at King Alfred's College, Winchester, UK.

Sisters of the Church (1996), *Peace till the Moon Fails*, London: The Community of the Sisters of the Church.

Sloboda, John (1985), *The Musical Mind*, Oxford: Clarendon Press.

Sloboda, John (1999), 'Music –where cognition and emotion meet', *The Psychologist*, 12, 9 September 1999, pp. 450–5.

Smith, Peter (ed.) (1967), *Faith Folk and Clarity*, London: Stainer and Bell.

Smith, Peter and Boyce-Tillman, June (1972), *New Orbit*, London: Galliard.

Smith, W.S. (1962), *Musical Aspects of the New Testament*, Amsterdam, unpublished dissertation.

Stevens, Denis (ed. and trans) (1980), *The Letters of Claudio Monteverdi*, Cambridge: Cambridge University Press.

Storr, Anthony (1993), *Music and the Mind*, London: HarperCollins.

Stuart, Elizabeth (1996), *Just Good Friends: Towards a Lesbian and Gay Theology of Relationships*, London: Mowbrays.

Subotnik, Rose Rosengard (1996), *Deconstructive Variations: Music and Reason in Western Society*, Minneapolis: University of Minnesota Press.

Sullivan, Lawrence E. (1997), *Enchanting Powers: Music in the World's Religions*, Cambridge MA: Harvard University Press.

Tambiah, Stanley J. (1979), 'A Performative Approach to Ritual', *Proceedings of the British Academy* 65, pp. 113–69.

Theobald, Elizabeth (1997), *Some criteria for assessing modern liturgical music*, Paper given a research seminar, King Alfred's College of Higher Education, 18th March 1997.

Thomas, Lisa Neufeld et al. (2003), *Voices Found: Women in the Church's Song*, New York: Church Publishing.

Tillman, June B. (1987), *Towards a model of the development of musical creativity: A Study of the Compositions of Children aged 3–11*. Unpublished PhD Thesis, University of London Institute of Education.

Tillman, June B. (1976), *Exploring Sound*, London: Stainer and Bell.

Tillman, June B. and Percival, Allen (eds) (1980), *The Galliard Book of Carols*, London: Stainer and Bell.

Tomlinson, Gary (1993), *Music in Renaissance Magic: Toward an Historiography of others*, Chicago: University of Chicago Press.

Tracy, D. (1975), *Blessed rage for order: The new pluralism in theology*, Chicago: University of Chicago Press.

Treitler, Leo (1993), 'Gender and Other dualities'. Chapter in Solie, Ruth A. (1993), *Musicology and Difference*, Berkeley and Los Angeles: University of California Press pp. 23–45.

Turner, Victor (1969, 1974), *The Ritual Process: Structure and Anti-structure*, Baltimore: Penguin Books.

Unitarian/Universalist Hymnbook Resources Commission (1993), *Singing the Living Tradition*, Boston: Beacon Press.

Van der Weyer, Robert (ed.) (1997), *Hildegard in a Nutshell*, London: Hodder and Stoughton.

Vitz, Paul (1979), *Psychology as Religion: The Cult of Self Worship*, London: Lion.

Ward, Elizabeth Stuart Phelps (1896), *Chapters from a Life*, New York: Arno Press.

Ward, Hannah and Wild, Jennifer (eds) (1995a), *Human Rites*, London: Mowbrays.

Ward, H., Wild, J. and Morley, J. (eds) (1995), *Celebrating Women*, London: SPCK.

Werner, Eric (1959), *The Sacred Bridge: The Interdependence of liturgy and music in Synagogue and Church during the first millennium*, London: Dennis Dobson and New York: Columbia University Press.

Whitney, Rae E. (1995), *With Joy our spirits sing: The Hymns of Rae E. Whitney*, Kingston, NY: Selah Publishing.

Wilson Dickson, Andrew (1992), *A History of Christian Music: from Gregorian Chant to Black Gospel, An authoritative illustrated guide to all the major traditions of music for Worship*, London: Lion/SPCK.

Winkett, Lucy (2010), *Our Sound is Our Wound: Contemplative Listening to a noisy world*, London: Continuum Books. <https://vulpeslibris.wordpress.com/2010/02/17/our-sound-is-our-wound-by-lucy-winkett-a-prophetic-voice-in-a-world-of-noise/> accessed Dec 30th 2013.

Winter, Miriam Therese (1987), *WomanPrayer, WomanSong*, MeyerStone/Crossroad.

Wootton, Janet H. (2000), *Introducing a Practical Feminist Theology of Worship*, Sheffield: Sheffield Academic.

Wootton, Janet (2003), *The Future of the Hymn*. Chapter in Darlington, Stephen and Kreider, Alan (2003), *Composing Music for Worship*, Norwich: Canterbury Press pp. 117–40.

Wootton, Janet (2010), *This is our song – Women's Hymn writing*, London: Epworth.

Wootton, Janet, Watson, Derek et al., eds (1997), *Peculiar Honours*, London: Stainer and Bell.

Wren, Brian (1989), *What language can I borrow*? London: SCM Press.

Zuesse, Evan M. (1987), 'Ritual'. Entry in Eliade, Mircea (1987), *The Encyclopaedia of Religion Vol 12*, New York: Collier Macmillan pp. 405–22.

Discography

Abtei St Hildegard, *The Music of Hildegard*

Anonymous Four, *11,000 Virgins*

Boyce-Tillman, June (1999), *Voice of Experience*, London: Hildegard Press

Dekker, Chris (199?), *Return to the Source – The Chakra* Journey, London: Return to the Source and Pyramid Records

Farrell, Bernadette (no date available), *Christ be our Light*, Brandon: Decani Books

Fulmer, Colleen (no date), *Her Wings unfurled: Original Songs of Challenge and Comfort calling forth Courage and Compassion*, Albany, CA: Loretto Spirituality Network

Gothic Voices, directed by Christopher Page, *Feather on the Breath of God*

McDade, Carolyn (1999), *We are the Land we sing*, WRA8–1313, Canada: Carolyn

Oliveros, Pauline (1989), *Deep Listening*, San Francisco: New Albion Records

Sequentia directed by Barbara Thornton, *Canticles of Ecstasy* and *Voice of the Blood*

Sherman, Kathy (1998), *Beyond Words; Original Instrumental Music by Kathy Sherman*, Illinois, Sisters of St Joseph of LaGrange II, Musings from the sleeve notes

Silvestro, Marsie (1993a), *Circling free*, Gloucester, MA: Moonsong productions Cassette

Silvestro, Marsie (1993b), *On the other side: Songs that celebrate Many Ways of Knowing*, Cassette Gloucester, MA: Moonsong productions

Tavener, John: A Portrait, NAXOS 8.558152–53

Vox Animae, *Ordo Virtutum*, Videotape

Women as composers and performers of mediaeval chant (1998) JARO 4210–2

Interviews

Bringle, Mel (2003), Brevard, North Carolina, June 3rd 2003

Catlin Reid, Pauline (1997), London, June 1997

Charleston, Bishop Stephen (2003), Episcopal Divinity School, Boston, May 25th 2003

Darr, Mother Carolyn and Frances, Sister Christina (2003), Society of St Margaret, Boston, April 2003

Daw, Carl (2003), Boston University, 27th April 2003

Erney, Mary (2003), Hildegard Community, Austin, TX, June 2003

Hernandez, Ana (2003), following a workshop in the Episcopal Divinity School, Cambridge, MA, January 11th 2003

Hildegard Community (2003), Interview with members, Austin, TX, June 2003

Kirk, Martha Ann (2003), European Women's Synod in Barcelona, August 8th 2003

Kiskun, Laime (2003), European Women's Synod in Barcelona, August 2003

Knoll Hicks, Flois (2003), European Women's Synod in Barcelona, August 2003

Lucozzi, Elisa (2003), Episcopal Divinity School, Cambridge, MA, January 2003

Medina, Margarita (2003), European Women's Synod in Barcelona, August 9th 2003

Methodist Women (2004), Birmingham, UK, May 2004.

Michaels, Pat (2003), St James' Episcopal Church in Porter Square in Cambridge, MA, January 31st 2003

Neu, Diann (2003), Washington DC, April 2003

Neufeld Thomas, Lisa (2003), Philadelphia, May 2003

Reynolds, Sister Robyn (2003), Nungalinga College, Darwin, Australia, July 4th 2003

Ring Frank, Jane (2003), Episcopal Divinity School, Cambridge, MA, January 16th, 2003

Silvestro, Marsie (2003), Gloucester, MA, May 2003

Vilstalmsdottir, Rev Audur (2003), European Women's Synod in Barcelona, August 9th 2003

Webb, Joy (2003), London, June 2003

Wilkins, Caroline (2003), First Church, Cambridge, MA, January 12th 2003

Woods, Rev Patricia (2003), Cambridge, MA, January 2003

Wootton, Rev Dr Janet (2003), Union Chapel. Islington, London, July 2003

Index

accompaniment 92, 172, 173, 223, 279
acoustics 53
aesthetics 7, 14, 36, 46–7, 57
Alleluias 82–3
altar 81
alternative liturgy 171, 194, 197, 213–61, 267, 270, 273, 285, 287, 290
Ambrose 69, 76, 77, 79
analysis 17, 37, 41, 264
angels 49–50, 123, 135, 155
anger 2, 175, 239; in God 281
Anglican Church 187, 211, 228, 229, 233, 235, 289
anointing 217
anthems 270
antiphonal singing 69–70, 72, 84
architecture 128, 144
aristocracy 78, 106, 115, 266, 274, 280
audience 33, 222, 233, 259
Augustine 75, 92
authority 76, 100, 162, 211, 240, 261, 272

Bach, J.S. 15, 26
Badalla, R.G. 121, 124, 130
baptism 68, 199, 251
Barthes 18, 34
Basil 70, 75, 89
Beethoven, Ludwig van 15
beliefs 35, 57, 62, 142, 165, 289
bells 51, 73, 90, 91
Benedictines 107, 288
Berger, T. 78, 80, 81
Bible 15, 19, 121, 189, 273, 279
birthing 169, 217, 251, 256

bishops 115, 116, 117, 125, 127, 130, 135, 173
blessing 148, 215, 217
blood 67, 72, 90, 103–4, 108
body 33–4, 35, 54, 93, 109, 112, 133, 161, 205–6, 251, 258, 259, 288–90
Borromeo, Bishop C. 119, 123, 125, 128
Borromeo, Bishop F. 123, 125–6, 131, 132
Bowers, J. 18, 41
boys 68, 81–2, 106, 210, 233–4
brides 89; of Christ 120, 122, 133, 137; of the Lamb 141
Bynum, C.W. 131, 132, 134

Campion, N.J. 140
candles 52, 77, 256
cantors 69, 78, 82, 172, 227, 228, 241, 267
carols 190, 242
Carter, S. 183, 197, 283
cathedrals 53, 210–11, 232, 233–5, 238, 239, 272
Catholic Women's Network 171, 245
celibacy 93, 141, 162, 228, 260, 283, 289
cemeteries 79–80
chants 28, 55, 72, 41, 82, 98, 130, 194, 197, 232, 246, 248, 252, 254
chaos 40–1, 269, 271
children 5, 38, 48, 87, 142, 187, 221–4, 242, 264, 277
choirs 8, 38, 70, 85, 220, 225, 233–6
chords 40, 114, 122, 223, 276
Christianity 33, 66–8, 73, 78, 93, 206, 226, 265, 274, 279, 288, 290
Christina Frances, Sr 241

Chrysostom, John 69, 72, 74, 80, 89, 90, 91, 92

Church, the 20–1, 165, 213, 239, 245, 255, 265, 282, 283; early Church 65–93

Citron, M. 45, 59, 60

city, the 71, 117, 126, 129, 133, 136

classical music tradition 4, 15, 29, 37, 38, 40, 44, 57, 223, 267, 269

clothes *see* robes

compassion 251

composers 5, 15, 29, 31, 32, 45, 107, 113–37, 223, 237, 247–8, 284

composition 37, 203n, 215–16, 286

confidence 201, 209–10, 248, 254, 268

congregations 69, 82, 179, 220, 248, 266, 275

consciousness 55, 58

controversy 2, 66, 77

cosmos 57, 107, 110–11, 266

Council of Laodicea 72, 81

Cozzolani, C.M. 121, 123, 130, 134

creation 107–8

creativity 14, 49, 183, 203, 249, 270, 273, 283, 293

Crosby, F. 194, 280, 287

cymbals 86, 90, 91

dance 33, 51, 67, 68, 75, 79, 89, 146–8, 155, 205–6, 250–1, 255, 257–8, 263, 289, 290

darkness 3, 4, 108, 184, 203–4, 251

Darr, Mother C. 241

Daw, C. 174, 178, 182, 193, 204, 242

deaconesses 75, 80, 142

deacons 142

dead, the 68, 73, 74–7, 166

democracy 29n, 222, 256–7, 260, 267, 268

devil, the 104–5, 146–7

devotion 120, 126, 130, 187

dirges 73, 74

diversity 76–7, 182–6, 221, 225, 230, 269–71

Divine, the 7, 61–2, 135, 163, 164, 166, 206, 255, 268

Drinker, S. 11–12, 59

drums 6, 30, 197, 228, 245–7, 278

earth, the 179–80, 216

ecotheology 172, 179

ecstasy 132, 160, 277

education 178, 268

Egeria 69, 82

Elliott, C. 187, 191

embodiment 33–4, 88–92, 255–9, 289–90

emotion 43, 159

empathy 224

empowerment 239, 247, 259, 260, 268, 282

enchantment 25, 252

enclosure 114, 116

ensembles 41, 53–4, 117, 223, 277

Ephrem 70, 81, 82

Ermey, M. 240, 253

ethics 35, 36, 276

ethnomusicology 9, 17, 32, 51

Eucharist 26, 75, 132–3, 217, 232, 250, 289–90

experience 57, 62–3, 111, 287–8

expertise 8, 214, 220, 243, 261

faith 135, 140, 166

family 44, 137, 142

Farrell, B. 198–9, 229

feelings 23, 61, 146, 162

feminine, the 3, 7, 13, 40, 134, 184–5, 216, 217, 230, 253, 271

feminism 18, 173, 205, 213, 248–9, 255, 258–9

feminist theology 28, 171, 172, 206, 219, 264

Ficino, M. 36, 61
Fiorenza, E. Schüssler 15, 93
flutes 87, 109, 219
folksong 154, 229
food 57, 131, 132–3
Foucault, M. 18, 36, 61
funding 31, 39, 238
funerals 72–3, 89, 93, 165

gatekeepers 30
gender 1, 17, 19, 42, 44, 80, 176, 182, 265
girls' choirs 210–11, 233–4
Gnosticism 68, 81, 87–8, 93, 240
God 36, 108, 166, 175, 180, 182–6, 188,
        193, 219, 230, 248–51, 271
goddess, the 67–8, 186, 259
gospel, the 85, 200, 258, 287
Graeco-Roman thought 33, 61, 286
Green, L. 43, 51, 60
Gregorian chant 87–8, 98, 252
guitar 195, 196, 280

harmony 99, 108, 114, 226, 274
Harper, M. 209–10
Harris, D. 39, 234–5, 237
Harvey, S. 79, 84–5
healing 195, 246, 247, 256
heresy 76–7
Hernandez, A. 232, 246, 248–9, 254
Herndon, M. 17, 41
hero/heroine 28, 32
Heyward, C. 21
hierarchy 63, 218, 249, 267, 269
Hildegard of Bingen 23, 26–8, 45, 95–112,
        203, 222, 247, 265, 274, 293
history 15, 16, 201, 264
Holloway, R. 36, 276
Holy Spirit 82, 133, 253
hymnbooks 171, 178, 284
hymnody 8, 21, 81, 86, 169–207
hymns 84–5, 154, 164, 176–7, 286–7

identity 44, 47
idolatry 73, 180
imagery 28, 34, 35, 36, 101, 184–5, 195,
        250–1, 271
imagination 56, 57
immanence 36, 62, 166, 292
improvisation 4–5, 36, 37–8, 82–3,
        103–4, 150, 226, 233, 242, 258,
        276, 286
incantation 11, 87–8
incarnation 109, 185
inclusive language 8, 169, 172–8, 238,
        249–52, 257
instruments 50–2, 91–2, 109, 119, 143–4,
        245, 282; *see also individual
        instruments*
intercession 69
interfaith work 232, 260–1
intuition 86–8, 91, 100, 112, 203, 252,
        254, 286
Iona Community 195, 214, 245

jazz 243–4
Jesus 8, 88, 108, 140, 188, 192, 199, 250,
        285
Judaism 66, 67, 77–8, 91
Julian of Norwich 3, 190, 203
justice 100, 189, 197–202, 226, 261, 283

Kendrick, R. 116, 117, 123, 130
Kirk, M.A. 239, 250–1, 258
Kristeva, J. 33–4

laity 118, 181–2
Lamb, R. 16, 46–7
language 29, 174, 175, 176
Latin 98, 115, 172, 178
leadership 212–13, 268; of worship 172
Lee, Mother A. 22, 139–66, 264, 265,
        283, 286
liberation theology 172, 206

light 3, 108, 184, 203
liminality 25, 54, 59, 61, 110, 260
Lindley, M. 66–7
literacy 38, 107n, 229, 274
liturgy 85, 105–6, 127, 148, 155, 174,
    239–40, 248, 265, 270, 272, 287
Lucozzi, E. 245–6
Lutheran Church 188, 219, 220, 256

McClary, S. 30, 34, 35, 40–1, 48
McDade, C. 179–80, 195–6, 198, 229
magic 86–7
male voice choir 61, 210–12
manuscripts 39, 107
marriage 81, 92, 272
martyrs 74, 95
Mary Magdalene 120, 124, 134, 191, 205,
    240
Maslow, A. 56, 58
Mass *see* Eucharist
meaning 34, 36, 43–4, 48, 102
Medina, M. 256–7
meditation 103, 247, 259
melisma 105, 124
melody 98, 105, 109, 124, 226, 277
Mendelssohn, Fanny 15, 45, 248
menopause 261
metres 194, 201
Michaels, P. 185, 193
midwife 16, 184, 271
mind 6, 33, 35, 59, 62, 161, 288, 290
ministry 67, 155, 228
Miriam 67, 91, 190, 191
misogyny 20, 211, 233–4, 238, 255, 260
modes 102, 153
monody 115, 121
monophony 114, 272
motets 123, 124
mother image 68, 95, 142, 161, 169, 176,
    184, 251, 271
Mother's Union 235

motherhood 11, 19, 93
mourning 72–4
Murray, S.E. 172, 180, 189, 193, 201–2
music education 16, 46, 51–2, 210–11,
    223–4, 236, 277
musical canon 12, 14–15, 29, 33, 37, 38, 41,
    47, 49, 51, 53, 59, 60, 123, 273, 277
musical score 37, 39, 104, 274
musicology 29, 30, 62, 88, 266, 293
mystery 89, 270, 292
mysticism 109, 131–2
mystics 57, 130, 134, 160, 251
myths 18–19, 59–60

narratives 55, 62
nature 53, 60, 179–80, 221–2, 260, 266–7
Neu, D. 242–3, 246, 248n, 255
New Age 6, 41, 53, 252
Ni Riain, N. 7, 254–5
notation 38–40, 98–9, 145, 274
nurture 33, 84–6, 111, 199, 202, 247, 250,
    261, 284–5

obedience 139
Offices 105–6, 237–8
opera 12, 35, 46, 114
oracy 38–40, 111, 192, 242, 244, 274, 275,
    277
orchestras 51, 115, 264
ordination 213, 217, 226
organ 118–19, 144, 196, 219, 244
organists 37, 119, 196, 234, 267
ornamentation 146, 277
Orthodox tradition 189, 191, 211, 227
Oxford Movement 289

paganism 67–8, 72, 74–5, 86–7, 89–90,
    231, 279
Passover 77, 261
patriarchy 21–2, 63, 88, 93, 213, 260,
    264–5

Paul, St 76, 290
peace 151, 157, 165, 206, 246
Pentecostal tradition 32, 278, 286, 290
performers 29, 34, 43, 45, 103, 125,
        212–13, 222, 258, 270
philosophers 52, 61, 90
piano 220, 227, 257
polyphony 113, 114, 129, 130
popular music 35, 37, 39, 43
power 21–2, 24, 135–6, 163, 224, 282
prayer 69, 161, 174, 175, 219, 224, 259,
        277
prejudice 18, 47, 211
priesthood 4, 10, 67, 181, 217–18, 220,
        249, 266, 269
priests 96, 231, 233, 249, 267
progress 15, 33
protest song 5, 30, 198
Protestant tradition 137, 187–8, 190, 207,
        237, 266, 279, 289
psalms 69–70, 71, 76, 77, 78, 81, 92
publication 171, 186, 237, 284
publishers 187–8

Quakers 140–1, 155–6

rattles 51
Reardon, C. 118, 122
recording 31, 39, 43–4, 53, 237
religion 19, 66
religious 75, 86, 107, 114–37, 228, 236,
        239, 241, 252, 260, 272
Renaissance 36, 49, 61, 113–37, 265, 280
resurrection 73–4, 190
Reynolds, Sr R. 232, 252, 257
rhythm 50, 88, 98–9, 161–2, 246, 278
Ring Frank, J. 33, 44, 46, 230
rituals 56; healing 246; of the dead 75–6;
        shaker 146–7, 149, 155–6
robes 97, 133, 147
rock music 267, 279

role models 44, 45–6, 210–11, 238–9
Roman Catholic Church 211, 217, 228–9,
        239–40, 273, 284, 289–90
Rusca, C. 120–1

sacraments 250, 253
saints 106, 118–19, 136–7
salvation 110, 141, 156
Salvation Army 220–1, 226, 264, 287
Sarah 84, 175, 190
Schumann, C. 45, 248
Second Coming 141, 165
self-policing 22, 23, 24, 48
sex 93, 141, 162, 163
sexuality 34, 35, 49, 89, 246, 283
Shakers 139–66, 277
Sherman, K. 204, 206
silence 83, 98, 149, 278
Silvestro, M. 176, 214–18
simplicity 79, 145, 165
singing 55–6, 68, 69–70, 110, 143, 146,
        151–5, 163–4, 245, 247, 254, 277,
        281
sistrum 73, 91
Sloboda, J. 31, 43
Smyth, E. 50, 59, 280
solo singing 69, 126, 133, 220, 227, 287
soul 33, 35, 104–5, 109, 112, 288
spaces 53, 80, 135, 213, 241, 272–3
speed 43, 83, 1111, 144, 279
spirits 157–8
spiritual frames 7, 58–9
spirituality 54–62, 107–10, 126, 134–5,
        206
spontaneity 158, 277
stereotypes 46, 49–50
story 19, 29–30
strings 109, 219
Subotnik, R.R. 17, 42
Sunday School 187, 227
synods 272

taboos 45, 81
Taizé chanting 192, 197, 214, 219, 253, 267
tambourines 51, 96, 89, 91
text 12, 28, 29–30, 103, 105, 170, 175, 284
Theobald, E. 267–8, 275
theology 12, 109–10, 148, 164, 177, 193,
        233, 264, 293; *see also* feminist
        theology; liberation theology
therapy 9, 256
Thomas, L. Neufeld 173, 213
Thornton, B. 99, 235
trance 56, 153
transcendence 36, 40, 56, 58, 62, 110, 217
transformation 162–3, 216, 222
Trinity 7, 66–7, 93, 106, 293
trumpet 73, 91, 109, 119, 244
tunes 87, 143, 144, 150, 154, 161, 195, 201

Unitarian/Universalist tradition 178, 226
US 172, 198, 212, 229, 241, 252–3, 285

Van Alstyne, F.J. *see* Crosby, F.
Vatican II 172, 228, 266–7, 284
veils 75, 119
Vespers 82, 123
Vilstalmsdottir, A. 219–20
violence 19, 22, 175, 195, 216, 247
Virgin Mary 84, 106, 120, 134, 182–3,
        187, 192

virgins 75, 86
visions 99–101, 111, 140, 158, 160
voice, the 50, 51, 108, 223, 236, 256
volume 43, 83, 279

wailing 74n
Wales 212
Webb, J. 220–1, 253–4, 267
wedding ceremonies 72, 89
Werner, K. 82–3, 87–8
White, E. 198, 229, 283
Wilkins, C. 243–4, 249–50
Winkett, L. 85, 120, 278
Wisdom 3–4, 109, 185, 197, 202, 206,
        207, 247, 261, 264, 269, 276, 282,
        290, 293
witchcraft 157
women 20, 39, 40, 48, 59, 81, 87, 93, 115,
        151, 157, 175, 186, 189–92, 201, 211,
        218, 227, 238, 258–9, 263–5, 280
women's voice choirs 34–5, 50, 67, 68, 70,
        85, 93, 179, 272
Wootton, J. 171, 174, 178, 184, 196, 199
worship 80, 143, 167, 197, 243, 248, 259,
        268, 278
worship songs 179–80, 196, 229, 236,
        267, 284
Wren, B. 177, 185, 190–1

Music and Spirituality

Edited by

JUNE BOYCE-TILLMAN

Music and Spirituality explores the relationships between spirituality and music in a variety of traditions and contexts including those in which human beings have performed music with spiritual intention or effect. It will address the plurality of modern society in the areas of musical style and philosophical and religious beliefs, and give respect to different positions regarding the place of music both in worship and in the wider society. It will include historical, anthropological, musicological, ethnomusicological, theological and philosophical dimensions and encourage multi-disciplinary and cross-disciplinary contributions.

It looks for well-researched studies with new and open approaches to spirituality and music and will encourage interesting innovative case-studies. Books within the series are subject to peer review and will include single and co-authored monographs as well as edited collections including conference proceedings. It will consider the use of musical material in either written or recorded form as part of submissions.

The Series Editor

The Rev Professor June Boyce-Tillman is Professor of Applied Music at the University of Winchester where she runs the Centre for the Arts as Well-being. She has wide experience in education, spirituality and music and has published widely in these areas. She is a self-supporting ordained Anglican Priest and received an MBE for her contribution to music and education.

Proposal submissions should be sent to oxford@peterlang.com

Vol. 1   June Boyce-Tillman
         In Tune With Heaven Or Not: Women in Christian
         Liturgical Music. 2014. ISBN 978-3-0343-1777-1

Praise for *In Tune With Heaven Or Not*

'Making music is the ultimate expression of embodied cognition. We use all of our senses, all of our being. Yet for too long it has been overly theorised and made unnecessarily academic, often by men. June Boyce-Tillman shows how music is bigger than any gender, how it is an outpouring of our minds and bodies which defies much of the traditional ways in which it is viewed. *In Tune With Heaven Or Not: Women in Christian Liturgical Music* corrects many of the myths surrounding contemporary views of music. It rebalances and retunes an imbalanced and historically discordant view of what matters in a highly readable and elegant way.'

— DR BILL LUCAS, Professor of Learning and Director of the
Centre for Real-World Learning, University of Winchester

'This book restores the presence of womanly wisdom and spirituality to the Christian musical tradition. Combining rich scholarly insights with fascinating personal vignettes and a wealth of practical suggestions, June Boyce-Tillman brings to life the forgotten and neglected capacities of music to serve as a bodily expression of love for the divine.'

— DR TINA BEATTIE, Professor of Catholic Theology,
University of Roehampton

'In this new book – possibly her greatest so far – June Boyce-Tillman truly brings out of the treasure-store "things ancient and new." What is ancient is the bringing to the light of the contribution – frequently obscured – that women have made to musicology from the very beginnings of Christianity. Those familiar with her work cherish the way she has already brought Hildegard of Bingen's unique genius to global recognition; less well-known are female voices from the earliest Christian communities, Renaissance Italian sisters and the beginnings of the Shaker movement. What is new is that to each example – even to contemporary struggles – are applied rigorous categories of challenge and scrutiny. From a contemporary scholar with rich experience on a global scene, herself a major contributor to the performance field for over thirty years, this book will be widely appreciated and influence both Church liturgy and the wider musical scene.'

— DR MARY GREY, Professor emeritus of Theology,
University of Wales